The War for Lebanon, 1970–1985

Itamar Rabinovich

The War for Lebanon, 1970–1985

REVISED EDITION

Cornell University Press

ITHACA AND LONDON

First edition published 1984 by Cornell University Press.
Revised edition first published, in cloth and paper, 1985.
Second printing, cloth and paper, 1986.

International Standard Book Number (cloth) 0-8014-1870-4
International Standard Book Number (paper) 0-8014-9313-7
Library of Congress Catalog Card Number 85-14891
Printed in the United States of America
Librarians: Library of Congress cataloging information
appears on the last page of the book.

The paper in this book is acid-free and meets the guidelines
for permanence and durability of the Committee on Production
Guidelines for Book Longevity of the Council on Library Resources.

In memory of my father,
Gutman Rabinovich,
1913–1983

Contents

Preface to the Revised Edition

CORNELL UNIVERSITY PRESS's decision to publish a paperback edition of *The War for Lebanon* in the summer of 1985 confronted me with several choices. Clearly the book had to be updated, but how much did it have to be revised? The events of the past three years do put those of the preceding twelve in a different perspective; memoirs and other kinds of books have been published, and I have had occasion to learn more about many of the issues, episodes, and personalities discussed here. Surely if I were to write the book now, parts of it would be written differently; but I came to the conclusion that the changes in perspective and fuller information afforded by the passage of time do not warrant revisions in the text itself. I rather chose to delete the postscript and to add a full chapter dealing with the Lebanese crisis during the past three years.

I. R.

June 1985

Preface

THE TITLE OF THIS BOOK may be somewhat misleading. The war for Lebanon—a conflict of domestic and external forces seeking to shape and control the Lebanese entity—began long before 1970 and unfortunately did not end in 1983. But these years form a particularly significant phase in the history of both Lebanon and its immediate environment.

The events of the period unfolded through four distinct stages: the collapse of the Lebanese political system between 1970 and 1975, the civil war of 1975–76, the lingering crisis of the years 1976–82 and the war of 1982. A new postwar phase began in September 1982 and is dealt with in chapter six and in the postscript.

Lebanon became Lebanon because of its relative insulation—for centuries rugged Mount Lebanon attracted minority communities escaping governments bent on enforcing orthodoxy and uniformity. And yet the history of modern Lebanon reflects a continuous interplay between domestic forces and external actors whose intervention has ranged from intellectual and economic influence to forceful occupation. The existence of the independent Lebanese republic during the thirty years following World War II was based on a delicate balance of domestic and external elements. In this respect the play of events between 1970 and 1983 represents a historical continuity. But there are three significant differences. One, the scope and intensity of external intervention were very much greater during these years. Two, the crisis in Lebanon had left the periphery and become central to Middle East politics. Three—and most striking—is that the three main external actors have themselves been profoundly affected. The Palestine Liberation Organization found an advantageous base in Lebanon, but its establishment brought the organization to clash twice with Syria and made it vulnerable to a concentrated Israeli attack. It survived the fighting with Syria in 1976, but Syrian pressure in 1982–83 is proving more fateful. For the Syrian Ba'thi regime, its intervention in Lebanon triggered the domestic crisis of 1977, which nearly brought the regime down. In 1983, it made a remarkable recovery from the military defeat of June 1982 and used its standing in Lebanon in order to build a position of regional and international influence. But its sense of achievement must have been tempered by a realization of the precariousness of Syria's standing in Lebanon and of the possibility that all might change with another swing of the pendulum.

In the early 1970s Israel was a marginal actor in the Lebanese crisis, which, in turn, did not rank high on its own agenda of priorities. Twelve years later, the evolution of the crisis and of Israel's domestic politics and regional policies led Israel into a principal role. The long-term significance of the 1982 war in Lebanon for the state of Israel has yet to be measured, but its short-term effect on the government that launched the war was disastrous. The minister of Defense was forced to resign his post eight months later, and the prime minister resigned in September 1983 against a backdrop of continuing deep Israeli involvement in Lebanon with no satisfactory end in sight.

It is this interplay of the past few years between Lebanon's domestic politics and developments in the larger Middle East that this book primarily seeks to explore. Special emphasis has been laid on the 1982 war and the events leading to it for a number of reasons— their significance, their intrinsic interest, and the absence as yet of authoritative works, which are available for the earlier phases of the crisis. For the same reason the chapters that deal with the years 1977–82 seek to combine an interpretation with a narrative account while those that deal with earlier periods and with the subject as a whole put a greater emphasis on interpretation.

A book on a still unfolding crisis raises a number of obvious questions and difficulties. Is there a perspective from which these recent events can be judged and evaluated? Are there sources available for a proper understanding of military moves, political ties, and diplomatic initiatives, many of which are still shrouded in secrecy? Can the author rise above the passions and controversies that the war for Lebanon has aroused?

I obviously believe that all these questions can be answered in the affirmative, but a few words about approach and method seem to be in order. The writing of contemporary history is hampered by limited information and by the certainty of changes in perspective that the passing of time, new events, and fresh revelations are bound to produce. These can be offset only by firmly grounding the interpretation and the narrative in a historical perspective. I am aware that the full story of the war for Lebanon in the years 1970–83 cannot yet be told. We still do not know exactly how the Lebanese civil war broke out in April 1975, what political and diplomatic moves preceded Syria's entry into Lebanon, or what the American and Israeli governments agreed upon in May 1982. But the book does not purport to tell the story in such a fashion; rather, it suggests an outline of events which fits into an analytical framework.

The sources for this study vary with the subject and the period. Some are well documented through memoirs, secondary sources, press coverage, and the rich polemical and apologetic literature that the parties to the conflict have produced during the years. Some of the other aspects particularly of more recent ones are scantily documented. Among the sources used for writing about contemporary Middle Eastern history, radio broadcasts occupy a special place. Radio is often the medium through which speeches, political sermons, and raw information are transmitted. Arab and Israeli radio broadcasts are faithfully recorded by three monitoring services: the BBC service, Foreign Broadcast Information Service (FBIS) in Washington, and the Israeli monitoring service. They have all been extensively used in researching the subject of this volume. Then too, I was able to discuss the events of the past few years with Israeli, American, and Lebanese participants. These were not formal interviews and they are not referred to as such in footnotes, but they did provide me with insight into attitudes and outlooks for which I am indebted to my interlocutors.

My thanks are due to many others as well. The Shiloah Institute at

PREFACE

Tel Aviv University has in the past twelve years been much more than my work place. I thank my colleagues at the Institute, Hanna Zamir, in particular, and the Institute's staff, Amira Margalith, Edna Liftman, Tali Mor, Lydia Gareh, Maggie Mahlab, and Ami Salant and his staff at the documentation system. Hanna Ben Artzi has been an effective research assistant in this and other projects.

Much of the writing was actually done while I was on leave in the Department of Near Eastern Studies at Cornell University. The faculty, staff, and students all helped in the effort. Part of the manuscript was read and discussed during the Middle East seminar at the Lehrman Institute in the winter and spring of 1982–83. I thank Robert Tucker and Nick Rizopoulos for organizing an excellent seminar and them and the other participants for their criticism and suggestions. Walter Lippincott, Jr., now the director of Cornell University Press, and Fouad Ajami, Carl Brown, and Elie Kedourie read the manuscript and made numerous suggestions that contributed to its improvement. I remain responsible for the lingering deficiencies. The Ford Foundation through Israel's Foundations Trustees facilitated much of the research that underlies this book. And finally, my gratitude and love go to the other members of the team—my wife, Efrat, and my daughters, Iris and Orna.

ITAMAR RABINOVICH

Tel Aviv, Israel

Chronology

August 31, 1920	Establishment of Greater Lebanon by France.
May 23, 1926	Establishment of a Lebanese constitutional republic under French mandatory control.
1936	French-Lebanese treaty (suspended in 1939).
June 1941	Anglo–Free-French invasion of Lebanon and formal declaration of independence.
1943	Lebanese National Pact; Lebanese-French clashes.
1946	Completion of French evacuation of Lebanon.
September 1952	Bloodless coup d'etat ends Bishara al-Khuri's administration and begins Camille Chamoun's administration.
1958	First Lebanese civil war; end of Chamoun's administration, beginning of Fu'ád Shihab's administration.
1964	Beginning of Charles Helou's administration.
December 1968	Israeli raid on Beirut airport; beginning of conflict in Lebanon over Palestinian issue.
November 1969	Cairo Agreement between Lebanese Government and the PLO.
1970	Beginning of Suleiman Faranjiyya's administration; the PLO transfers its main base from Jordan to Lebanon.
May 1973	Confrontation between the Lebanese army and the PLO.
April 1975	Opening phase of the second Lebanese civil war.
January 1976	Indirect Syrian intervention in the civil war.
February 1976	Syrian effort to formulate a political compromise in Lebanon.

March 1976	Failure of Syrian effort; abortive coup d'etat by General Aziz al-Ahdab.
June 1976	Full-fledged Syrian invasion, stiff Palestinian opposition.
September 1976	Second Syrian offensive in Lebanon; formation of Lebanese Front and Lebanese Forces.
October 1976	The Riyad and Cairo agreements, which end the Lebanese civil war.
July 25, 1977	The Shtura Agreement between Syria, Lebanon, and the PLO—another attempt at implementing the Cairo Agreement.
February 2, 1978	The Fayadiyya incident, which marks the beginning of Syria's conflict with the Lebanese Front.
March 16, 1978	Israel's Litani Operation in southern Lebanon.
June 13, 1978	Killing of Tony Faranjiyya by a Phalangist squad.
August 31, 1978	Disappearance of Musa al-Sadr, the Shi'i Imam, during a visit to Libya.
January 22–31, 1980	First phase of Syria's redeployment in Lebanon.
July 7, 1980	Phalangist raid on the Chamounist militia.
December 20–27, 1980	First phase of Syrian-Phalangist fighting in Zahle.
April 2, 1981	Second phase of Syrian-Phalangist fighting in Zahle; developed into the missile crisis.
July 1981	Israeli-Palestinian fighting; cease-fire negotiated by U.S. Ambassador Philip Habib.
June 6–11, 1982	Israel's Operation Peace for Galilee and the Syrian-Israeli cease-fire.
August 1982	Bashir Jumayyil elected president of Lebanon; the PLO evacuates Beirut.
September 1982	President Ronald Reagan's Middle East peace initiative; assassination of Bashir Jumayyil; massacre at Sabra and Shatila; beginning of Amin Jumayyil's administration.

The War for Lebanon, 1970–1985

CHAPTER 1

The Lebanese Paradox

THE OUTBREAK OF the second Lebanese civil war in 1975 and the subsequent collapse of the Lebanese state can be studied from two diametrically opposed vantage points. From one, the independent Lebanese republic appears to be artificial and archaic, built on shaky demographic and political foundations, and therefore doomed to be destroyed by the domestic and external foes of its political system. Consequently, the first thirty years of its history are simply the working out of prophecy: that tension and contradiction are inherent in Lebanese politics. From the other vantage point, the Lebanese political system is seen as an impressive and unique attempt in the Middle East to develop a pluralistic polity, a state able to contain a heterogeneous population against difficult odds. This view derived encouragement from the system's capacity to endure for thirty years—in an unstable environment—through its imaginative responses to successive challenges.[1]

The Nature of the Lebanese State

Underlying these contradictory interpretations of Lebanon's recent history is the more fundamental debate on the nature of the Lebanese state and on the degree of continuity between historic Lebanon and the post–World War I Lebanese state. Was the independent Lebanese republic of the years 1945–75 an essentially

Christian state, the successor and perpetuator of a long tradition? Or was it a new entity, shaped by but never fully adjusted to the demographic realities of its 1920 boundaries?[2] The notion of a Lebanese political entity was officially embodied for the first time in 1861 when, under European pressure and guarantee, an autonomous province (Mutasarifiyya) was established in Mount Lebanon. Its establishment was the product of several historical processes, the complexity and subtleties of which are reflected also in the subsequent history of the Lebanese polity. In tracing the evolution of the Lebanese entity, it is useful to distinguish between its territory, its population, and its political system.

The name Mount Lebanon applied originally only to the northern part of the Mountain. With the migration of the growing Maronite population, the name gradually encompassed the whole mountain. The rugged Mountain had traditionally attracted minority communities—heterodox Muslims and Christians—that in the later Middle Ages and early modern period sought refuge from the governments of the Sunni empires (Mameluk and Ottoman) that dominated the region. The Druze and Maronite were the two principal communities on Mount Lebanon, but Shiʿis, Melchites, and Sunnis became associated with the Lebanese entity either through living at the Mountain's edges or by coming under the authority of the Lebanese emirates of the Maʿnids (1516–1697) and the Shihabis (1697–1841).

The Maʿnid emirate (*imarah*) developed out of the protofeudal social stratification, land tenure, military service, and system of tax collection in the Shuf Mountain, the original mountain of the Druze. In its heyday, under Fakhr al-Din (1585–1635), the emirate was characterized by (a) virtual autonomy within the framework of the Ottoman Empire, (b) Druze-Maronite cooperation, which transcended the rigid religious and communal lines known elsewhere in the region, (c) the extension of the emir's authority into other parts of Ottoman Syria, and (d) the development of Lebanon's relationship with Latin-Catholic Europe.

When the Maʿnid male line became extinct in 1697, it was replaced by the Shihabis. The latter were Sunni and not Druze, but the emirate was already clearly losing its distinct Druze bias. The trend was accentuated in the eighteenth century by two separate developments—the migration of a large part of the Druze to southern Syria

18

because of intracommunal fighting, and the territorial expansion of the Maronites. This process was to a large extent led by the Maronite church, whose predominance in the community was acquired at the expense of Maronite feudatories. The Shihabi family in fact converted to Maronite Catholicism; but it was characteristic of the ambiguous relationship between religion and politics in the Lebanese entity that the religious affiliation of the Shihabi family remained opaque.

The long reign of Emir Bashir II (1788–1840) reinforced the tradition and legacy of a strong central authority exercised over Mount Lebanon and the areas adjacent to it. His fall, and the end of the Shihabi emirate (1841), were followed by twenty years of social and political upheaval: a revolt by Maronite peasants against their Maronite landlords (1858), and a Druze-Maronite civil war (1860), in which the less numerous but more warlike Druze at first routed their enemies, who were then saved by the intervention of a French expeditionary force. The events in 1860 brought to the surface and nourished a new ingredient in Lebanese politics of the nineteenth century—religious solidarity and religious hatred.

France's intervention and European pressure brought about the creation of an autonomous Lebanese province within the Ottoman Empire. The autonomous Lebanon of the late nineteenth and early twentieth centuries had a clear Christian majority and character and a political system that offered representation and a share of political power to minority communities. It was an exceptional entity in its Muslim environment, and its tentative existence owed much to Europe's support. Indeed, when World War I broke out, the Ottoman government abolished the 1861 arrangements and established its direct rule over Mount Lebanon (1915).[3]

A sizable segment of the Maronite community refused to reconcile itself to the "smaller Lebanon" of the 1861–1915 period and demanded that all the area united by the Lebanese emirate be included in the new Lebanese entity. (See Map 1.) Without Beirut and much of its agricultural and commercial hinterland, the mutasarifiyya appeared to these Maronite nationalists as a poor and weak version of the Lebanon they aspired to. Their time came after 1918, when France secured a mandate for Syria and Lebanon. Some of the authors of French policy in the Levant supported the Maronite militants' demands, arguing that Lebanon's Catholic population was

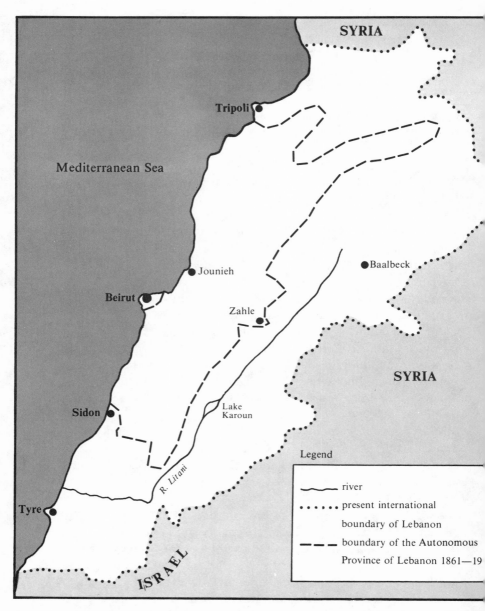

Map 1. Smaller and Greater Lebanon. The Autonomous Province 1861–1915 and Leba since 1920.

France's one reliable ally against the hostile Arab nationalists and Muslims in the hinterland and that Lebanon's economic viability should therefore be bolstered. Thus, when on September 1, 1920, the French added parts of Ottoman Syria to the original territory of the autonomous province of Lebanon, they created a completely distinct state—Greater Lebanon.[4]

The consequences of this measure were clear at the time to at least one perceptive and prescient French official, Robert de Caix, who in his internal memoranda warned of the dangers inherent in the creation of Greater Lebanon. De Caix was an architect of the policy that sought to break the French-mandated territory in the Levant into a patchwork of ethnic units and to prevent the crystallization of a large, anti-French, Syrian Arab entity. A larger Christian Lebanon would be a mainstay of France's position, but the expansion of Lebanon's territory should be done with prudence and moderation. "We know of no reason to annex Tripoli to Lebanon," he wrote in July 1920. "It is a Sunni Muslim center, rather fanatic, and not wishing at all to be incorporated in a country with a Christian majority." In the same vein, de Caix argued that "it is most questionable whether such a large city as Beirut, which will no doubt contain half the Lebanese population in a few years, is the most desirable capital for the Mountain, whose character might be greatly altered by the move."[5]

Indeed, the net effect of the creation of Greater Lebanon was Syrian irredentism and the disruption of the demographic balance in the new state, resulting in discord between the traditional Maronite Christian ethos, which underlay its creation, and the heterogeneous composition of its population. How was this discord to be resolved? One school of thought among the Maronites saw the solution in continued reliance on French support. As long as French or other external support was certain, the Lebanese state could be preserved as a Christian entity against domestic and external Muslim and Arab nationalist opposition. Another school of thought, headed by Emile Eddé (Lebanon's president, 1936–41), was convinced by the 1932 census that the Muslims were about to become the majority in the Lebanese state and that the possibility of France abandoning the Lebanese Christians had to be taken seriously. Eddé concluded that it was essential to "expedite the territorial reduction of Lebanon in order to enable the latter state to have a more consistent Christian majority." By "amputating" Tripoli and southern Lebanon from the Lebanese state, "Lebanon will be rid of almost 140,000 Shi'i and Sunni Muslims and will be left with a Christian majority equalling about eighty percent of its population."[6] (See Map 2.) Eddé tried to win the support of the French government, which was not unimpressed with his reasoning but which in the end chose to preserve the territorial status quo. Still, Eddé did not abandon his idea, and in 1946 he sent an emissary to Chaim Weizmann, the Zionist leader, to attempt to persuade Weizmann to seek the incorporation of southern Lebanon and its predominantly Muslim population into the Jewish national home.[7]

Alongside these comparatively straightforward solutions, other, more subtle approaches were developed. In the more complex political arena and atmosphere of the post-1920 Lebanese state, Christian intellectuals and politicians tried to devise a formula that would enable the non-Christian minorities to find their place in an essentially Christian Lebanon. Thus the Catholic banker and intellectual Michel Chiha saw the modern Lebanese state as a successor to the ancient Phoenicians, a merchant republic, bearer of a Mediterranean culture, illuminator of its environment, and an interpreter between East and West. Chiha's notion of Phoenicianism was further developed and given a Christian flavor by two Maronite poets, Charles Corm and Sa'id 'Aql. Later, the concept of l'asile de Liban, Lebanon as a haven for persecuted minorities—Druze and Shi'a as well as Christian—was put forth. But neither concept appealed to Lebanon's Muslim population, and rather than mobilizing support among Greater Lebanon's opponents, each concept served only as a legitimizing tool for its defenders.[8]

Chiha's stronger impact on the development of the Lebanese state came from his contributions to the drafting of the 1926 constitution and to the shaping of the Lebanese republic's political institutions. Some flexibility was built into the constitution and the governmental structure, which enabled the Lebanese political system to adapt to the changes that occurred in the 1930s and 1940s.[9] During most of the interwar years, Lebanese politics were dominated by the conflict between Lebanese Catholic communities sup-

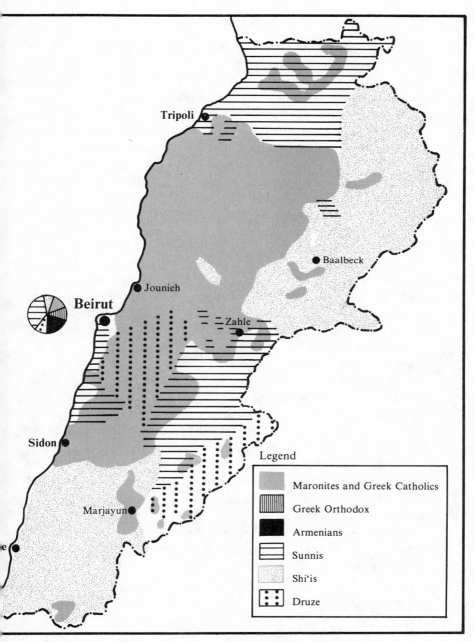

Tripoli

Baalbeck

Jounieh

Beirut

Zahle

Sidon

Marjayun

Legend

Maronites and Greek Catholics

Greek Orthodox

Armenians

Sunnis

Shi'is

Druze

2. Lebanon: Approximate concentration areas of major communities.

ported by France and the Sunni and Greek Orthodox communities, which rejected the legitimacy of the Lebanese state, objected to the Maronites' political supremacy, and demanded that Lebanon (or part of it) be added onto a larger Arab state. But by the 1940s, the Lebanese political spectrum had altered because of the integration of the Shi'i community into the Lebanese state; the rise of ideological, extraparliamentary parties; and the crystallization of distinct political groups within the Maronite and Sunni establishments, groups shaped by differences of policy orientations as well as by personal and regional conflicts.

World War II, France's political decline, and the apparent ascendancy of Pan-Arab nationalism facilitated the victory within the Maronite community of Bishara al-Khuri and other leaders, who urged an accommodation with Lebanon's Muslim communities and the Arab world and the abandonment of the traditional aspiration and demand for a Christian Lebanon. This development was matched by the crystallization of a Sunni leadership, headed by Riad al-Sulh, that despite its ritualistic commitment to Arab nationalism and unity was willing to share power with a senior Maronite partner in a Lebanese state.

In 1943, these two groups reached an oral agreement known as the National Pact, which made possible the establishment of an independent Lebanon. The Muslim political establishment recognized the legitimacy of a sovereign Lebanese entity in return for the Christian communities' willingness to share power and recognition of at least partial Arab character of this entity. The distribution of power among the various communities according to their presumed numerical strength—by then a traditional pattern in Lebanon—was also agreed upon. Christian supremacy in the state was exemplified in the decision to elect a Maronite as its powerful president and to establish a ratio of six Christian deputies to every five Muslim deputies in parliament. The Lebanese polity was not based on the presumed existence of a Lebanese nation but on a confederation of protonational communities, each of which claimed the ultimate allegiance of its members. This unique political system, which acknowledged the primacy of its constituent religious communities and vested them with political power, came to be dubbed *confessional*.

The Muslim establishment's willingness to accept Christian

hegemony in Lebanon, when Christian numerical strength was clearly declining, was induced by a number of factors whose influence continued in later years. The Muslim leadership could not ignore the historical basis for the Christian claim to a special status and a special role in Lebanon, nor could it disregard the American and European support for this claim. The Sunni establishment was fully aware of the significant concessions made by its Maronite counterparts in 1943, as well as of their common interests. Changing the status quo might, after all, play into the hands of more radical Sunnis and the Shi'is, whose share of power in the government no longer reflected their numbers. This process of political accommodation was characteristic of a widespread tendency in the Arab world during the interwar years, as the states created by the 1918–20 settlement acquired vitality and as local elites with vested interests in perpetuating the territorial status quo emerged. Yet not all Muslims and Christians accepted the 1943 compromise, and segments of the major communities continued to harbor dreams either of an Arab union or of a purely Christian Lebanon.

The political system of post-1943 Lebanon was based on the political institutions of the mandatory period and on the National Pact. It was unique, complex, and its inherent flaws were quite evident. It was conservative by definition, as an ascriptive system based on the preservation of the status quo. With confessionalism as a cornerstone of the political system, religious leaders and other traditional leaders and interests kept their prominence within their respective communities. This conservative bias was further reinforced by other characteristics of the political system, such as the electoral system, which served to preserve the position of community notables (Zu'ama) and to hinder the development of parliamentary political parties across communal and regional boundaries.[10] By electing parliamentary members through regional lists, the Zu'ama were practically assured of election and could often carry with them into parliament a number of clients. Often the Zu'ama would function alongside the formal and bureaucratic structures, offering services and protection and demanding allegiance, votes, and sometimes participation in violent conflicts.[11] In describing the phenomenon known as Wasita (mediation and the exercising of influence), Peter Gubser says:

These personal services take many forms and subsequently create various ties to the *za'im*, which he may in turn use for his benefit. Because
of the administrative reforms, the leaders can no longer easily obtain
employment for their clients in the state bureaucracy but they can
exercise influence on where a man is posted. If a Zahlawi who is
assigned to Tripoli wants to work in Zahlah, the easiest way to effect
this change is to use his *za'im*'s influence. As a result of this service, the
za'im has not only insured the man's support at the polls, but also put a
man in a bureaucratic position who will be able to help him in the
future.[12]

The Lebanese parliament thus reflected the web of relationships
among the traditional foci of power in the country. And moreover, it
was for a rather long period virtually closed to new contenders.
Furthermore, in upholding the principles of confessionalism and
playing down the notions of nation and class, the Lebanese political
system acquired an archaic complexion, and from the mid-1960s it
found itself challenged by the political attitudes prevailing in most
of the outside world.

But the system had important merits, not least of which was that it
was based on an awareness of the fundamental conflict in Lebanon
and attempted to come to grips with it. In this respect, Lebanon was
significantly different from Syria and Iraq, whose political systems
were ostensibly built on the assumption that communal differences
had given way to an allegiance to Arabism. Furthermore, the Lebanese political system contained mechanisms designed to blunt intercommunal rivalries and to require intercommunal cooperation.
The historical roots of the system and its gradual evolution gave it
significant advantages over possible alternatives. And whatever the
system's obvious deficiencies, it did not seem that any other could
preserve the Lebanese state as a pluralistic polity. Furthermore, it
was the only genuine parliamentary system that survived and functioned in the post–World War II Arab world.[13]

The 1958 Civil War

The challenges to the status quo in Lebanon since the 1940s have
come primarily from three sources. First, some Muslims rejected the

1943 compromise and its political system as unrepresentative of its population. Second, a variety of ideologically inclined groups and individuals (Arab nationalists, Communists, and other advocates of social and economic change) viewed the existing system as a barrier to the implementation of their ideas. Finally, external forces (such as Syria, Egypt, and the Soviet Union) sought to establish influence in Lebanon and to weaken Western presence and influence.

Until the second half of the 1950s, the Lebanese system warded off these challengers with relative ease. Supporters of the status quo controlled the government, and the opposition was relegated to a marginal position outside or on the fringes of the parliamentary system. In these circumstances, it was quite natural for members of the traditional elite to adhere to a strict interpretation of the status quo. Their sense of security was in fact reinforced by the 1952 crisis, which ended in the forced resignation of Bishara al-Khuri and the election of Camille Chamoun. When compared to the military take-overs in Syria and Egypt, the assassination of King Abdallah in Jordan, and the violent conflicts between government and opposition in Iraq, the Lebanese crisis was merely a matter of bickerings among the ruling elite. The Lebanese took pride in the fact that the army refused to intervene in the crisis and that it was resolved peacefully through constitutional channels.[14]

The first major crisis to threaten the existence of the Lebanese state erupted in 1958, under the combined pressure of domestic and regional developments. The upsurge of messianic Pan-Arab nationalism under the leadership of Gamal Abdel Nasser, plus the Egyptian-Iraqi rivalry (and the Great Power rivalry superimposed on it), set the regional scene for the explosion. Nasserism offered an external focus of loyalty for Lebanon's Muslims, to the detriment of their attachment to the Lebanese state. Why accept a secondary position in a state dominated by Christians with ambivalent attitudes to Arabism, when Arabism was about to enjoy its finest hour?

Christian leaders were sharply divided as to the best response to these developments. Some favored a conciliatory and flexible policy which would enable Lebanon to weather the storm. Others, headed by Chamoun, advocated a resolute policy based on unambivalent cooperation with the West and the conservative Arab states against the wave of revolutionary Pan-Arab nationalism. The problem was further compounded by Chamoun's decision to modify the constitution to enable his reelection for a second consecutive term. Some Christian and Muslim politicians opposed this, and during the 1957 elections Chamoun sought to exclude them from the new parliament. He was successful in several cases, and the new parliament was much more supportive than its predecessor. But it was a Pyrrhic victory, for several important politicians ousted by Chamoun thereafter pitted themselves against the Lebanese parliamentary system.

Tension mounted after the formation of the United Arab Republic in February 1958, and a civil war broke out between Chamoun's supporters and his opponents, most of whom were Muslims. This conflict mainly involved Phalangist militias and the Lebanese Syrian Nationalist Party (a radical party advocating a united Greater Syria, but acting at that time to defend the Lebanese entity against the onslaught of Pan-Arabism). The Lebanese army, led by Fu'ád Shihab, maintained a neutral line. The fighting ended with the landing of American marines in Beirut, while the political war subsided after another historic compromise had been devised. Chamoun renounced reelection, and Shihab was elected president. Under the slogan "no victors and no vanquished," it was decided to restore the status quo. The marked improvement in the position of the Muslims and the rebel leaders, shown in the composition of the first postwar cabinet, brought the Phalanges out on the streets. This threatened to reactivate the crisis and forced the formation of a new and more balanced government.

The Lebanese civil war of 1958 had manifold causes, but the overriding issue was undoubtedly a Christian-Muslim struggle over the nature of the Lebanese state. The compromise that ended the struggle had important consequences in the following years.[15]

The Years 1958–70

The lessons of the 1958 crisis and the general regional developments had a salutary influence on the stability of the Lebanese political system. The civil war demonstrated to both Christians and Muslims that extremist policies in the delicate circumstances obtaining in Lebanon were bound to lead to violent crises. It also showed that whatever the shortcomings of the existing system, the alternatives were still less attractive. With the checking of the messianic wave of Pan-Arab nationalism and the gradual decline of the Nasserite movement, the pressure on Lebanon was alleviated. Developments in the Arab Middle East after 1958, especially in Syria, showed that the Lebanese political system and way of life had distinct advantages over the patterns in other Arab countries.

Fu'ád Shihab's leadership was instrumental in steering Lebanon out of the crisis. The new president (1958–64) was favored with a number of assets: an authoritative personality, family prestige, a basis of power in the army, and neutral posture throughout the crisis—appearing at the end as a savior-hero. Although he was a Maronite, he adopted a moderate line, advocating a healthy balance between Lebanon's Christian identity and an Arab nationalist orientation. Shihab manipulated the Lebanese political system dexterously and conducted a slightly pro-Nasserite foreign policy. But while Shihab was successful in restabilizing the Lebanese system, he was far less successful in coping with the more fundamental questions. What was the nature of the Lebanese political community, some twenty years after the 1943 National Pact? Was Lebanon's political system still suited to the country's realities? Did it afford the degree of flexibility needed for dealing with domestic and external problems and changes?

Conservatives among the Maronites and other Christians continued to view Lebanon as the embodiment of the notion of a Christian Catholic entity closely linked to the West, a Christian haven and fortress in the midst of a hostile Muslim environment. They argued that the political arrangements made in 1943, although themselves a compromise that diluted Lebanon's original character, should be kept, even in the event the Christians lost their numerical superiority. By accepting the principle of accommodation and adaptation now, the Christian communities would undermine the system that guaranteed their hegemony and security. Nor should the social and economic system—based on a free economy, a small bureaucracy, low taxation, and minimal government intervention in social and economic processes—be reformed. This state of affairs served the interests of the elite and further widened the gap between Christian communities (which enjoyed private and parochial education and other social services) and Muslim communities, particularly the Shi'is (which lagged behind in their social and economic development). The conservatives naturally resisted changes that were bound to adversely affect their immediate interests. They also feared that reform would mobilize the Muslim communities and poorer classes, with unfortunate political consequences.

Moderate Christian leaders, while sharing the concerns and aims of the conservatives, advocated reform and adaptation as the only way to address these concerns. They strove for a redefinition of the relation between state and community, which would acknowledge a Lebanese political community above the communities that constituted it. Doubtless this Lebanese community was to have a Christian character, but it could be implicit rather than explicit. Political institutions and practices should be adapted to new realities, and social and economic reforms should be instituted lest the "benign neglect" of the traditional politicians lead to a social and political explosion.

Shihab's policies reflected many of these ideas. He was a practical politician rather than the formulator of doctrines and ideologies, and when he encountered serious difficulties in reforming the traditional system through traditional political channels, he tried to circumvent the political system by building a powerful state apparatus. Government bureaucracy and the *deuxième bureau* (military intelligence) were developed as an alternative system of government, designed to split or crush those groups powerful enough to resist the president's efforts to impinge on their privileges. Shihab's strategy produced a series of reforms and changes but did little to resolve Lebanon's fundamental dilemma. This failure was largely concealed during Shihab's term by his dominant personality and the relatively smooth functioning of the political system under his stewardship.[16] But when he stepped down in 1964, the failure of his more ambitious plans exposed that fundamental dilemma. The inherent flaws in the Lebanese entity became evident. But it was equally apparent that attempts at extensive reforms or revisions were certain to upset the delicate balance on which the whole system rested. Furthermore, modernization and social mobilization were weakening the position of conservative elements and strengthening extraparliamentary and other opposition groups that sought to join, to modify, or to overthrow the political system.[17]

But in the years immediately following Shihab's presidency, Lebanon's politicians focused less on underlying issues and more on immediate problems, which the existing system was hard put to solve. Some of these derived from the way power was transferred to the new president, Charles Helou. Shihab left the presidency rather reluctantly, and together with his entourage he sought to perpetuate his influence through his meek successor. The president plays a vital role in the Lebanese political system, which was affected by the weakness of the new president. Unlike the Shihabi period, there was no stable majority in parliament, and the relationships among the president, the prime minister, and the parliament were far from satisfactory. Rivalries among Arab states in the years 1964–67, the rising tension in the Arab-Israeli conflict, and finally the Six Day War forced the Lebanese government to make decisions harmful to the stability of the political system. Still more ominous pressure was felt at the end of 1968, when the presence and activities of the Palestine Liberation Organization (PLO) and its constituent organizations became a cardinal issue and a catalyst for other developments.

The full impact of these developments was not absorbed until the mid-1970s. In the late 1960s and very early 1970s, conservative Lebanon enjoyed an Indian summer of sorts. In the parliamentary elections of 1968, the three large Maronite parties (Pierre Jumayyil's Phalange, Camille Chamoun's National Liberals, and Raymond Eddé's National Bloc) coordinated their campaigns and enhanced their collective influence.[18] Partly as a result of this, the Shihabi bloc (Nahj) was defeated in the 1970 presidential elections, and a traditional, conservative Maronite leader from northern Lebanon, Suleiman Faranjiyya, was elected president.

Faranjiyya was very much the traditional Za'im, a leader of the clan, and an important political and economic force in Zugharta. In 1957, Faranjiyya was implicated in the "Ziyara incident," in which several members and followers of the rival Duwayhi clan were killed. Faranjiyya had to flee to Syria. It was only in 1960 that Faranjiyya inherited the position, held previously by his brother Hamid, as the principal national representative of northern Lebanon's Maronites.[19]

Favorable circumstances and his initially successful cooperation with the Sunni leader of Beirut, Sa'ib Salam, resulted in a relatively smooth functioning of the political system. But the early phase of Faranjiyya's presidency did not actually signify a revival of Lebanon's traditional politics. By 1973, a series of domestic and external developments converged to produce a crisis that Faranjiyya and the groups he represented were incapable of coping with.

How is the transition from the controlled tension of the late 1960s to the civil war of 1975 to be explained? It is hardly surprising that most analyses originate in their authors' view of the essential Lebanese system. Some prophets of doom saw the collapse of the system as inevitable, expedited perhaps by extraneous factors. The sociologist Halim Barakat, who in 1973 predicted the collapse of the Lebanese system, wrote in 1976–77 that "according to the framework employed in this study, the current civil war in Lebanon is a culmination of a confrontation that has been building up between the forces of change and the forces for maintaining the established order against all odds and quite often in opposition to the professed principles of the society and government."[20] Those who take a positive view of the post-1943 Lebanese state and political system offer different interpretations of the 1975–76 civil war. Political scientist Iliya Harik argues that social and economic tensions in Lebanon were manageable, that the system was undergoing a transformation, and that power was subtly shifting from Christian hands to Muslim hands. Contemplating the same data as Barakat, Harik argues that his "survey of social and economic factors did not reveal any conditions serious enough to inspire such a degree of violence over such a protracted period of time." His thesis is that the Lebanese system did not collapse under its own weight but was rather the victim of extraneous influences: "it would have survived one way or another had it not been for the unusual regional violence in which it was trapped. A historical accident no doubt, but one of traumatic magnitude."[21]

The difference between these two vantage points is moot. Nor is the difference between their implications as stark as it may appear at first sight. After all, even those who argue that the collapse of the Lebanese system was inevitable agree that the events of the early 1970s precipitated the crisis. The following account of the 1975–76 civil war will, indeed, be preceded by an interpretation of the domestic and external changes that affected Lebanon in the early 1970s.

CHAPTER 2

The Second Civil War, 1975–76

THE COURSE OF LEBANON'S modern history can, as we have seen, be interpreted as the inevitable outcome of conflict between contending concepts of the Lebanese entity and the Lebanese state. Alternatively, it can be viewed as the product of a permanent effort to maintain a subtle balance among domestic and external forces, a balance often preserved by external protection (the European powers until 1914, France during the mandatory period) and intervention (the United States in 1958). But in independent Lebanon, it was primarily the political leadership that had to keep domestic and external balance. The balance was upset temporarily in 1958, restored during the Shihab presidency, and maintained against increasingly difficult odds through the 1960s and early 1970s. It was then shattered by the continuous influences of the domestic and external changes that converged during Suleiman Faranjiyya's presidency.[1]

Prelude to Crisis

In 1972–76, several events had an unsettling effect on Lebanon. The establishment of the PLO's principal base is particularly important. It is examined separately, below. Among other events were the oil embargo and the consequent accumulation of immense financial resources in some Arab countries. The collective power of the Arab

34

world—and, within the Arab world, the influence of Saudi Arabia and other distinctly Islamic oil-producing states—grew. Thus Islam and Islamic solidarity assumed a clearer political role. There was a new sense of Arab and Muslim power, which in moments of high enthusiasm led various Arab leaders and writers to refer to the Arab world as a new superpower in a new international order.

This new feeling was less overwhelming than Nasserism in its heyday, but its effect on Lebanon's Muslims was comparable. Why should they continue to accept Christian hegemony in Lebanon, when elsewhere Islam and Arabism were triumphant, or nearly so? The new assertiveness of Lebanon's Muslims was evidenced by the political prominence of the leaders of the Sunni and Shi'a religious establishments. The mood was accentuated by a growth of Lebanon's Muslim majority as well as by the altered position of the Western powers in the region. In 1958, when the United States landed marines in Beirut Lebanon perceived the intervention as a manifestation of the West's commitment to the preservation of Lebanon's political status quo. Fifteen years later, however, the repercussions of the 1958 intervention had faded, and the position of the United States and its attitude to Lebanon had changed considerably. In the mid-1970s, the United States was not very likely to intervene on behalf of a political system that many influential Americans viewed as outdated. The United States and Western Europe were seeking friends and influence in other parts of the Arab world and were not likely to jeopardize these interests for the sake of the vague notion of a Christian Lebanon.

The Middle East oil revolution in 1973–74 also added to social and economic tensions in Lebanon. The case has been argued persuasively that these social and economic gaps were not as wide as had once been believed.[2] But gaps did exist, and they were widened by the influx of oil revenues and by the weakness of the state mechanisms that might have mitigated their impact. The political significance of these gaps was heightened by events in Beirut and in the area of the Israeli border. Only fifty miles separate the border villages from Beirut. People and ideas made that trip in both directions in the early 1970s, as Tawfiq Yusuf Awwad's novel *Death in Beirut* so vividly illustrates: Through the story of a young girl drawn from her small village in southern Lebanon to Beirut, the author sketches a gallery of characters woven into the stories of Lebanese politics and southern Lebanon during these years.[3]

Political life in overpopulated Beirut—a capital much too large for a country as small as Lebanon (as Robert de Caix had predicted)—was affected by the juxtaposition of a new, poor district to affluent districts, by a sharp demarcation between a predominantly Christian (eastern) part of the city and a predominantly Muslim (western) part, and by the presence of Palestinian refugees. Migration to Beirut tended to arouse or intensify sectarian animosities among people used to more homogeneous environments.[4] The nature and patterns of political organization and activity changed among both Muslims and Christians in Beirut. The influx of a large number of Muslims and the radicalization of Beirut's Muslim residents undermined the authority of the traditional political bosses in Beirut's Muslim quarters. Many Muslims shifted their allegiance to newer, more radical parties, movements, and militias. In the 1972 parliamentary elections, Najjah Wakim, a twenty-six-year-old lawyer who ran as a Nasserite, defeated a traditionalist rival. Wakim's victory was indicative of a new mood and a new balance of power among the opponents and critics of the status quo. These trends were matched by the growth of Christian militias, particularly the Phalange, whose role as protector of the Lebanese Christian entity and of a threatened way of life became much more pronounced.

Another change stemmed from Syria's newfound political stability, which was the basis for an ambitious foreign policy, with Lebanon as one of its main targets.[5] Syria had never given up its implicit claim over Lebanon, or at least the parts added to it in September 1920. Still, the weakness of the Syrian state during the first twenty-five years of its independence prevented Syria from exerting effective pressure on Lebanon; the emergence of a comparatively stable and effective regime made such pressure possible. Syria had both political and security concerns in Lebanon. Lebanon, as an open political society, was a threat to the closed political society of Syria. And Lebanon could be used militarily by Israel to outflank Syria's defenses or by Syria to open a new front against Israel.

But Syria's leaders also fitted Lebanon into a larger design, intended to capitalize on Egypt's declining position in the Arab world and to develop an independent power base for Syria that was to rely on its military strength and the extension of Syrian influence over the immediate environment: Jordan, Lebanon, and with the Palestinians. As the PLO's principal base as well as the center for several Arab political parties and movements, Lebanese territory was vital to a regime with Pan-Arab ambitions. Syria also developed a peculiar interest in Lebanon's Shi'i community. This was not merely the single largest community, but one that could have a soothing effect on Syrian domestic politics. The Syrian regime calculated that if Lebanon's Shi'i leaders acknowledged the Alawis as part of the Shi'a sect, it would help Syria's minority Alawi rulers legitimize their rule. This the Lebanese Shi'is did on a number of occasions in the summer of 1973, following the Sunni challenge to the Syrian Ba'thi regime in the winter and spring of that year. Lebanon's Shi'i leader, Musa al-Sadr, not only recognized the Alawis in Lebanon as part of his community but accused Syrian Sunnis of trying to monopolize Islam.[6]

The means employed by Damascus to interfere in Lebanon and to exert pressure on the government were commensurate with the importance attached by the Hafiz al-Asad regime to its Lebanese policy. Syria could mobilize the support of at least some of the Palestinian organizations, its Shi'i community, the pro-Syrian wing of the Lebanese Ba'th party, and Lebanon's half-million Syrian workers. Syria could also resort to such measures as cutting Lebanon off from its commercial hinterland by closing its border with Syria. And, ultimately, Syria could threaten military intervention. The cumulative effect of Syria's presence, pressure, and intervention became visible by 1973. Syria had intervened discreetly in the Lebanese elections in 1972. A year later, Damascus replaced Cairo as the external center of allegiance and guidance for Lebanese Muslims and acquired virtual veto power over major decisions concerning Lebanon's domestic and foreign policies. It became customary for Lebanese politicians to go to Damascus (in the same fashion they used to go to Cairo in the 1960s) and for the Syrian foreign minister, Abdul Halim Khaddam, to go to Beirut to mediate and arbitrate.

Syria's influence accelerated a related development in Lebanon's domestic politics—the political mobilization and radicalization of its Shi'i community. In previous decades the Shi'i community had played an important role in the consolidation of Greater Lebanon. The French government had skillfully exploited Shi'i distrust of Arab nationalism, with its distinct Sunni flavor, and had given the Shi'i community privileges denied by Ottoman and earlier Sunni administrations. In 1926, during the Syrian revolt, the French mandatory authorities recognized formally the separate judicial status of the Shi'i community, thus demonstrating to its leaders the advantages of the Lebanese entity. The Zu'ama of the Shi'a in southern Lebanon and the Beqa (As'ads, Himadehs, and Usayrans) were content with their community's share of power and wealth and did not agitate for the larger share it was entitled to on the basis of its numerical strength. Nor did the Shi'i Mujtahidun (men of religion) challenge either the lay political leaderships' supremacy in the community or the wider political order in Lebanon.

Several developments combined in the late 1960s and early 1970s to transform Shi'i quietism and passivity. In 1967, the Shi'i community was for the first time placed on the same formal footing as the Sunni community, when the parliament approved the formation of the Supreme Islamic Shi'i Council. In 1969, Imam Musa al-Sadr was elected its president, and he immediately set out to fortify his position as leader of the Shi'i community and to improve his community's position in Lebanon.

Sadr's swift rise was not solely a result of his Lebanese experiences. He was born in Iran (to a Lebanese father, who had emigrated to the Shi'i centers in Iran) and was educated in Iran and Iraq. His relationship with the shah's regime and with the regime that toppled it is obscure, but he and his movement must have been influenced by the revolutionary ideas of the Iranian Mujtahidun and other Shi'i activists. Some of the latter, it should be mentioned, found temporary refuge in southern Lebanon in the early 1970s. Sadr's relationship with Hafiz al-Asad's regime in Syria was another asset. Within five years of his election, Sadr had built a powerful movement—the Movement of the Disinherited (Harakat al-mahrumin)—which undermined the traditional Shi'i leadership and articulated and presented the community's main grievances and demands: a larger share of power and more positions in the Lebanese political system, protection of Shi'i border areas, funds and development projects for Shi'i areas, and the remedying of various specific complaints.[7]

Musa Sadr's speeches to Shiʻi mass rallies in the early 1970s offer an interesting blend of demands, threats, and Shiʻa motifs: "This revolution did not die in the fields of Karbala; it flowed into the life stream of the Islamic world and passed from generation to generation, even to our day. It is a deposit placed in our hands so that we may profit from it, that we draw out from it as from a source a new reform. . . . We do not want sentiments, but action . . . from today on I will not keep silent . . . we want our full rights completely. Not only posts, but the twenty written demands in the petition [submitted by the Supreme Islamic Shiʻi Council]. . . . Eighteen million pounds are destined for the improvement of roads. The south has received none of this and the Beqa only one-hundred thousand pounds. O rising generations, if our demands are not met, we will set about taking them by force: if this country is not given, it must be taken."[8]

The complex and delicate mechanisms of the Lebanese polity depended on the leadership and political wisdom of the communal leaders; the political system was ill equipped to deal with the changed mood of the Shiʻi community. The system had functioned through manipulation and intrigue, the eternal tools of the weak, during the presidency of Charles Helou (1964–70). His predecessor, Shihab, never quite relinquished hopes for reelection and sought to perpetuate his influence and to preserve his political camp (the Nahj). Helou, who lacked a political base of his own, sought to maximize the powers of the presidency against the Sunni prime minister. Helou's successor, Faranjiyya, though beginning auspiciously, found it increasingly difficult to get his Muslim partners to cooperate in forming cabinets and maintaining a parliamentary majority, especially after the 1972 parliamentary elections, in which Syria's influence and the rising power of the Lebanese left were apparent. Faranjiyya resorted to a variety of unorthodox measures, such as the nomination of a second-echelon Sunni leader (Amin al-Hafiz) to lead the cabinet, in defiance of the traditional Sunni leadership. But rather than solve the problem, these measures only aggravated frictions within the political establishment and inflamed communal tensions.

Furthermore, the politicians' traditional bickerings over the daily business of government were symptomatic of much graver underlying problems. Their preoccupation with preserving or achieving influence and position evidenced a failure to read the writing on the wall and an incomprehension of the qualitative change that had taken place in Lebanese politics. A show of unity and restraint by Lebanon's traditional politicians may not have stemmed the tide, but its absence compounded the difficulties and added a mournful touch to the course of events that in retrospect is seen as a prelude to the civil war. Older politicians, some of whom had begun their political careers thirty or forty years earlier, were clearly incapable of coping with the most serious threat to the Lebanese system; and yet, in the best tradition of *anciens regimes*, they were powerful enough to block access to others.

The Palestinians

The unsettling effect of the changes mentioned above was magnified by the presence in Lebanon of the chief bases and headquarters of the PLO and most of its constituent organizations.[9] Until 1968, the Lebanese polity viewed the Palestinian problem as essentially one of refugees—some 180,000 of them came to Lebanon during the Arab-Israeli war of 1948–49. Successive Lebanese governments refused to integrate the refugees into Lebanon's own population, both because this was the policy decreed by the Arab consensus and because of Lebanese Christian opposition to such an increase in Lebanon's Muslim population. Although the Palestinians provided most of the membership of the country's radical extraparliamentary opposition movements in the 1950s, the refugees seemed not to be a danger to the foundations of the Lebanese political system. A decade later, however, the Palestine Liberation Movement developed into the first effective autonomous Palestinian national movement since the collapse of the Palestinian Arab community in 1949. It established its headquarters in Beirut and began to construct military and operational bases there and elsewhere in Lebanon. It organized the Palestinian population in the camps and in other centers in Lebanon into autonomous extraterritorial entities. And, with the blessing and support of Egypt and Syria, it launched raids against Israel from southern Lebanon and against Israeli targets outside the Middle East from Beirut.

Egypt and Syria saw the Palestinians as a strategic component in the Arab-Israeli conflict and preferred them operating from Jordan and Lebanon. Jordan had become the PLO's principal territorial base, and the Jordanian-Israeli border and cease-fire lines became an active front during the 1968–70 Arab-Israeli War of Attrition. In the late 1960s, Lebanon's and Jordan's relations with the Palestinians evolved along parallel lines. In Jordan, controlled cooperation between the Hashemite regime and the Palestinians was replaced by virtual Palestinian autonomy, which defied Jordanian sovereignty and threatened the survival of the Jordanian state. In Lebanon, the severity of the PLO challenge to the existing order was revealed in December 1968: Palestinians from Beirut attacked El Al planes, and an Israeli commando unit retaliated by raiding Beirut's international airport.

The raid on Beirut's airport was in line with the thesis underlying most of Israel's retaliatory actions since the early 1950s: that the neighboring Arab states, as sovereign states, were responsible for activities originating in or carried through their territories. In this case, the purpose was to demonstrate to Lebanon the price it would pay for the freedom of operation given to or seized by the Palestinians. But the Israelis should have realized that the Lebanese state was too weak to resist the pressure of PLO supporters. In November 1969, Gamal Abdel Nasser, the leader of Arab nationalism, hosted a meeting of the supreme commander of the Lebanese army and a PLO delegation, and they signed the Cairo Agreement, intended to regulate PLO presence and activities in Lebanon. But only a magic formula could have achieved its stated aims—to preserve both PLO autonomy and Lebanese sovereignty. In reality the Agreement legitimized PLO freedom of action and did little to protect Lebanon's interests.

In 1970, the respective courses of Jordan's and Lebanon's relations with the Palestinians diverged. In September 1970, Jordan's military and political elites decided to stop the corrosion of their state's authority by the Palestinian organization. Taking advantage of the PLO's mistakes and provocations, the Jordanians precipitated a confrontation with the Palestinian organization and drove it out of Jordan. But Lebanon did not have the advantages of a cohesive ruling elite, a strong army, and unambiguous external (American and Israeli) support. Jordan's success, moreover, resulted in greater pressure on Lebanon, as the only base contiguous to Israel now available to the Palestinians. Thus many Palestinians expelled from Jordan moved through Syria to Lebanon.

As events in December 1968 and their sequels show, this new reality was a manifold challenge to the Lebanese state. For one thing, the state's authority and sovereignty were subverted by extraterritorial enclaves and an armed force that, unlike the traditional Lebanese militias, was not integrated into the political system. Second, relations between Christians and Muslims were further exacerbated by their different attitudes to the Palestinian issue: many Muslims regarded the provision of a refuge for the Palestinians as a sacred duty as well as a litmus test for the country's adherence to the National Pact of 1943; but many Christians regarded it as a cynical abuse of Lebanon's weakness by Egypt, Syria, and other Arab states. (Christian opposition, however, refrained in the late 1960s from expressing its opinion explicitly, professing support for the Palestinians, and arguing only that other Arab countries should also allow the Palestinians to operate against Israel from their borders.) Third, the presence and activities of the Palestinian organizations, Marxist ones in particular, reinforced the weak Lebanese left, turning it into a formidable threat to the system. And finally, as southern Lebanon became a Palestinian base and a battleground for Israel and the Palestinians, the region's predominantly Shi'i population began to move northward, further disrupting Beirut's daily and political life. Lebanon enjoyed a brief respite in late 1970 and part of 1971. The Palestinians, weak and discredited, avoided a direct confrontation with the Lebanese government, now headed by Faranjiyya. His tough, conservative policies did not go unnoticed by the Palestinians. But their activities were renewed before 1971 was over.

The Lebanese political elite was aware of the toll exacted by the perpetuation of the status quo, but its members did not believe they could modify it significantly. Any attempt to impose new political conditions was bound to be opposed by the Palestinians, their Lebanese supporters and allies, and probably Syria as well. The conventional wisdom was that even if the Lebanese army could defeat or restrain the Palestinians—not a likely occurrence—the economic and political price for such a victory would be prohibitive. It seemed, therefore, preferable to put up with the gradual, less shocking damage that the Palestinians had been inflicting on the tissue of Lebanese public life since 1968. This view was bolstered by the Lebanese army's abortive attempt in the spring of 1973 to restrain the Palestinian organizations, stimulated by the outburst of PLO violence following the successful Israeli raid on PLO targets and leaders in Beirut. But the Lebanese army's siege of Palestinian bases had to be lifted when Syria closed its border with Lebanon, cutting Lebanon off from its Arab hinterland and thereby serving notice that even more alarming measures might be taken.

A new Lebanese-Palestinian agreement endeavoring to interpret and implement the 1969 Cairo Agreement was negotiated in the Malkert Hotel in Beirut, but it too failed to clarify or improve the situation. Furthermore, the political and diplomatic sequels of the October War—the rise in the PLO's status, the beginning of the Arab-Israeli peace settlement, and the acrimonious inter-Arab bickerings—exacerbated the pressure that the Palestinian problem exerted on Lebanon and hastened the outbreak of the 1975 war.

Four Phases of the War

In the spring of 1975, the Lebanese political system finally collapsed under the persistent pressure of rival internal and external forces. The endless demands and ultimatums, acts of political violence, transgressions against the state's authority and sovereignty, and other manifestations of social and political tensions developed into a civil war that lasted eighteen months. The course of the war can be divided into four distinct phases.

Transition, April to June 1975

An armed clash between radical Palestinians and the Phalange militia in the Beirut quarter of Ayn al-Rumani opened this phase. The fighting between the Phalanges (who were joined later by the militia of the National Liberals) and the Palestinians, who have since been identified mostly as members of the Popular Front for the

43

Liberation of Palestine, continued despite various mediation efforts and cease-fire agreements. The bone of contention seemed to be the Palestinian organizations' freedom of action in Lebanon. The two essentially Christian militias were defending not so much the violated authority of the Lebanese state as the pattern of life in the Christian neighborhoods of Beirut. Their Palestinian rivals were protecting not merely the position and privileges they had seized in recent years but also the political environment that had facilitated their acquisition. Much of the political and diplomatic activity in April was devoted to an attempt to reach a Palestinian-Lebanese modus vivendi based on the Cairo and Malkert agreements. A compromise was announced on April 29, and a joint Lebanese-Palestinian committee was formed to implement it. Its effort turned out to be yet one more abortive attempt to devise a workable Palestinian-Lebanese modus vivendi.

Violent clashes also occurred in Tripoli between supporters of President Faranjiyya and his traditional rival, Rashid Karami, that city's Sunni political leader. Prime Minister Rashid al-Sulh's cabinet was torn by controversy, and he resigned on May 18. The president tried to resolve the crisis by resorting to an unorthodox procedure, nominating as prime minister a reserve officer, Brigadier General Nur al-Din al-Rifai and appointing a cabinet composed of seven other officers and one civilian. It was of no avail, and Faranjiyya had to ask Karami to form a government. On June 30, Karami formed a "government of communal balance," in which he himself held the defense portfolio, while Camille Chamoun became minister of the interior. But by that time the crisis had developed into an all-out civil war.

All-out War, June 1975 to January 1976

By the end of June 1975, Lebanon was in a full-fledged civil war, and the protagonists had crystallized into two broad coalitions. The definition of these two coalitions and the terminology used have become one of the most controversial aspects in the literature dealing with the Lebanese civil war. The coupling of *right wing* with *Christian* and *left wing* with *Muslim*, which characterized much of the doctrinaire and simpleminded writing on the war, has by now been practically discarded.[10] But there remains a tendency and a temptation to define a camp of mostly Christians as *Christian* and one of mostly Muslims as *Muslim*. Such definitions obscure the fact that neither camp was constituted on a truly communal or religious basis and reduce their aims to communal or sectarian ones. Rather, it should be realized that these camps have political aims; the largely Christian camp, a status quo coalition, sought to preserve the traditional Lebanese political system, and the largely Muslim camp, a revisionist coalition, sought to transform or overthrow that system.

Several developments in July and August highlighted the severity of the civil war's new phase. Fighting between various Lebanese factions, but primarily between Christian and Muslim groups, took place in Beirut, Zahle, Tripoli, Akkar, and other localities (see Map 3). Shi'i leader al-Sadr announced the formation of a Shi'i militia, al-Amal (Hope). And on the political front, the Muslims announced that Karami intended to run for the presidency and then demanded a change in the electoral system and the abolition of confessionalism.

In September and October, the fighting continued while "a national dialogue committee" established by Prime Minister Karami tried in vain to reach an agreement on social and political reforms and on the PLO's status in Lebanon. The cabinet, despite its frequent and often acrimonious disagreements, served as another forum for leaders of the two camps to meet. President Faranjiyya and Minister of the Interior Chamoun represented the hard core of the status quo coalition. Prime Minister Karami found himself in an ambivalent position. Although he was an important member of the revisionist coalition which demanded far-reaching reforms in the Lebanese political system, his position like that of other traditional politicians of his generation and standing was being undermined by younger and more radical Muslims. Karami and his coalition escalated their demands, but they were seeking to restructure rather than destroy the Lebanese political system.

One of the sharpest points of contention between Karami and his rival Maronite partners in the government concerned the role of the Lebanese army. Its senior officers were mostly Christian and were close in outlook to the leadership of the status quo coalition. Yet the

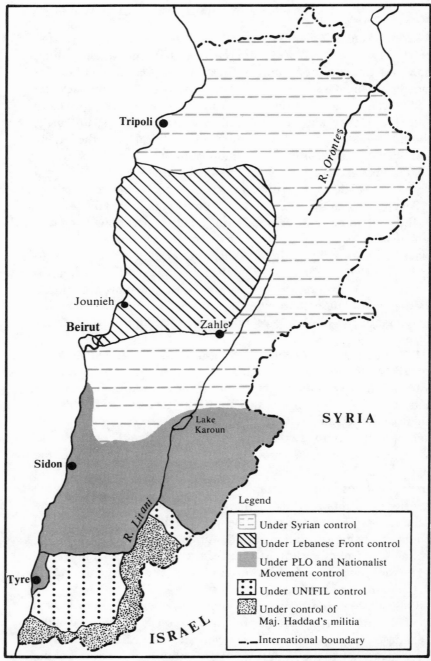

Map 3. Lebanon's virtual partition into areas of control following the 1975–76 civil war.

army did not intervene in the civil war. This was the result not only of a lesson learned in 1958—that a nonpoliticized army could be built—but a realization that the army's intervention on the side of the status quo coalition would split the coalition, would provoke Karami to resign, and would lead to all-out civil war and the probable intervention of the Palestinians and Syria. A compromise formula was tried whereby Faranjiyya and Karami agreed (1) to appoint a new commander-in-chief (General Hanna Said, who was considered less political than his predecessor, (2) to give Karami greater authority over the army, and (3) to allow the Lebanese army a limited military effort to try to bring an end to the fighting. But this was not successful. The army's intervention in September and October did not prevent further intensification of the fighting. The army's protracted passivity in the face of an acute crisis together with political pressure led to the army's disintegration in 1976.

By the end of 1975 a number of political patterns could be picked out in the apparent chaos. Having realized that they could neither end nor win the armed conflict, the leaders of the status quo coalition began to contemplate and then to discuss publicly the notion of partition. This was hardly a status quo position, but rather a return to the idea of a small, predominantly Christian, Lebanon. The Maronite political leadership did not relish such a course of action but raised it as a last resort should the preservation of the Lebanese political system prove utterly impossible. The Maronites' last resort was anathema to Lebanese Muslims, Palestinians, and Syrians, because a compact Christian state in a partitioned and smaller Lebanon was bound to be a "second Israel," a "Maronite Zion," and its establishment was to be opposed with all means. Although the Palestinians were appalled by the possibility of partition, their growing involvement in the fighting on the revisionist side strengthened the Maronites' conviction that the old Lebanon could no longer be sustained. It also helped to bring about a change in Syrian policy.[11]

Until December 1975, Syria's role in the Lebanese crisis and civil war was essentially similar to that of the Palestinians. The Syrian regime had also contributed to the collapse of the traditional order in Lebanon, and thereafter it pursued a policy of extending support to the revisionist elements while occasionally mediating between the warring parties in an effort to prevent a total collapse of the Lebanese political system. But by December that policy was no longer tenable. Asad was determined to prevent both Lebanon's partition and a clear-cut victory by the radical revisionists and their Palestinian supporters. Such a victory would have sandwiched Syria between two radical neighbors, one of whom, Iraq, was a bitter enemy and would, moreover, probably provoke Israeli intervention on the side of the beleaguered Christians. Were such an intervention to take place, Syria would have to choose between two equally unappealing alternatives—to fight Israel or to suffer the humiliation of failing to do so.

To obviate such a choice, Asad decided to intervene militarily in the Lebanese civil war, but his decision also had broader political implications. This was not a conspiracy, which many contributors to the polemical literature on the Lebanese civil war claimed as an explanation of the complexities of Syria's policy in Lebanon and its about-face in 1976. Nor was it then a drive to realize the vision of a Greater Syria centered in Damascus. It was the product of a new Syrian foreign policy devised in the aftermath of and under the impact of the October War. Mention has already been made of Asad's determination to develop an independent power base and of Lebanon's place in that vision. Its new resources—a strong army and influence over Lebanon, Jordan, and the Palestinians—enabled Syria to diversify its foreign policy and, while keeping a close relationship with the Soviet Union, to develop advantageous relations with the United States and the rich oil-producing Arab countries. By intervening in Lebanon and resolving the crisis, Asad would not only end a situation that threatened Syrian interests but would also demonstrate that Syria was the most effective Arab power in that part of the Middle East.[12]

Moreover, the move was acceptable to the United States, which weighed it against the prospect of taking a more active role itself and also against other risks of a worsening crisis. Washington's endorsement was essential for Asad, a ruler capable of bold, not to say reckless, decisions, but who usually took them after lengthy consideration. American acquiescence in Syria's intervention in Lebanon actually meant that the intervention would be supported by Lebanon's Western guarantor. Even more important perhaps was U.S.

mediation between Syria and Israel, which resulted in securing Israel's tacit agreement to Syria's intervention in Lebanon in return for some limitations on the scope of that intervention. The indirect Syrian-Israeli understanding was further elaborated in 1976 and came to be known in Israeli political parlance as "the red line" in Lebanon.

Syrian Intervention, January to May 1976

Syria's military intervention in the Lebanese civil war proved to be one of its most intriguing and consequential aspects. In addition to altering the course of the Lebanese crisis, it had far-reaching repercussions for Syria's domestic politics and for the pattern of Middle Eastern regional politics. Its scope and effect on Syria's relations with the superpowers make it an instructive case study in interventionism. And Syria's conflict with the PLO and the Lebanese left was one of the decade's most significant developments in Arab politics.

Syrian intervention in Lebanon unfolded in six successive stages—the initial intervention and the confusion it created, Syria's actual support for a moderate reform plan, the ensuing conflict with Syria's former allies, their attempted rapprochement, its failure, and the Syrian regime's decision to launch a direct all-out military offensive against its former Lebanese allies.

Syria's participation in the fighting in Lebanon began in the second week of January, when it dispatched units of the Syrian Palestine Liberation Army (PLA), composed of Palestinians theoretically affiliated with the PLO but which for all practical purposes were part and parcel of the Syrian army. The intervention occurred as the fighting grew worse, particularly in Beirut. The warring parties had clearly adapted their respective strategies to the possibility of partition. The Phalanges and their allies besieged Palestinian camps sited in Christian areas in Beirut and destroyed Karantina, a predominantly Muslim quarter, which separated the Christian area just north of Beirut from the port area. The Palestinians, and the revisionist and leftist militias allied with them, captured and devastated the Christian town of Damour, just south of Beirut, which dominated the coastal road to Sidon and Tyre.

At first Syria's involvement was perceived as support of Syria's traditional allies and clients and as designed to obstruct plans for partition. The Syrian regime's newly acquired leverage encouraged it to formulate plans to resolve both the Lebanese domestic conflict and the controversy over the PLO's status in Lebanon. Thus, while the first PLA units to enter Lebanon fought on the side of the revisionist coalition, the Syrians were soon urging a cease-fire (January 21), and on February 7, in a formal joint communiqué with President Faranjiyya, Syria guaranteed the implementation of the Cairo Agreement. It was also announced that the two coalitions had agreed on the broad lines of political reform for Lebanon.

Syria had already, on January 21, published a reform plan for Lebanon. It was apparently well received by Kamal Junblatt, the most prominent leader of the Lebanese left, and subsequently by the Lebanese "Muslim summit," which met at the end of January to decide the Muslim position toward a new national pact. At a comparable Maronite summit, Faranjiyya exerted a moderating influence over his colleagues and was given a mandate to reach an agreement with Syria. This was accomplished on February 7, and on February 14 the Lebanese president released the Reform Document. The document retained Christian supremacy through the presidency but reduced the president's power vis-à-vis the Sunni prime minister and equalized the number of Christian and Muslim deputies in parliament. The confessional system was to be limited (but not entirely abolished), and electoral and socioeconomic reforms were promised. A cryptic promise to amend the citizenship law implied the possibility of profound changes in the future, including possibly the integration of more Palestinians into the Lebanese system.

The reforms were moderate and acceptable to the bulk of the Maronite leadership, with the notable exception of Raymond Eddé, who emerged as the most outspoken Maronite critic of Syria's new role and position in Lebanon. His colleagues, however, viewed the reform plan as a tolerable compromise, judging Syria's influence to be a lesser evil than the other likely alternatives. Syria's own acceptance of the compromise formula was a telling sign of the changes that had prompted the Asad regime's intervention in Lebanon. A Syrian government that had become involved in Lebanon in coordination with the United States could not support, let alone take an active part in, a radical transformation of the Lebanese system. By 1976, the Ba'thi regime, pursuing a domestic policy of economic and political liberalization and seeking cooperation with the rich oil-producing Arab states, had abandoned many of the radical features it still retained after 1970. If the purpose of the Syrian intervention was to preserve a workable Lebanese system, the status quo coalition had to have an important role in it.

Syria already had comfortable, even intimate, working relations with several Maronite leaders. A dialogue had developed between the Syrian Ba'thi regime and the Phalanges, mainly through Karim Pakradouni, a lawyer of Armenian descent. On the Phalangist spectrum, Pakradouni was a prominent member of the moderate wing, which advocated social and economic reforms in Lebanon and a dialogue with the Lebanese Muslim communities, the Palestinians, and the Arab states. The Syrians had an even closer relationship with Faranjiyya, who during his exile in Syria in the 1950s found refuge in the Alawi area, close to the Lebanese border. His and his family's friendship with the Asad family dates back to that period. Later, the friendship between Asad and Faranjiyya, as the respective presidents of Syria and Lebanon, became an important political fact. It was also a curious turn of events in the modern history of the Levant. In the 1920s and 1930s it was often suggested that France, incapable of coming to terms with the Sunni Arab nationalism prevalent in the Syrian interior, ought to base its position in the Levant on a coastal "rampart" or "anvil" of Alawis and Maronites. In the 1970s, the Alawis ruled in Damascus and were trying to develop an alliance with the Maronites, particularly with those in the coastal region contiguous to the Alawi region.[13]

All this did not escape the notice of Syria's traditional friends and allies, who for various reasons became increasingly suspicious and critical of Syrian motives and conduct. The compromise that was acceptable to the defenders of the status quo was rejected by many of their opponents as offering too little to a cause which to them was not only just but also victorious. Syrian arguments that in the long run victory was assured primarily by Syria's presence and new role in Lebanon were to no avail. They rather sharpened the fears of Syria's rivals in the Arab world (notably Iraq), the PLO, and such leaders of the Lebanese left as Kamal Junblatt, that Syria was in Lebanon to stay. Syria's Arab rivals saw this as further self-aggrandizement by a hostile regime. For Palestinians, the danger was still greater. Syria, unlike most of the Arab states, claimed a special position with regard to the Palestinian issue, arguing—meekly at that stage—that Palestine was, after all, a part of southern Syria.[14] Syria's leadership did try in fact to extend its control over the Palestinians as part of Asad's new regional policy. In 1975, a Syrian proposal to unify the PLO's political and military commands was gently but firmly rejected by the Palestinians. Syrian domination of Lebanon, the PLO's only autonomous territorial base, was therefore seen by its leaders as a grave threat to their independence. As for Junblatt, his fear of Syrian domination was reinforced by his strong criticism of the Ba'thi regime's drift away from the ideas and principles of the party and the adoption of what he saw as personal, pragmatic, corrupt, and sectarian policies. In his posthumously published "legacy," Junblatt deals at length with Syria's and Asad's personal policy in the Lebanese crisis. But his criticism extended beyond this. It was the criticism of an Arab leftist, disenchanted with the pragmatism of those Arab regimes that a decade earlier had constituted the progressive or revolutionary Arab camp. "And the truth is," wrote Junblatt, "that we can ask whether all these 'progressive' Arab regimes in the region were genuinely interested in the establishment of democracy and socialism."[15]

The first challenge to Syria's policy came from rebellious Lebanese officers. First a Muslim lieutenant, Ahmed al-Khatib, deserted from the Lebanese army and formed Lebanon's Arab Army. Composed mostly of Lebanese Muslims, Khatib's army broke the January 21 cease-fire. On March 11, Brigadier General Aziz al-Ahdab, the Sunni commander of the Beirut area, announced a coup d'etat, which, he said, was directed primarily against President Faranjiyya, but which was in fact aimed at the latter's Syrian allies. Faranjiyya's political future now became a bitterly contested issue. The revisionist forces were united in demanding his immediate resignation. He refused to resign, especially in circumstances which would have depicted him as the chief culprit in his country's tragedy. He enjoyed the support not only of his Maronite government partners but also of the Syrians, who refused to agree to his departure before the successor of their choice was elected—Elyas Sarkis. Sarkis had been the chief aide to former president Shihab and later the governor of Lebanon's central bank. In 1970, he was the presidential candidate for the Shihabi bloc, but he was defeated by Faranjiyya. In the spring of 1976, he resurfaced as a Maronite politician, trusted and supported by the Syrians.

Syria's disagreements with the Palestinians and the Lebanese left soon degenerated into an uninhibited political and military conflict. Since Asad had intervened in Lebanon not only to avert an imminent worsening of the crisis but also to demonstrate his ability to do so, the collapse of his mediation and settlement threatened to become a humiliating defeat. The American mediation effort by Dean Brown, and Egypt's, Iraq's, and Libya's efforts to obstruct Syrian policy, seemed to underscore that point. And so in March, April, and May, Asad dispatched al-Sa'iqa and PLA units to Lebanon to aid those who accepted his policy—the conservative status quo coalition—against those who rejected it—the Lebanese left and the Palestinians.

The one agreement between Syria and the Palestinians to end the fighting, reached on April 15, failed, and the Ba'thi regime encountered great political difficulties in explaining to Syrian and Arab public opinion how an Arab ideological party, successor to one of the great legacies in the history of the Arab left, could fight on the side of conservative pro-Western militias against the Lebanese left and the PLO. Damascus developed an argument that the Lebanese left (under Junblatt, who was also the leader of the Druze community) was actually pursuing a traditional sectarian policy and that the PLO had arrogated to itself the right to represent the Palestinian cause (of which Syria was no less a custodian) and had become embroiled in Lebanese affairs that should not have concerned an organization dedicated to the liberation of Palestine. The need to justify and legitimize a controversial intervention and a controversial policy in Lebanon induced Asad and his regime to develop and emphasize themes that were either implicit or inconsequential during the early phases of Syria's intervention. Most notable among them was the notion of a Greater Syria. As we saw, Asad's decision to intervene in Lebanon was not made in order to implement that notion. But when the conflict with the Palestinians and the Lebanese left developed, this vision became useful to justify their subjugation. The development of this concept can be traced in Asad's own speeches in 1976 (culminating in the speech of July 20) and in the pronouncements and writings of other spokesmen for his regime. It was given its fullest expression a few months later by a knowledgeable and sympathetic British journalist:

> Asad has been a member in the Ba'th party, dedicated to Arab unity for 30 years. Moreover, the fact that he rules in Damascus, the heartland of Arabism, makes him heir to a remorseless drive to reach out beyond Syria's boundaries. His current unionist campaign is two-pronged. First he sees Syria's two immediate neighbors, Lebanon and Jordan, as a natural extension of its territory, vital to its defence. This three-nation grouping is already a *fait accompli*, although in the low-profile Asad manner, without fanfare. Asad now rules by proxy in Lebanon, while the progressive integration with Jordan is well advanced. If the Palestinians ever recover a West Bank homeland, they will inevitably join the complex.[16]

Syrian Invasion and an All-Arab Settlement, May to October 1976

Unable to impose his will with the limited power of the PLA and al-Sa'iqa units, Asad decided at the end of May to dispatch a powerful Syrian column into Lebanon and put an end to the agonizing dilemma. This was not an easy decision to take, and Asad struggled with it for quite some time. His conclusion did not escape his Soviet allies, who objected to the contemplated invasion both because it would result in a conflict between their local allies and because they interpreted it as a move oriented more toward the United States than toward them. Prime Minister Aleksei Kosygin decided to come to Damascus on June 1, but this only prompted Asad to launch his invasion into Lebanon on May 31 so as to present his visitor with a fait accompli. It was then characteristic of Syria's attitude to the Soviet Union that Asad was ready to jeopardize his relations with Moscow to preserve the sovereignty of his government's decision-making.[17]

The invasion of Lebanon was a military failure. Both in Mount Lebanon and in the urban areas of Beirut, Tripoli, and Sidon, the Palestinians and Lebanese left were able to inflict heavy casualties on the Syrian forces, who were ill prepared for the nature of the terrain and the ferocity of the opposition. An invasion calculated to put a swift end to an embarrassing political situation thus served in fact to aggravate it. The political difficulties inherent in Syria's direct offensive against her Palestinian and Lebanese allies were compounded by the Syrian units' poor performance and ultimate failure.[18] The cooperation between Syria and the Maronite militias was now overt, as the latter took advantage of the failure of the Syrian forces and took the lead in the offensive. Their main effort was directed at the Palestinian refugee camp of Tel al-Za'tar in Beirut, which fell in August after a two months' siege. To the Sunni majority in Syria, this was an intolerable collusion by two minority groups, the Syrian Alawis and the Lebanese Maronites, against oppressed Sunni majorities. So harsh was the criticism of his Lebanese policy in Syria, that Asad had to address it in an atypically direct fashion and in great and revealing detail in the remarkable speech he delivered on July 20.[19]

As long as the fighting continued indecisively, no other Arab state intervened in Lebanon, although a small Arab peacekeeping force eventually arrived, which exercised no influence over the course of events. Small Libyan and Iraqi contingents joined Syria's opponents. Southern Lebanon and the area of the Lebanese-Israeli border were unusually calm, and a direct link was established between the region's isolated population and Israel.

On July 29, yet another attempt to reach a Syrian-Palestinian agreement was made, but it too failed. Subsequently Syria and its Lebanese allies directed their energies to achieving a military victory before September 23, when Sarkis, whose election to the presidency was secured by Syria in May, was to begin his term of office. Damascus launched a second all-out military offensive against Palestinian and leftist strongholds in Mount Lebanon and the coastal areas. The military lessons of Syria's debacle in June were applied, and resistance to the Syrian onslaught was far less effective; in two weeks the opposition was on the verge of total defeat. But rather than consummate its military victory, Syria attended the Six Parties

Summit, convened by Saudi Arabia in Riyad between October 16 and 18 to find a solution to the Lebanese crisis. The Saudis argued that it was time to put an end to a trauma that had shamed and paralyzed the Arab world for such a long time. The 1976 American presidential elections were to take place within a month, and the new administration should be pressured to pursue a settlement of the Arab-Israeli conflict more favorable to the Arabs than Kissinger's step-by-step diplomacy. But to accomplish that, the Arabs should settle their differences and revive the cooperation that had facilitated their achievements in 1973 and 1974. For that purpose, Saudi Arabia and Kuwait invited Syria, Egypt, Lebanon, and the PLO to join them in Riyad.

Asad went to Riyad primarily in response to Saudi Arabian pressure. But he may also have realized that a total humiliation of the PLO by Syria and its Lebanese allies would be unacceptable to Syrian and Arab opinion. He emerged from the Riyad conference and its immediate sequel in Cairo with impressive achievements. The six participants decided (and their decisions were accepted by most of the Arab states) on an immediate cease-fire and a gradual normalization in Lebanon. Arab troops (the Arab Deterrent Force), some thirty thousand strong, composed mainly of Syrian troops, were to maintain peace and order in Lebanon. They would be under the nominal authority of Lebanon's president and would be financed by the oil-producing states. The Cairo Agreement was to be implemented; all armed forces were to return to their pre-April 1975 locations and all heavy weapons put under the control of the Arab Deterrent Force.

Shooting, other acts of violence, and political quarrels continued during the next few weeks, but the all-out fighting of the previous eighteen months came to an end. President Sarkis began to form his administration, and in December Salim al-Huss, the Sunni president of the development bank, formed a cabinet composed of four Christian and four Muslim members. It was defined as a nonpolitical technocrats' cabinet, Foreign Minister Fuad Butrus being the only known politician in its ranks. These beginnings of political normalization and the decline in the level of violence encouraged a gradual return to everyday life and the restoration of services, economic activities, and the infrastructure.

Consequences of the Civil War

A year and a half of civil war and foreign military intervention resulted in a terrible loss of human life (well over ten thousand, according to some estimates), the wounding of many others, and massive physical destruction. The atrocities committed during the war and the conviction that Christian Lebanon was destroyed led many, particularly Christians, to emigrate. The flow of money to support various militias and factions and Lebanon's interaction with Syria's black market had preserved, paradoxically, not only a certain affluence in Lebanon but even a stable rate of exchange for the Lebanese pound. But notwithstanding this paradox and the rapid rate of rehabilitation, Lebanon lost many of its functions as a financial, cultural, and communications center.

Despite many predictions made in the course of the civil war and its immediate aftermath, the Lebanese state and political system were not destroyed; but they were exhausted. The war had turned the state into an almost empty shell. The authority of Lebanon's president, government, parliament, and central bureaucracy was limited to a small part of Beirut. Lebanon's territory was in fact divided among external forces and local baronies. Syria controlled and administered directly large parts of eastern and northern Lebanon; an autonomous Christian entity developed north of Beirut, with its capital in Jounieh; a comparable protostate dominated by the Palestinians and their Lebanese allies existed south of Beirut; in the southernmost part of Lebanon, along the Israeli border, Major Saʿd Haddad and his pro-Israeli militia vied with the PLO and leftist militias for control; in the far north, the Faranjiyya family and the Sunni political bosses and militia leaders maintained their respective fiefs.

Nor did the Lebanese state have the power to impose its authority. The Lebanese army had disintegrated in 1976, and its remnants were divided between pro-Syrian elements and supporters of the Christian militias. All efforts to reconstruct the army led in a vicious circle, characteristic of Lebanon's political life in the postwar period: the army could not be restored without a consensus, this required political normalization, which could not proceed in the absence of an effective and credible state system, which needed the backing of an apolitical, militarily effective army. The course of the civil war and the interaction between rival domestic and external forces set up a balance that prevented both the Lebanese state's transformation and its restoration. It remained an entity in abeyance, one which those same forces, each according to its own outlook, would try either to preserve as an indispensable political framework or to modify.

Yet even greater harm was done to the delicate fabric of the Lebanese political system. The 1958 civil war had been shorter, less violent, and its sectarian component was mitigated by other more urgent issues. Most important, despite the role played by the United States in ending that crisis, the compromise solution in 1958 was an authentically Lebanese formula, based on the prestige of a national leader and national institutions and on a common belief in the merits of the Lebanese system, which the lessons of the crisis had strengthened. These elements were conspicuously absent in 1976. The war was long and brutal, and despite the mixed composition of the two rival coalitions, it had distinct communal and religious dimensions. Religious hatred and fanaticism manifested in the "identity card killings": individuals were kidnapped or arrested at roadblocks and executed if the religion designated on their identity cards was not in accord with their captors'. Christians and Muslims fled isolated and besieged areas to areas where their communities predominated. The sectarian character of the war was accentuated by the fact that many Greek Catholics and some Greek Orthodox Christians came to accept the hegemony of the Maronites and their militias as the effective protectors of a larger Christian community.

The failure to implement any structural reforms, as well as some of the changes brought about by the war, widened the gap between the institutional framework and the reality of Lebanese politics. In both Christian and Muslim communities, power shifted from traditional politicians and factions to new groups, particularly to armed militias and their leaders. Since the early 1970s, and even more so after 1975, a political leader or grouping devoid of military power was irrelevant. The parliamentary elections scheduled for 1976 could not be held that year (or, for that matter, later), so the parliament elected in 1972 was prolonged. This provided the Lebanese state and political system with a legitimate formal institutional framework, but the membership of the 1972 parliament was far from representative of those actually engaged in Lebanese politics at the end of 1976. Lebanon's political life was actually conducted through other channels, many of them not purely Lebanese. The Lebanese system's reliance on a balance of outside forces and its vulnerability to extraneous intervention were noted above as traditional characteristics. The events of 1975–76 altered the external balance and enabled a foreign power, Syria, to acquire an actual hegemony over Lebanon. The United States and Israel both demonstrated their unwillingness to interfere militarily on behalf of Lebanon's Christian communities and acquiesced, the latter more reluctantly than the former, in Syria's intervention. During the Arab summit conferences in October 1976, the Arab leadership came to tolerate and even to finance Syria's new role in Lebanon. As part of the same settlement, the Syrian government had to accept the PLO's political role and continued autonomy in Lebanon. Although the PLO was weakened and discredited by its involvement in a second Arab civil war in six years, it remained a crucial actor in the Lebanese system, one that had to be taken into consideration in any attempt to resolve the Lebanese crisis.

The Syrian and PLO positions in Lebanon stimulated Israel to greater interest and involvement. Syria's implicit recognition of Israeli interests in Lebanon was the quid pro quo for Israel's conditional acceptance of Syria's intervention in Lebanon. Israel provided military aid to the militias of the status quo coalition and developed a relationship—initially humanitarian and subsequently political and military—with the population in the Lebanese-Israeli border area. In the conditions created by the settlement in October 1976—a subtle continuation of the conflict over Lebanon's future and a prominent role for Syria and the PLO—Israel was likely to increase its involvement in order to affect the outcome of the struggle for Lebanon and to limit both Syria's and the PLO's influence. Their triangular conflict was to constitute an important aspect of the Lebanese crisis in the years 1977–82. But before turning to it, a more systematic survey of the Lebanese political scene is called for.

CHAPTER 3

Political Parties and Factions

THIS ANALYSIS OF the domestic Lebanese conflict, which developed into civil war in the summer of 1975, distinguishes the two warring camps as status quo and revisionist. The same distinction provides a useful framework for a closer scrutiny of the parties and factions of these two camps. But it should be noted that about a year later, in the early summer of 1976, Syrian intervention resulted in the formation of a third grouping, Syria's clients and supporters.

The Status Quo Coalition

The status quo coalition relied on the Maronite leaders, for neither the Maronite community as a whole nor all other Christian communities supported its political line. In the summer of 1976, these Maronite leaders formalized and institutionalized their cooperation by establishing the Lebanese Front.[1] The dominant political groups within the Maronite community, deriving from traditional outlooks and reflecting responses to the latest crisis, fall into five categories.

Parties with Christian-Maronite orientation and their affiliated militias were the backbone of the Maronite community's political and military power. They included the Phalanges, headed by Pierre Jumayyil, Camille Chamoun's National Liberals, and Suleiman Faranjiyya's political clientele. In each of these groups, prominent roles were played by the leaders' sons (Bashir and Amin Jumayyil, Dany and Dori Chamoun, Tony Faranjiyya), which accentuated their traditionalist image. Despite their different policies and personal interests, the three groups and their leaders acted with relative harmony during the height of the crisis. In the late summer of 1976, when military victory seemed certain and the president elect, Sarkis, was about to begin his term, signs of friction and renewed competition appeared.

The other four categories were the Maronite religious establishment; recently formed communal Maronite groups; Christian leadership in the army; and accommodationist Christian leaders, of whom Sarkis was the most prominent.

The Phalange

The Phalanges Libanaises (Kataib) was clearly the single most important actor among Lebanon's Christians in the events leading to the crisis.[2] The party was established by Pierre Jumayyil in the mid-1930s as a radical, vigilante youth movement in defense of the Lebanese entity. As its name suggests, the movement's original ideology and structure were influenced by the ultranationalist and fascist models of the decade. But other elements proved more durable and important in the party's and Jumayyil's later career. Jumayyil, a pharmacist by profession, came from Bikfayya, a small town in the Northern Metn section of Mount Lebanon, just outside and above Beirut. The location is significant; although they were Maronites of the mountain, the residents of Bikfayya lived close enough to the more cosmopolitan atmosphere of the city to feel its influence. Jumayyil was the scion of an important local family (hence the title Sheikh). The militant Maronite populism of Mount Lebanon was a crucial element in the party's make-up, but it was mitigated by the more complex views of the Lebanese entity emanating from Beirut and by Jumayyil's political pragmatism. In the early years, when the Phalanges took to the streets against the Parti Populaire Syrien (PPS) and the Muslim foes of Christian Lebanon, the party was also anxious to establish good connections with the president of the republic and to ensure its place in the mainstream of Lebanese politics.

For more than forty years the erect and impressive figure of Pierre Jumayyil has dominated the party he has led. During this long period he has persisted in his original purpose and mission but has been remarkably flexible in adapting the party to the changing circumstances. In the early 1950s, the Phalange became a parliamentary party and a participant in the traditional game of Lebanese politics. But, the party retained its militia and constructed an elaborate party hierarchy and bureaucracy that set it apart from most other Lebanese parties. A similar tactical flexibility was apparent in the party's doctrinal and political line, in the development of which Maurice Jumayyil, Pierre's cousin, apparently played an important role. The line advocated a Lebanonism that would transcend Christian-Muslim rivalries and social and economic reforms and recruited non-Christian and non-Maronite members. Yet the Phalange remained an essentially Maronite party, and the Lebanese entity it envisaged was in reality Christian. Political expediency required that this issue remain latent but in times of crisis, when Lebanon's future was to be decided, the ambivalence would be set aside and the historical role as the armed protector of a Christian Lebanon, haven and fortress in the midst of a hostile Muslim environment, assumed once more.

In the 1958 civil war, the Phalange fought on the side of President Camille Chamoun and later did not shy away from a showdown with his successor, Fu'ád Shihab, when it seemed that the latter had deviated from the compromise formula that ended the crisis. But during the rest of Shihab's presidency, he enjoyed the party's support and cooperation. The similarity of outlook was reinforced by the Phalange drive for a share in power and political influence. An interesting light on the Phalangist evolution after 1958 is shed by an anthropological study of Shiyah, a Beirut suburb, where many Maronite immigrants from the Mountain settled. Their new role in the central government helped the Phalanges change their image from that of tough boys to that of reasonable men, mature enough to be entrusted with serious and delicate national affairs. Locally, the Phalange introduced new standards of political organization and a new system of political values. They challenged the traditional family-oriented political structure and sought to replace it with a modern, bureaucratic, and (Maronite) community-oriented organization. Thus one Phalangist official told an interviewer that

We decided to run for the municipal elections of 1964 neither to defeat an opponent nor to score a petty victory; rather we wanted to change the mentality of the people here. . . . They see that the country is torn by serious crises that may threaten its very existence while they are busy dishonoring one another. . . .[3]

If the Phalangist cooperation with President Shihab and Pierre Jumayyil's quests for the presidency in the 1960s portray the Phalange as devoted to the pursuit of power and influence, the crises of the early 1970s show it in its original vigilante role. As the Lebanese state, army, and political system seemed increasingly incapable of dealing with the challenges posed by the Palestine Liberation Organization and domestic opposition groups, the Phalange became, in the words of a sympathetic and perceptive observer, "the super-vigilantes . . . builder, surrogate and defender of the state." While some party ideologues continued to plan the reforms deemed vital for the preservation of the Lebanese political system, others were planning in great detail the defenses of fortress Lebanon—that part of Mount Lebanon and the coastal plain in which the Lebanese Christian entity could be upheld. Phalange conduct in the early 1970s, particularly after the army's abortive effort to check the PLO in May 1973, mirrored the party's split personality. It continued to participate in Lebanese politics, took part in the governing coalition, and maneuvered for the presidency in 1976. But it also began to prepare militarily for a clash with the Palestinians, which by then seemed to be unavoidable. It was indeed a skirmish between the Phalange and radical Palestinians that marked the beginning of the civil war. The Phalangist militia recruited and trained new members and acquired additional and heavier weapons, which enabled it to bear the brunt of the fighting on behalf of the status quo coalition in the spring and summer of 1975.

In the course of the civil war, the Phalange had to make two crucial decisions, radical departures from the traditional party line. In the late summer of 1975, when it appeared that the preservation of Christian hegemony and of the traditional political system in Greater Lebanon was no longer feasible, the party, or at least its radical wing, opted temporarily for the less desirable goal fore-shadowed in the early 1970s—a smaller Christian Lebanon based in East Beirut, the northern part of Mount Lebanon, and the coastal area north of Beirut. The temporary change in the party's goal was reflected in an interesting pamphlet, published by the Maronite intellectual center in Kaslik, under the title *Greater Lebanon—A Half Century's Tragedy*.[4] As the title suggests, the pamphlet expressed disenchantment with the experience of a pluralistic Greater Lebanon and recommended a retreat to the homogeneity, security, and comfort of a smaller Christian Lebanon. The Phalanges thus became temporary successors to the philosophy represented in the 1930s and 1940s by Emile Eddé.

The other change concerned the party's attitude toward Syria's intervention in Lebanon. The Phalange took a position between Faranjiyya's eager cooperation with the Syrian Ba'thi regime and Chamoun's deep-seated distrust and hostility. Phalangist willingness to acknowledge Syria's supremacy and to cooperate with its regime against common rivals was a radical departure from tradition for a party that began its career as a staunch defender of Lebanon's territorial integrity against those who sought to submerge Lebanon in a Greater Syria, but the Phalanges did not lose sight of the precarious and temporary nature of their new and strange alliance with Syria. Syrian and Phalangist visions of Lebanon's long-term future were incompatible, and the Phalanges were prepared for the inevitable parting of the ways. In anticipation of that future situation, and indeed as added security in the present one, alternatives such as the Israeli connection were explored.

There was no unanimity on these matters among the Phalanges. In the years preceding the outbreak of the civil war, three distinct orientations crystallized in the party's hierarchy: a conservative one, which upheld the party's traditional line on domestic and external affairs; a reformist one, which hardly resembled the stereotypic Phalangist outlook; and the inevitable middle-of-the-road outlook. Pierre Jumayyil himself stood above these divisions, an appropriate position for such a historic leader and one befitting his own pragmatism. But his two sons came to be identified with the two extreme attitudes, which hardened during and after the civil war. The school of thought represented by Jumayyil's elder son, Amin, (and by Karim Pakradouni) believed that Lebanon's Christians could only survive by coming to terms with their environment, and it therefore sought an accommodation with Syria, with Lebanon's Muslims, and with the larger Arab world. The other school of thought was exemplified by Amin's younger and more assertive brother, Bashir, who in the summer of 1976 became commander of the party's armed forces. This school, skeptical of Arab and Muslim willingness to tolerate a Lebanese Christian entity in their midst, believed in the need to develop that entity's resources—an alliance with Israel, mobilization of the Lebanese Christian diaspora, and American support. But in 1976, a period of satisfactory Syrian-Phalangist cooperation, and in view of American and Israeli reluctance to become more involved, the differences in outlook remained obscure.

The National Liberal Party

The Phalanges' principal ally in the Lebanese Front, Camille Chamoun's National Liberal Party and its Tigers militia (Numūr), was a markedly dissimilar political formation.[5] A small party organized around the person and personality of its leader, it lacked the coherent doctrine, elaborate structure, and large membership of its senior partner. There were significant differences in the members attracted to the two parties. Since the 1930s, the Phalange had appealed mostly to the Maronite lower and middle classes, for whom it was not only a protector of the community and Lebanon's Christians, but also a movement, responding to the social and economic dislocations of the time. The National Liberals, apart from representing Chamoun's constituency in the Shuf region, in Mount Lebanon to the south and east of Beirut, attracted a more patrician, and obviously smaller, group of members and supporters. (The name Tigers does not, it must be admitted, evoke particularly patrician associations.)

Chamoun, an unusually elegant figure and the consummate pragmatic politician, first made his mark on the Lebanese political scene during the final years of the French mandate, as a promising, open-minded politician of the Bishara al-Khuri school, who sought an accommodation with Lebanon's Muslims and their coreligionists across its borders. His preferred version of Arab nationalism was the conservative Hashemite brand, and he kept a close relationship with the Hashemite regimes in Iraq and Jordan. In 1952, Chamoun played a dominant role in terminating Khuri's corrupt administration and was elected his successor. Within five years, he had become a controversial figure in domestic politics, a bitter opponent and critic of Pan-Arab nationalism, and the only Arab ruler who accepted the Eisenhower doctrine. This transition is well-illustrated by the differences between his first two books of memoirs, *The Phases of Independence*, published in Arabic in the 1940s, and *Crise au Moyen Orient*, published in French, in which he presents his interpretation of the 1958 crisis.

Chamoun remained active in Lebanese politics after his presidential term, but his successor, Shihab, and the latter's supporters sought to ostracize him for his excessively pro-Western and anti-Arab nationalist position and for violating the rules of the Lebanese political game. Chamoun's chief castigator was Kamal Junblatt, whose bitter hostility was nourished by ideological differences, personal antipathy, and a long-standing competition for the votes of the Shuf constituency. Chamoun's influence increased with Shihab's departure and Helou's accession to the presidency in 1964. His cooperation with the Phalange and Raymond Eddé's National Bloc in the 1968 parliamentary elections resulted in a strengthening of the Maronite representation in parliament and subsequently in Faranjiyya's election to the presidency. Chamoun's position was accordingly enhanced, but Junblatt was still able to obstruct his full rehabilitation by vetoing his party's participation in government coalitions. Only in June 1975, well into the civil war, was Chamoun given a cabinet portfolio. As minister of the interior, he was Faranjiyya's strongest supporter in the government during most of the war, which he spent in the Ba'abda presidential palace and not in the Ministry of Interior. His role in the war was many-sided: a central figure in the government, a chief protagonist in the conflict, he was also the leader of his party[6] and of the militia it had to build in order to remain an influential political force. The militia was in fact led by his two sons.

The Suleiman Faranjiyya Camp

Suleiman Faranjiyya's pre–civil war presidency discloses the main components of his political makeup—a traditional Za'im relying on his family's and his own following in the Zugharta region, a willingness to resort to violent and unorthodox methods to protect his own and his community's position, a long-standing rivalry with the Sunni politicians from Tripoli, and a recent but significant rela-

66

tionship with Syria's President Hafiz al-Asad and his family.[7] Once the civil war broke out, Faranjiyya's ability to use his position as president to influence the course of events was severely curtailed. He was more active through the status quo coalition and his family's militia, the Zugharta Liberation Army. The militia was formed in 1969, during one of the early conflicts with the Palestinian organizations. (Like his two senior Maronite colleagues, Faranjiyya groomed his son, Tony, to be his political heir. Tony Faranjiyya, who had previously looked after the family's economic interests, was elected to parliament and held cabinet portfolios in the early 1970s. During the civil war, he led the family militia, which had a distinct regional orientation and was engaged mostly in fighting Tripoli's Muslim militias.)

Faranjiyya's personality and conduct became a focal point in the crisis in February 1976, when rebellious army officers and other opponents of the status quo made their demand for his resignation one of their main grievances. The president was saved from the humiliation and repercussions of such a forced resignation not so much by his Maronite colleagues as by his Syrian allies. The military intervention by units of al-Sa'iqa, the pro-Syrian Palestinian organization, to counter Ahmed al-Khatib's attempt to force Faranjiyya's resignation was, in fact, the first unmistakable indication of Syria's about-face in Lebanon. The growing Syrian political and military presence in Lebanon and Asad's efforts to form a distinctively pro-Syrian political bloc led to a still closer cooperation with Faranjiyya during the final months of his presidency, as well as upon his return to Zugharta.

The personalized style of Syria's relationship with the Faranjiyyas was accentuated by the special nexus between Rifat, Hafiz al-Asad's younger brother, and Tony Faranjiyya. They were friends and also partners in the commercial enterprises that were an important aspect of Rifat's activity in Lebanon. Rifat al-Asad was commander of the Defense Detachments, a military formation designed to protect the Syrian regime, which developed into a full-fledged army division with special privileges and something of the status of a Praetorian Guard. His role in the Ba'thi regime has gone beyond his unorthodox military position; he also helped formulate and execute Syrian policy in Lebanon. Rifat al-Asad's activities contributed substantially to domestic criticism of the Ba'thi regime, which proved to be a very significant by-product of Syria's intervention in Lebanon.[8]

The Maronite Religious Establishment

The political saliency of the Sunni Mufti and Shi'i Imam, a novelty of the 1970s Lebanon, was matched by the conspicuous role that Maronite clerics came to play at the other end of the political spectrum. This was less true of the Maronite patriarch, Bulus Khureysh. His three predecessors, Huwayyek, Arida, and Ma'ushi, had been active and influential in Lebanese politics, usually in a discreet fashion, but occasionally as visible and forceful participants. Khureysh, a humbler figure, had not acquired the same position and had not been very active in Lebanese politics before the crisis. His limited political activities and pronouncements after the outbreak of the civil war disclosed a moderate line, close to that of Raymond Eddé.

It was Father Sharbal Qassis, head of the order of Maronite monks and chairman of the Association of Lebanese Monastic Orders, who took the activist and militant line within the Maronite church. He advocated a "pure Lebanon" and rejected the notion of Lebanon's "Arab face," which had been incorporated into the compromise formula of the 1943 National Pact. Qassis was also more outspoken than other Maronites in voicing his opposition to the Palestinians and demanded, among other things, that their numbers in Lebanon be restricted. Quite naturally the Maronite lay leaders preferred Sharbal Qassis to the patriarch and his circle. Qassis was chosen to represent the church in such all-Maronite forums as the Maronite summit (December 1975) and the Lebanese Front. The Maronite monastic orders were the main intellectual and financial contributors to the Maronite academic and intellectual center in Kaslik. As the owners of a sizable portion of Lebanon's agricultural land, the monastic orders provided financial help to Maronite militias.

The line he took and the activities he pursued made Qassis a controversial figure. His critics charged that despite his professed allegiance to the patriarch, he was making "cracks in the unity of the church" and that by storing weapons, ammunition, and food for Christian militias in Maronite monasteries he was undermining their sanctity.[9] Qassis was later replaced as head of the monastic orders in the Lebanese Front by Father Bulus Naʿaman, another powerful, militant cleric.

Communal Maronite Groups

The long-standing and semi-Maronite groupings surveyed above were augmented in the course of the crisis by new groups and forums that sprang up in response to it. The Maronite League was a militant militia headed by Shaker Abu Suleiman, an ardent supporter of Qassis. Like the Guardians of the Cedar, it was a purely Maronite militia without the inhibitions of the politically sophisticated Phalanges and National Liberals. It therefore chose to fight alongside these groups rather than to merge with them.

Even more than the Phalanges, the Guardians of the Cedar manifest the tension between the notion of a supracommunal movement to defend a supracommunal Lebanese entity and the reality that the movement's membership has been largely Maronite. Furthermore, although they advocated a nonconfessional ideology, the Guardians have in practice been among the fiercest fighters for the Maronite cause. The political and military leader of the Guardians of the Cedar, Etienne Saqr (nicknamed Abu Arz), worked for the Faranjiyya administration in the early 1970s. But ideologically, the Guardians were inspired by the poet Saʿid ʿAql. ʿAql inherited from Michel Chiha the notions of Phoenicianism and Al-isha ʿāʾ al-lubnani (the Lebanese illumination), which Chiha devised as the ideological underpinning of the Lebanese entity. But unlike Chiha, ʿAql sought to draw a clear distinction between Lebanonism and Arabism. ʿAql's conception of Lebanon, originating in and inspired by a remote Phoenician past, and contributing to the development of civilization, minimizes the role of Islam and Arabism. A poet of note in the Arabic language, he developed a version of the Latin alphabet more suited in his view to render the language he and his circle called Lebanese. ʿAql's doctrines are related to other concepts of territorial nationalism that appeared in the Middle East in the interwar period and that were later discredited by the allure of Pan-Arab nationalism.

Although there were non-Maronite and non-Christian members in its ranks, the militia of the Guardians of the Cedar functioned in the predominantly Maronite quarter of Ashrafiyya and represented the most militant brand of Maronite political opinion. They were, among other things, atypically frank about the Maronites' relationship with Israel. While the Phalanges and the National Liberals sought to conceal their relations with Israel and avoided public discussion of them, the Guardians of the Cedar argued publicly in 1976 that should Syria's intervention fail, the Lebanese should turn to Israel to ask it to save what was left of Lebanon. Like the Maronite League, they maintained their separate organization but fought alongside the larger militias.

The Tanzim was a small secretive organization formed and led by George Adwan, which appeared soon after the outbreak of the civil war in April 1975. Adwan and his colleagues rapidly concluded that the severity of the crisis called for a new kind of Maronite effort and organization—hence the name Tanzim (organization). Despite their small number, the members of the Tanzim played an important role in the fighting in Beirut. Their numbers dwindled later in the 1970s, and the organization split in two, but it retained its position as one of the four partners in the Lebanese Front.

The Lebanese Front

In December 1975, when major changes in the Lebanese system were being discussed seriously and a Muslim summit was convened to formulate a joint position, a comparable Maronite summit was called. The major Maronite leaders of the status quo coalition—Jumayyil, Chamoun, Qassis, and Shaker Abu Suleiman among them—met in the Ba'abda presidential palace. Faranjiyya himself did not participate in the meetings, though he was briefed on their course and outcome, but the use of the presidential palace for partisan meetings was added to his opponents' list of grievances. The purpose of the meeting was not only to coordinate policies but to form a more unified leadership. The assembled Maronite leaders had no difficulty in defining the crisis as a Palestinian-Lebanese conflict rather than a civil war. The Palestinians, they charged, had joined forces with the Lebanese left in order to provoke a sectarian crisis in Lebanon.

In the spring of 1976, the Maronite summit was renamed the Kafur summit after the new location chosen for the meetings. In September 1976, the unification efforts met with a measure of success when the Lebanese Front was established. Camille Chamoun was chosen president of the Front. Its leadership included Pierre and Bashir Jumayyil, Bulus Na'aman, Edward Hunayin (who had previously worked with Raymond Eddé), and two noted Christian intellectuals, Charles Malik and Fu'ad Ephrem al-Boustani. It became the political backbone of the status quo coalition. A joint military command was formed for the various militias, whose new collective name was the Lebanese Forces. The Lebanese Forces were made up of four militias, the Phalanges, Chamoun's Numūr, the Guardians of the Cedar, and the Tanzim. Each was represented in the Forces' command by two members. Despite the nominal parity, it was clear that the Lebanese Forces were dominated and controlled by Bashir Jumayyil. Still, the formation of an apparently nonpartisan, all-Maronite forum proved very useful for the further development of the status quo coalition.

The Army's Christian Leadership

The Christian leadership within the army can be considered an important component of the status quo coalition. The Lebanese army's refusal to take sides during the crises of 1952 and 1958 was a rare phenomenon in the post-World War II Middle East, where political history has been largely shaped by military intervention and domination. But the Lebanese army did play a role in and was certainly the object of political conflicts prior to 1975.[10] For one thing the confessional system operated in it and communal balance was carefully monitored. The higher echelon of the professional officer corps was predominantly Christian, and the army was seen as one of the ultimate guarantors of both the Lebanese political system and its Christian character. In the 1950s and 1960s, Muslim politicians repeatedly demanded a national service law that would transform the army into a predominantly Muslim force, but it was essentially a political ritual. Of greater political significance was the discrepancy between the army's contrived image as an arbiter, standing above petty partisan squabbles, and its actual activity, both within the formal political system and as an alternative system of power and influence. The issue was first brought to the surface by Raymond Eddé in the mid-1960s; it was publicized in great and vivid detail when President Charles Helou purged the *deuxième bureau* and when the army's supreme commander, General Emile Bustani, fled to Syria in 1972.

Other political developments and events in the late 1960s and early 1970s—growing Muslim pressure to modify the system, confrontations with the Palestinians, Israeli preemptive and punitive raids, and the proliferation of armed militias defiant of the state—had an unsettling effect on the Lebanese army. Its officers still viewed the army as the arbiter of national politics, whose intervention could resolve the impending crisis. The supporters of the status quo were less certain, and after 1973 the Phalange began to build its own military force to perform the task the army seemed incapable of. The army played a very limited role during the early period of the civil war, and by the time it became vital for it to step in, the army had disintegrated, and its self-designated role was taken over by the Syrian army.

In the summer of 1976, the Lebanese army was divided into three distinct groups: Ahmed al-Khatib's rebellious Lebanese Arab Army, which was integrated into the leftist anti-Syrian militias; the vanguards of Lebanon's Arab Army, a thinly disguised pro-Syrian military force, organized in the Beqa Valley; and the bulk of the army, which was positioned in Beirut and the center of the country. The officers in these units were mostly Christian, and their sympathies were with the Lebanese Front. The competition for their support and loyalty figured in the next phase of the Lebanese crisis.

Accommodationist Christian Leaders

Somewhere between the status quo and revisionist coalitions there stood another group. The moderate Christian politicians and public figures who sought an accommodation with the opponents of the status quo were far from possessing the coherence of an actual political school or bloc. Much more moderate than the three senior Maronite politicians, these leaders were willing to concede a large share of power in the Lebanese system to the Muslim communities and to find a modus vivendi with the Palestinians in order to preserve the framework of a Lebanese state. They strongly opposed the notion of partition. In the spring of 1975, Elyas Sarkis, the former Shihabi politician, emerged as the most prominent representative of the accommodationists. Until then that role had been played by Raymond Eddé, the son of the former president. In an interesting shift of political legacies, the Phalange adopted, albeit temporarily, the traditional line of Emile Eddé, while his son pursued a policy close to that of his father's great rival, Bishara al-Khuri.

Raymond Eddé made his mark on Lebanese politics as an opponent of President Shihab and a vehement critic of the army's and intelligence services' interference in the political process.[11] Their common opposition to the keepers of the Shihabi legacy facilitated the cooperation in 1968 between Eddé's National Bloc and the two other large Maronite parties. But the new alignment soon foundered owing to political and personal differences, particularly Eddé's and Jumayyil's rival bids for the presidency in 1970. During Faranjiyya's presidency, Eddé drew closer to such traditional Sunni politicians as Sa'ib Salam and Rashid Karami, as well as to Kamal Junblatt, so that Eddé and his former partner drifted further apart.

Eddé's initial role in the civil war conformed to the policies he had formed in the early 1970s. He did not take part in the fighting but advocated compromise and moderation. He was particularly opposed to partition, which he denounced as an American Zionism design. In 1976, Eddé became the most prominent and persistent opponent among Lebanon's Christian politicians of Syria's intervention and ensuing supremacy. In May, he tried to compete with Sarkis, the Syrians' candidate, for the presidency, but he had no resources to counter the great resources of the Syrians. In the summer of 1976, he formed the National Unity Front, which agitated for Syria's withdrawal from Lebanon. The Front had an auspicious beginning, because apparently Eddé's Sunni friends had joined it. This suggested the formation of a middle-of-the-road coalition, a serious competition to the existing rival camps. But in the end, the

Front was little more than a platform for its founder. After Syria's presence in Lebanon had been sanctioned by the Arab consensus and following a number of assassination attempts against him, Eddé, like several other prominent opponents of Syrian hegemony, left Lebanon and settled in Paris.

It was ironic that Sarkis, a politician closely identified with the Shihabi search for a new Lebanese consensus, became president in circumstances that defined him as the representative of a narrow and controversial segment of the 1976 Lebanese political spectrum. Many of the erstwhile supporters of the Shihabi Nahj were active and bitter opponents of Syrian policies in Lebanon and refused to cooperate with a president imposed on Lebanon by the Syrians. The Lebanese Front was then cooperating with Syria, but in reality it could not reconcile itself to Syria's long-range plans for Lebanon and was wary of Sarkis, a veteran opponent of the Front's leaders and attitudes. Upon assuming office, President Sarkis did try to work for national reconciliation. He presented a plan for Lebanon's political and economic rehabilitation and sought to bring the rival Lebanese factions to a "round table conference." This may have been an altogether impossible task and it obviously was beyond the reach of the controversial president of an emasculated state. Nor was he helped by his patrons the Syrians, who having first delegitimized him by treating him as their instrument, continued to undermine his position by scrutinizing his cabinet and allowing him minimal freedom of action.

The Revisionist Coalition

This coalition was large and heterogeneous. It sought, most of the time in vain, to coordinate the efforts of many political groups and figures. Most of the fighting on behalf of this camp was carried out by Palestinian organizations and Muslim and leftist militias. Among the Palestinians, the rejectionist organizations had fought from the outset and without much ambivalence. Until January 1976, the leadership of the Palestine Liberation Organization had formally refrained from taking part in the war, but groups under its authority did join the fighting in earlier stages. Palestinian formations under

74

Syrian control participated in the war on both sides. In January 1976, the revisionist camp was reinforced by Khatib's forces. These were decimated by the fighting into a small force, which at the end of 1976 was located in southern Lebanon. Most of the traditional Muslim politicians failed to take part in the fighting, partly because of their ambivalent attitude but mostly because of their inability to create their own militias.

Within the revisionist coalition five major categories can be discerned: veteran leftist and opposition parties; organizations and militias formed on the eve of or in the course of the crisis; traditional Zu'ama and the Sunni establishment; the militant Shi'i leadership; and the Palestinian organizations.

Syria's intervention in 1976 contributed most to splitting the revisionist coalition. Its two most substantial elements, the leftist parties and the Palestine Liberation Organization, reacted differently to Syria's role and policies. The PLO leadership was free of the doctrinaire fervor and personal animosity that characterized Kamal Junblatt's attitude and at various times showed a desire to come to terms with Syria. Later, some of the coalition's supporters shifted their allegiance to Syria and became a rather weak third, or central, camp. A proliferation of other organizations, mostly ephemeral, also followed the revisionist split: Raymond Eddé's National Unity Front; the National Islamic Front, formed in the summer of 1976 by Khatib's supporters (who claimed it was above the conventional left and right); the revolutionary Druze Organization, which rallied some of Junblatt's opponents within his own community; and the Shi'i Revolutionary Organization.

In an effort to arrest the disintegration and to counterbalance the formation of the Lebanese Front, the Lebanese left sought to bolster the leftist National Front, which had existed since 1969. A supreme political council and a joint military command were established, as well as supportive "fronts"—a Front of Patriotic Christians and the Arab Shi'i Front, both defining themselves as leftist organizations.

Kamal Junblatt and His Party

Kamal Junblatt was indubitably the dominant leader of the established leftist groups, and his ascetic figure is one of the central and most intriguing personas in the history of the Lebanese crisis and civil war. Junblatt was the founder and leader of a genuine leftist party, the Progressive Socialist Party, but his influence derived from other sources: the support of the Druze community for its traditional leading family; his power base in the Shuf region; his personality; and his role as a leftist leader of national and regional stature.

Junblatt's long political career in and his crucial impact on Lebanese politics were marked by several incongruities and apparent inconsistencies, leading many observers to consider him either cynical or enigmatic. Junblatt was indeed a moody man, and he did form and lead a leftist party while remaining a large landlord and a prominent sectarian leader. But there was a fundamental consistency in his political career. He was genuinely hostile to the confessional system, which precluded him from achieving the highest office. In that respect, he was a true successor to his Junblatt ancestors, who had fought the Maronite Shihabi amirs, the heads of Lebanon's semifeudal hierarchy, whom they could hope to defeat but not to replace. And he was too astute to renounce positions that gave him influence in Lebanese politics. An examination of Junblatt's career from the early 1950s to his assassination in March 1977 reveals his persistent striving for political reform and the enhancement of his personal standing and the left's position in Lebanon.

His effectiveness increased as the system grew weaker. In 1969, he formed the National Front to provide leftist and Palestinian organizations with a common framework. In 1970, as minister of the interior, he published a decree legalizing the Ba'th, the Communist, the Syrian Nationalist, and other transnational parties. These parties, although illegal under previous Lebanese law, had been tolerated in practice; Junblatt's action was therefore largely (though not entirely) of symbolic significance. In the same vein, Junblatt lost or forsook the working relations he had with Pierre Jumayyil and other status quo politicians, and his political activities pivoted more and more around his relations with other leftist and Palestinian groups.

Junblatt's major demands for a reform of the Lebanese system were presented in a document published by Lebanon's leftist parties in the summer of 1975. They were (a) the abolition of the confessional system; (b) a constitutional amendment that would change the relationships among the branches of government; (c) a new electoral law; (d) the reorganization of the army; and (e) an amendment of the citizenship law. These demands, which constituted in fact the platform of the Lebanese revisionists, were strictly political and constitutional and made no mention of social and economic reforms. But even so, defenders of the status quo rejected them as tantamount to an outright abolition of the Lebanese system. Opponents from both ends of the spectrum tried to denigrate Junblatt's program, pointing to its limited scope and arguing that it was actually designed to enable him to gain the presidency.

The reform document of February 1976, which Syria endorsed and tried to implement, bore a superficial resemblance to Junblatt's demands, but he was right in claiming that it introduced only a moderate change in the political system. In his political testament, he explained that "[The Syrians] minoritarian military dictatorship made them hostile to any democracy. The 'presidential letter' on which President Faranjiyya and the Syrian foreign minister agreed sought to impose on us an illegal, distorted constitution and a caricature of a parliamentary democracy. We therefore rejected this pseudoconstitutional letter, which Faranjiyya (being ignorant in constitutional matters) announced on February 14."[12]

Junblatt's rejection of the Syrian reform plan and his refusal to comply with Syria's ambitions and to resign himself to the Ba'thi regime's pragmatism led to a bitter conflict. Junblatt could not win. He was defeated militarily by Syria and politically by an Arab world that recognized Syria's supremacy in Lebanon. In March 1977, he was assassinated. Junblatt's importance in the conflict with Syria was political rather than military. His militia had a limited local significance, and the firepower of his camp was provided by the Palestinians and by other Lebanese militias. But Junblatt's personality and leadership were indispensable to the preservation of a united anti-Syrian front, as the effect of his assassination showed.

It is now widely believed in Lebanon that Junblatt's assassins were inspired if not dispatched by the Syrian authorities. So it is sadly ironic that his followers' immediate response to the assassination was an attack on Maronite villagers in the Shuf. In a moment of tragedy, the old conflict with the Maronites was more enduring than a feud with Syria.

The Syrian regime's relations with Kamal Junblatt's son and followers were restored soon after his assassination, but the feud's influence on Syria's domestic politics continued to be felt. Junblatt's resistance to Syria's policies in Lebanon and the countermeasures taken by the Ba'thi regime had contributed to the outbreak of the crisis, which still threatened Asad's regime in the early 1980s. Both Asad's unusual speech on July 20, 1976, and Junblatt's posthumously published account of the crisis reflect the intensity of the rivalry between the two former allies and provide telling examples of the rhetoric and themes used in the polemics of the Lebanese crisis. Thus Asad, the Alawi president of Syria, whom Syria's Sunni majority refused to accept as their legitimate ruler, charged that while the Phalange wanted a secular Lebanon, Kamal Junblatt's Muslim allies rejected the notion of secularism "because it related to the foundations of Islam" (see appendix). As for Junblatt himself, Asad explained, "the matter was not between right and left, progressive and reactionary, or Muslim and Christian." It was rather a personal and a sectarian Druze vendetta, a desire to terminate and take revenge for a hundred and forty years of Maronite supremacy.

The Communist Party

The Communist party has existed in Lebanon since the late 1920s, and its appeal to members of the intelligentsia and to disaffected minority communities has provided it with a comparatively large membership.[13] Its base was further broadened by the party's control of several trade unions. But like their colleagues in other Arab countries, the Lebanese Communists discovered that they could not grow beyond a certain numerical size and measure of political influence. These were further reduced in the 1960s by schisms and by the attraction of noncommunist Arab leftist organizations. The Party tried to reverse this trend by assuming the character of a party of the masses and by pursuing the strategy of popular fronts. It cooperated with the groups attractive to its potential constituency—the Palestinian organizations, the Ba'th party, the Nasserite groups, and Junblatt's party. The Communist party realized, too, the revolutionary potential of the Shi'i community and recruited new members from its ranks. Like several other political groups in Lebanon, the Communist party decided in the early 1970s that without an armed militia it would lose its political relevance. Its militia, the People's Guard, took part in the civil war.

The Ba'th Party

The Lebanese branch of the Pan-Arab Ba'th party is one of the veteran leftist parties in Lebanon. It was established in the 1940s by Michel Aflaq, a Syrian Greek Orthodox, and the other historic founders of the Ba'th. Its membership characteristically came from the Sunni and Greek Orthodox communities, the traditional re-positories of Arab nationalist sentiment and hostility to the Lebanese state. The party was politically inconsequential until the change in the fortunes of its larger branches in Syria and Iraq.[14]

The history and structure of the Lebanese Ba'th reflected the course of the party's larger branches in Arab politics and particularly their schisms and secessions. From the late 1960s, the party was divided between pro-Syrians and pro-Iraqis, the former led by 'Isam Qansu and the latter by Abdul Majid al-Rafi'i. During the first phases of the war, both factions belonged to the National Front, but Syria's intervention and Iraq's efforts to subvert Syrian policies set the groups against one another. The pro-Syrian Ba'th, having failed in its attempt to mediate between its Syrian patrons and Junblatt, seceded from the National Front. While supporting Syria's policies in the spring and summer of 1976 they did not fight alongside the conservative militias against their former allies. The pro-Iraqi Ba'th, in turn, escalated its anti-Syrian campaign, particularly in Tripoli, al-Rafi'i's hometown.

The Communist Labor Organization

This small radical group seceded in 1968 from the Arab National-ist Movement, the pan-Arab party that reflected Arab ideological politics of the previous three decades.[15] Thus, from being a militant

79

pro-Nasserite movement, the Communist Labor Organization became in the mid-1960s a Marxist movement, the parent organization of the Popular Front and Popular Democratic Front for the Liberation of Palestine. Its leader, Musim Ibrahim, defined the Communist Labor Movement as Lebanon's true defender against the "danger of Zionist occupation" but insisted that it was a strictly political organization without a militia of its own.

The Najjada

The Najjada was formed as an Arab-Muslim paramilitary group in Lebanon and Palestine in the mid-1930s. The Lebanese Najjada presented itself as the Muslim equivalent of the Phalange, but it never acquired the same power and significance. The party's founder and leader, Adnan al-Hakim, had been a persistent advocate of a thorough reform of the Lebanese political system, and in 1970 he stood as a presidential candidate in defiance of the accepted political norms. He received one vote, his own, but his gesture was a harbinger of greater challenges. The Najjada's social program was rather conservative; its militancy focused on the demand for a redistribution of political power. Its small armed force (which, Hakim insisted, was not a militia) cooperated in 1975 with the Palestinians, but, following Syria's intervention, withdrew from the fighting and reduced its political activity as well.

The Syrian Socialist Nationalist Party

The Parti Populaire Syrien (PPS), the original name for this party, is one of the oldest and most intriguing political parties in Lebanon. It was founded in the early 1930s by Antun Sa'adeh, a Greek Orthodox. The party's structure, organizational patterns, and, to some extent, ideology were influenced by the ultranationalist and fascist movements of the 1930s, but the most important elements of its doctrine were formulated in response to the social and political conditions in Lebanon and the Fertile Crescent. Sa'adeh argued that Greater Syria was a national entity, the home and creator of a Syrian nation; the artificial states established in its territory by the 1918–21 settlement should be destroyed and integrated into a Syrian state. His views made him an enemy of the Lebanese Republic, Arab nationalism, Zionism, and French policy. Sa'adeh's personality and his bold views attracted an impressive group, especially in the Greek Orthodox community, which was hostile to the Maronite-Catholic hegemony in the Lebanese state.[16]

Sa'adeh was executed in 1949 for conspiring with the Syrian government to stage a coup in Lebanon, and his party has since undergone two transformations. In the mid-1950s, its hostility to Pan-Arab nationalism turned it into a pro-Western movement and a defender of the Lebanese state. It fought alongside President Chamoun and the Phalanges in 1958 and in 1961 staged an abortive coup d'etat against President Shihab, whose domestic and foreign policies it opposed.[17] A decade later, the party was transformed yet again, its militancy once more directed against the Lebanese state and system but this time in league with leftist and Palestinian groups. It renounced its opposition to Arab unity—then a waning ideology—and supported Asad's regime in Syria and its ambitions in Lebanon.

The PPS's relationship to the Ba'th party has a curious and ironic history. Both parties were founded by leaders trying to solve the problems of minority communities in a fragmented, pluralistic society and both used the secularist approach of Christian proponents of Syrian-Arab nationalism in the Levant in the 1860s and 1870s. But whereas Sa'adeh advocated a secular Greater Syrian nationalism, Aflaq formulated a doctrine of a reformist, secular (that is, not Sunni) Arab nationalism. The two parties were popular among Alawi youth in Syria during the 1940s and 1950s, but in the mid-1950s, as the Ba'thi regime led Syria toward neutralism, socialism, and union with Egypt, the PPS acted as the rear guard for conservative pro-Western forces. In 1955, Fuad and Ghassan Jadid, two Alawi brothers who were army officers and members of the PPS, masterminded the assassination of the leading Ba'thi officer in the Syrian army, Adnan al-Maliki, which led to the brutal suppression of the party in Syria. Ten years later, another brother, Salah Jadid, who had joined the rival party in the 1940s, became a leader in the Ba'thi regime in Syria.

By the early 1970s, the old rivalries became meaningless, and many Lebanese members of the PPS came to view Asad's regime and its regional ambitions as the first real opportunity to implement the party's original vision of Greater Syria. For other members, Ba'thi Syria was a source of support against their traditional Maronite rivals.[18] These two attitudes toward Syria helped divide the party in Lebanon, the faction headed by Ina'm Ra'd being closely allied to Syrian policy, the faction headed by George Abdul Masih keeping a distance. Following Syria's about-face in 1976, Ra'd's faction remained loyal to its patron (although it did not take part in the fighting), while Masih's continued to support the National Front.

Late-forming Revisionist Groups

Among the Lebanese (as distinct from the Palestinians), most of the fighting for the revisionist cause was by organizations that appeared on the Lebanese political scene in the first half of the 1970s. With the exception of the Movement of the 24th of October, all these organizations defined themselves as Nasserite. After Nasser's death, this identification implied the fundamental goals of Nasserism (Arab unity, social reform, a strengthening of the Arab world's power vis-à-vis Western interests, and affiliation with other bearers of the Nasserite legacy, primarily Libya's President Mu'ammar Kadhafi).

The Independent Nasserites, led by Ibrahim Qulilat, presented itself as a progressive socialist movement, supportive of the Palestinians and opposed to Lebanon's partition.[19] Its militia, the Murabitun (a Muslim organization, as its name implies) played an important role in fighting the Phalanges in that city. It was particularly close to the Fath. Qulilat claimed that his organization existed secretly since the early 1970s and fought Israel in southern Lebanon alongside the Palestinians. It remained allied to the Palestinians (and opposed to Syria) throughout 1976.

The Union of the Toiling People's Forces was the only Nasserite organization boasting parliamentary representation: as we saw, one of its two leaders, Najjah Wakim, won a seat in the 1972 elections,

POLITICAL PARTIES AND FACTIONS

the first in which members of parties made legal in 1970 took part. Of the Nasserite organizations, it was the closest to Syria. Its military wing, Firqat Nasir, fought in the Beirut area. The change in Syria's policy forced the Union to break ranks with the other Nasserites. Its other leader, Kamal Shatila, was among those who tried in vain to mediate between Syria and Junblatt. It then ceased its military activity but extended unreserved political support to Syria. A related group, the Corrective Movement, was formed by 'Isam Arab, who seceded from the Union on personal grounds. This small organization had its own militia, Quwwat Nassir.

Two other groups were essentially local. The Popular Nasserite Organization was a militia located in the town of Sidon. Its leader, Mustafa Sa'd, was the son of the parliamentary deputy Ma'ruf Sa'd, whose death in the violent events in Sidon in March 1975 was part of the prelude to the civil war.[20] The Movement of the Twenty-fourth of October crystallized in Tripoli at the end of 1969 during the clashes between the Lebanese authorities and the Palestinians.[21] Its leader, Faruq al-Muqaddam, was a scion of an intensely nationalistic family, which had opposed the traditional Sunni establishment led by the Karamis. While eschewing a Nasserite label, Muqaddam was consistently anti-Syrian. His movement supported the Palestinians, opposed the Lebanese political system, and agitated for radical social reform. It was impelled, however, not so much by ideology as by traditional animosity to the Maronites of Zugharta and by impatience with the Sunni leadership in Tripoli. Muqaddam's opposition to Syria was reinforced in the mid-1970s by Syria's cooperation with the Faranjiyyas and its cultivation of Syrian temporary workers, many of them Alawis, in Tripoli.

The Sunni Establishment

The outbreak of the civil war brought the established political leadership of Lebanon's Sunni community—the object of Faruq al-Muqaddam's wrath and scorn—face to face with an inescapable dilemma. During previous decades, Sunni politicians like Sa'ib Salam, Rashid Karami, and Abdullah al-Yafi had recognized that their

83

interests overlapped with those of their Maronite counterparts.[22] In the late 1960s and early 1970s, this community of interests eroded, and Sunni leaders were demanding a greater share of power for their own sake and in response to the mood and pressure of their constituents. Still they stopped short of adhering to the far-reaching demands of the National Movement, fearing a crisis like the one which finally erupted in 1975. The crisis polarized Christian-Muslim relations and forced leaders like Salam and Karami to embrace the cause of their more radical colleagues, even though they did so reluctantly, realizing that the tremors of radicalism were undermining their own position as well.

It was a measure of their ambivalence and ill-preparation for the new conditions in Lebanon that the Sunni Zuʿama took almost no part in the fighting and persistently used their influence to try to reach a compromise. Salam did form a conservative militia intended to defend West Beirut. But he and his friends were out of tune with Lebanon's street politics; their clientele had come under the influence of the new militias' leaders.

The Sunni religious leadership, headed by the Mufti, Sheikh Hasan Khaled, pursued an intermediate course. Without endorsing violence, it supported the reform proposals raised by the National Front. The Mufti argued that no just demands should be withdrawn just because they had been raised by Marxists. The Mufti's newly acquired political role and saliency were illustrated by the convening of the Islamic Summit at his residence in Aramun in December 1975. Other Muslim leaders (the Shiʿi Imam and the Sheikh of the Druzes), conservative Sunni politicians (Saʾib Salam, Rashid Karami, and Abdullah al-Yafi), as well as Yasir ʿArafat, leader of the PLO, participated in the meeting. These participants, according to Asad's July 20, 1976, speech, telephoned Asad, asking Syria to intervene in Lebanon. That intervention widened the gap between the conservative and pragmatic Zuʿama and the radical Muslims, who refused to come to terms with Syrian policies. The radicals' defeat at the hands of the Syrians and the indefinite prolongation of the 1972 parliament then helped the traditional politicians to preserve a measure of political influence, which at the height of the civil war seemed to have been eliminated by the radicals and their militias.

The Shiʿi Establishment

The military role played by the militant leadership of the Shi'i community in the civil war was hardly commensurate with its part in the developments leading to it. Imam Musa al-Sadr's Movement of the Disinherited did form a militia, al-Amal (also known as the Battalions of Lebanese Resistance), defining itself as a force defending southern Lebanon from Israel and combatting social injustice at home. It organized secretly, surfacing in the summer of 1975. While Shi'is in Beirut fought hard along the dividing line between al-Shiyah and Ayn al-Rumani (the Maronite quarter), their contribution to the overall military effort of the revisionist coalition was limited, a consequence of the leadership's complex relationship with Syria and perhaps also of a feeling that the community's quarrel was with the Lebanese political system and not with the Maronites.

But Sadr was very active politically. He participated in the Lebanese Muslim summit, took part in several mediation efforts between Syria and its opponents, and visited Arab capitals. During one of these visits, to Libya in August 1978, Sadr disappeared in mysterious circumstances. He was probably killed by political rivals, whose identity has remained a contentious matter. The traditional leaders of the Shi'i community, Kamel al-Asʿad, Kazem al-Khalil, and Adel Usayran, faced a dilemma similar to that of the Sunni Zuʿama: their hold over their constituents had eroded, and they were wary of a conflict that might jeopardize the Lebanese system and play into the hands of the radicals. Yet their efforts at compromise and mediation had little influence on the course of the crisis, nor did their efforts restore their positions.

The Palestine Liberation Organization

It is misleading to speak of one PLO role in the Lebanese civil war, which was significantly influenced by divisions and disagreements within the Organization.[23] Rather, distinctions should be made among three Palestinian groups: the PLO establishment, George

Habash's Popular Front for the Liberation of Palestine (PFLP), and Zuheir Muhsin's al-Sa'iqa.

From the PLO establishment's perspective, embodied in the policies of the Fath and to a lesser extent the Popular Democratic Front for the Liberation of Palestine (PDFLP), the situation in prewar Lebanon was optimal. The Palestinians had an autonomous territorial base contiguous with Israel, and the Lebanese government was too weak to restrain them. And Israel, although it made raids into Lebanon, did not launch an all-out offensive because of Lebanon's close ties to the West. Thus, despite their criticism of the Lebanese political system and their affinity with its domestic foes, until January 1976, these Palestinians resisted being dragged into the fighting. Their reluctance was strengthened by the lessons learned after September 1970, when meddling in Jordanian politics had brought the PLO to the verge of catastrophe. Furthermore, in the summer and fall of 1975 the Organization was engaged in a political offensive that had already achieved impressive results in the United Nations and promised additional gains in the January 1976 Security Council discussions of the Palestinian issue. Involvement in the civil war was, therefore, officially shunned, and the Organization publicized its policy of nonintervention and sought the statesman-like roles of mediation and cease-fire supervision.

Reality, however, was more intricate. Units affiliated with the Organization did take part in the fighting, and the PLO leadership itself took advantage of the gains made by its Lebanese allies to improve the terms secured in the 1969 Cairo Agreement. The policy of nonintervention collapsed in 1976. Syria's intervention in Lebanon and its conflict with the Palestinians produced an entirely new situation. The issues at stake were no longer Lebanon's political future and PLO diplomatic ventures but the Syrian challenge to PLO autonomy and its status as "the sole legitimate representative of the Palestinian people." The Syrian Ba'thi regime had asserted that Syria was not just another Arab state extending support to the Palestinians but that it had a special nexus with the southern part of Greater Syria (that is, Palestine).

The PLO obstruction of Asad's policy in Lebanon provoked Syria to assail the PLO position and was a justification for Syria's determination to punish the PLO leadership. Asad referred to this leadership in July 1976 as "those who are now speaking in the name of Palestine, who are absorbed in their imaginations, and ignore all the efforts we have invested on their behalf." In the same speech, he denied the PLO's right to take unilateral decisions on how and where the struggle for Palestine should be waged: "The Palestinians fighting in Mount Lebanon are by no means fighting for Palestine. He who wants to liberate Jounieh and Tripoli does not want to liberate Palestine, even if he claims to." And finally, "All talk about war, about the liberation of Palestine without Syria, is ignorance and a misleading of the masses." These themes were stated even more explicitly in private. According to Junblatt's testimony, Asad told Yasir 'Arafat that "you do not represent Palestine more than we do . . . and don't you forget one thing—there is no Palestinian people and there is no Palestinian entity—there is Syria."[24]

Here, then, was 'Arafat's dilemma in the spring and summer of 1976. Syria had claimed a special role in Lebanon and, regarding the Palestinian issue, had challenged 'Arafat's status. Furthermore, it had acted in apparent concert with the United States. Would Syria now try to force the PLO to fit into the settlement scheme? And if so, should the PLO fight against superior Syrian troops without the benefit of real support from Syria's Arab rivals? The PLO was finally saved by Saudi Arabia, which exerted a moderating influence on Syria and summoned the conference that brought an end to the fighting. The Riyad conference also prepared the ground for a new effort to produce a comprehensive Arab-Israeli settlement in which the PLO and the Syrian-PLO connection would play a crucial role.

The notions of "conspiracy" and "liquidation," which 'Arafat and the PLO establishment adopted after the Syrian invasion, were formulated at the outset of the crisis by George Habash, the leader of the PFLP and his rejectionist colleagues. This being the case, they argued, they had to fight the war alongside their Lebanese partners. But their whole-hearted participation in the war had still deeper roots: most of the Marxist elements in the PLO believed in the ultimate futility of a political and military struggle. Social conditions had to be transformed and conservative regimes had to be overthrown before the full resources of the Arab world could be mobilized for the decisive battle against Israel. Amman in 1970 was seen as the equivalent of Hanoi; by 1975, the liberation of Tripoli and Jounieh was seen as essential for the liberation of Palestine.

The PLO's predicament was compounded by the activity of al-Sa'iqa, its large constituent organization, which was controlled directly by Syria. It fought on the side of the Syrians and its leader, Zuheir Muhsin, faithfully echoed the political line in Damascus. He even went beyond his Syrian masters when he told a Dutch interviewer: "Between Jordanians, Palestinians, Syrians, and Lebanese there are no differences. We are part of one people, the Arab nation. . . . only for political reasons do we subscribe to our Palestinian identity. . . . Palestinians must work together with Syria in the first place, and only after that with the other Arab states."[25] Among Palestinians, al-Sa'iqa was regarded as merely a tool of Syrian policy, but for the larger audience watching the Syrian-Palestinian conflict, al-Sa'iqa's challenge to the PLO's established leadership added yet another question mark to a very confusing story.[26]

CHAPTER 4

The Lingering Crisis

THE SETTLEMENT OF October 1976 ended the Lebanese civil war but not the Lebanese crisis. Both the underlying and the immediate problems that had unsettled the Lebanese political system and had led to the outburst in April 1975 remained unsolved and were in fact exacerbated and compounded by the war and its repercussions. The issues, problems and actors concerned in this ongoing crisis can best be examined in terms of four facets: the continuing domestic conflict, Syria's quest for hegemony, the Palestinian issue, and Israel's policies.

These components were closely intertwined. Syria stayed in Lebanon for the stated purpose of preventing a resumption of the civil war, which was a likely possibility as long as the internal Lebanese conflict remained unresolved. But its very presence, while certainly helping to prevent a resumption of all-out fighting, seemed also to perpetuate the domestic conflict. Syria had a set of goals in Lebanon and a policy designed to achieve them. But the actual steps taken to gain them generated greater antagonism in those whose interests they threatened. Furthermore, Syria's presence in Lebanon—and that of the PLO—stimulated greater Israeli involvement. And although Israel argued that it had to support the local militias in southern Lebanon since there was no proper Lebanese army to police the border area, that support contributed to the further humiliation of Elyas Sarkis's weak central government.

But the interaction among the four components that stalemated the Lebanese crisis also had a balancing effect: no single factor could impose its will. Syria could not crush the PLO in 1976 nor the Maronite militias in 1978, but it did thwart the militias' attempt to expand their territorial base in 1981. Thus the period was marked by an unstable equilibrium among hostile and reluctant partners; each could seek to improve its position within the terms of the Lebanese equation but not to revise its contours.

This situation will be made clear in the ensuing account of political developments in the Lebanese crisis between October 1976 and May 1982. But first the international and regional context of the crisis and its four facets should be briefly explored.

The International Setting

From 1976 to 1982, despite two changes of administration in Washington and many changes in the region, the essence of U.S. policy toward Lebanon did not change. The United States did not think an acceptable fundamental change in Lebanon likely, and did not give the Lebanese issue a high priority on its Middle East agenda. Instead it was inclined to encourage the consolidation of the status quo. The United States wanted primarily to prevent an acute crisis that would threaten regional stability and the success of its policies elsewhere in the Middle East.[1]

The Gerald Ford administration, which opened the dialogue with Syria and sanctioned its intervention in Lebanon, was replaced soon after the Riyad and Cairo conferences by the Carter administration. The latter revised several aspects of its predecessor's policies in the Middle East but adhered to its policy toward the Lebanese crisis. During most of 1977, the Carter administration tried to sustain the dialogue with Syria and to open one with the PLO to prepare the way for a comprehensive settlement of the Arab-Israeli conflict. This fact, the importance attributed by Washington to Saudi Arabia, and the Carter administration's ideological biases combined to support the view that the framework developed in October 1976 was the most propitious for dealing with the Lebanese problem. No immediate solution appeared feasible, but hope for the future lay in the gradual consolidation of the central government. Since Syria supported the Sarkis government and prevented a resumption of the fighting, it was perceived as playing a constructive role. The Palestinians, once integrated into the comprehensive settlement, should relax their pressure on the Lebanese political system. Although the Carter administration frowned upon Israel's support of the Lebanese Front and Sa'd Haddad's militias, it concentrated its influence with Israel on the Palestinian issue, and it thought it unwise to add yet another point of friction to an already strained relationship. The United States considered the Maronite militias, much to their chagrin, retrogressive, voices from the past, quite unlike their self-image, as described by Bashir Jumayyil: "A small population . . . fighting alone for liberty, democracy, for the dignity of man against peoples and groups that deny these values . . ."[2]

In the autumn of 1977, the Carter administration abandoned its original Middle East policy and replaced it with a reluctant endorsement of the Egyptian-Israeli dialogue and peace negotiations, putting aside its dialogue with Syria and its hoped-for dialogue with the Palestinians. But still the Lebanese crisis remained a marginal issue for the United States, completely overshadowed by the Camp David accords, the Egyptian-Israeli peace treaty, and the events in Iran. In the euphoria immediately after the Camp David conference, resolution of the Lebanese crisis was mentioned; but the idea was abandoned as difficulties arose in the Camp David accords.

Subtle changes occurred in Washington's policy toward Lebanon when the Reagan administration began its term of office.[3] The new president and his first secretary of state, Alexander Haig, saw the Middle East primarily through the prism of Soviet-American rivalries. From this angle, Syria and the Palestinians were seen in a negative light, in Lebanon and elsewhere, while the militias of the Lebanese Front, a conservative pro-Western force, were viewed more favorably than they had been by the previous administration. Accordingly, the new administration agreed early in 1981 to receive Bashir Jumayyil for a visit in Washington.

In the spring of 1981, the United States seemed to be considering trying to end Syria's military presence and political influence in Lebanon. This was the significance attached at the time to Secretary Haig's specific denunciation of Syria's role in Lebanon during his first official tour of the Middle East. In a press conference held with

Prime Minister Menachem Begin in Jerusalem on April 6, Haig addressed himself to the Syrian-Phalangist clashes in Zahle: "With respect to the situation in Lebanon, I think there are few differences [between the United States and Israel] that I am aware of. We view the brutality of the Syrian action against the Christian enclosure as a very very serious turn of events, which is unacceptable by any measure of appropriate international standards of conduct . . . and the consequences of a failure to return to a cease-fire of course are most, most serious."[4]

But if Haig did accurately reflect the Reagan administration's intentions in Lebanon, these intentions were abandoned when the Syrian-Israeli missile crisis erupted later in April. A Syrian-Israeli war would divide the United States—which would be seen to be supporting Israel—from its conservative Arab allies—which would support Syria (albeit without enthusiasm). Moreover, Syria's Treaty of Friendship and Cooperation with the Soviet Union might force a U.S. confrontation with the Soviets. And then there were influential members of the administration, the secretary of defense in particular, whose outlook on the Middle East (and consequently on the Lebanese crisis) differed radically from that of the secretary of state.

Aiming to avert a Syrian-Israeli war, Washington sent Philip Habib to mediate the missile crisis. The scope of his mission soon expanded as it became evident once again that no one aspect of the Lebanese crisis could be addressed in isolation, and Habib tried with Saudi Arabia's help to reach a settlement of the broader crisis. Given Saudi Arabia's active role, this attempt was conducted within the framework first devised in 1976–77. Thus, during the latter part of 1981 and the early months of 1982, it was generally believed that the indications of change in early 1981 had been a passing episode and that the Reagan administration's Lebanese policy was essentially a continuation of the policies of its two predecessors.

It is significant that despite the collapse of the American-Syrian dialogue and the reverses sustained by the United States in Iran and Afghanistan, it was the United States that drew the external contours of the Lebanese crisis. America's position was based on its influence in several important Arab countries, on Syria's and the PLO's desire for a dialogue with the United States, on a residual belief in America's interest in and concern for Lebanon, and, most important, on the widely held view that the United States was the only power capable of influencing Israel. Egypt's gradual disengagement from the military dimension of the Arab-Israeli conflict, which culminated in the Egyptian-Israeli peace treaty had given Israel a decisive military advantage over Syria, and Israel now could conceivably seek a military solution to the Lebanese crisis. Although America's capacity to prevent, moderate, or condone Israeli military activity in Lebanon generated much Arab criticism, it strengthened American influence over the course of the Lebanese crisis.

However, as a case study in the superpower-client relations in the region, the Lebanese crisis more often than not disclosed the limitations and disappointments inherent in such relationships for the senior partner. American and Israeli outlooks on the crisis often diverged, and the American government discovered it could not always compel its junior partner to act in accordance with its wishes in matters that Israel considered to be vital and the United States to be inconsequential. But Washington's occasional consternation was mild compared with Moscow's sustained discomfiture. The Lebanese crisis clearly demonstrated the limits of Soviet influence in the Middle East and the extent of the United States's success in the mid-1970s in restoring its ascendancy in the core of the area. Although clients and friends of the Soviet Union played important roles in the civil war, they spent the crucial phases of it fighting each other. Syria, the Soviet Union's most important client in the Arab world after Egypt's defection, acted in coordination with the United States and blatantly rejected Moscow's advice.

Even the eventual Soviet-Syrian rapprochement and the disruption of the incipient Syrian-American dialogue failed to improve Moscow's standing. Syria's continued presence in Lebanon endangered the very existence of the Ba'thi regime and risked a Syrian-Israeli war, in which the Soviet Union would be identified with the weaker side, which would be fighting outside its frontiers.

President Hafiz al-Asad's precarious domestic position and the prospect of a Syrian-Israeli war in Lebanon seem, indeed, to have been two of the considerations behind the Soviet Union's change of mind regarding a treaty relationship with Syria. During most of the 1970s, the Soviet Union had sought to formalize its relations with Syria through a treaty of friendship and cooperation, while Ba'thi

Syria evaded Soviet overtures. In 1980, it was the weakened and discredited Ba'thi regime that wanted the treaty, while the Soviets appeared reluctant to risk their prestige.[5] When the treaty was finally signed in October 1980, the clauses that could apply in the eventuality of Syrian-Israeli fighting in Lebanon were, indeed, carefully drafted to be imprecise and vague. And when such combat seemed imminent during the missile crisis in 1981, the Soviets indicated that the 1980 treaty did not apply to Syrian forces in Lebanon. Only later, when the crisis was nearly over, did Soviet statements vis-à-vis Israel assume a more threatening tone.[6]

The Regional Setting

The outbreak, the course, and the outcome of the Lebanese civil war were all influenced by the changes in the system of inter-Arab relations in the early 1970s: primarily the decline in Egypt's position and the concomitant rise in influence of the oil-producing states and Syria.[7] But these convulsions did not produce a stable new order. Hegemonies and alliances were short-lived, and the pattern of inter-Arab relations was altered often and abruptly. Saudi Arabia and Syria, whose regional policies seemed so influential and successful in 1976 and 1977, were weakened by 1979—Syria by the crisis in Asad's regime and Saudi Arabia by the ramifications of the Islamic revolution in Iran. For a brief moment in October 1978, Iraq appeared to be the leading state in the Arab system but was soon incapacitated by domestic problems and the Iranian challenge. Most important, in 1977 Egypt opted out of formal inter-Arab relations for a few years in order to complete the peace process with Israel, and regain all Egyptian territory. The other Arab states were unable to force Egypt to renounce this policy, or to suggest an effective alternative.

This state of affairs had two important repercussions for the Lebanese crisis in the years 1977–82. For one thing, the crisis was pushed to one side on the Arab agenda, overshadowed by the issues that preoccupied the principal Arab states: the stability of their own regimes, the Egyptian-Israeli peace process, the Islamic revolution in Iran, and the Soviet invasion of Afghanistan. This decline of Arab interest and the absence of a durable pattern of alliances and hegemony in the Arab system helped to perpetuate the status quo in the Lebanese crisis during this period. Various Arab states were unhappy that the crisis continued, or with some particular aspect of it, be it Syria's policy or the Lebanese Front's relations with Israel, but they lacked the motivation or the capacity to translate their dissatisfaction into sustained and effective policies. All efforts to devise a solution to the crisis in Arab summit conferences during these years ended in failure.

The profound changes of the late 1970s in the Arab-Israeli conflict, however, had an immediate bearing on the Lebanese crisis. As has already been mentioned, the Egyptian-Israeli peace process (and the failure to form an eastern Arab front) contributed to a crucial change in the Syrian-Israeli balance of power. But while some consequences of this change emerged gradually, others were already apparent in 1977.

For one thing, Syria and the PLO were driven to paper over their differences and jointly oppose Sadat's policies. The bitterness of 1976 did not fully disappear, nor did the underlying causes of Syrian-Palestinian tension in Lebanon; but they became less important, and a period of cooperation ensued.[8]

It was Lebanon's misfortune that the Egyptian-Israeli detente did not ease the broader Arab-Israeli conflict, but tended rather to telescope it and focus it on the Palestinian issue. While Israel was making peace with Egypt, it was fighting a bitter war with the PLO, primarily in the West Bank and in Lebanon. In the West Bank the conflict was over land and political influence; in Lebanon it was governed, until June 1982, by military action. Having by and large renounced terror outside the Middle East and being barred from Israel's Syrian and Jordanian borders, the PLO concentrated its efforts on launching raids along Israel's land and sea borders with Lebanon. Earlier Palestinian-Israeli violence in Lebanon was dwarfed by the military build-up, raids, counterraids, and preemptive raids of 1977–82.

One other regional issue affected the Lebanese crisis, though less significantly than the foregoing: the rise of a revolutionary Islamic regime in Iran, its efforts to "export" the Islamic revolution, and the ensuing Iraqi-Iranian war. Iran is a Shi'i country; it has traditionally

95

influenced the Lebanese Shiʻi and since 1979 has been an ally of Syria and an enemy of Iraq. Iranian meddling in Lebanon contributed to violent conflict between Lebanese who supported Iran and those who supported Iraq. Its impact on the strength and politics of the Shiʻi community was twofold. While further splintering the community, it also helped to fashion within its ranks a cadre determined to go to great lengths to enhance Shiʻi power and standing.

The Continuing Domestic Conflict

It has already been noted that the partial settlement in October 1976 failed even to consider, let alone remedy, the root cause of the Lebanese crisis: the conflict between two rival camps over the identity of the Lebanese entity and the distribution of power within the Lebanese state and political system.

In the absence of reconciliation and consensus, the term of Lebanon's 1972 parliament was extended in 1976 and again in 1980. Even by-elections for seats that became vacant could not be held. The cabinets of Salim al-Huss and then of Shafiq al-Wazzan were defined as technocratic and as such won approval from a parliament whose functions were primarily ceremonial. Several attempts were made after October 1976 to devise a formula that would enable a gradual return to normal political life, but Lebanon's politicians, divided and under pressure from external forces, were unable to agree. Nor could the army or the presidency act as a focus for consensus and stability. The Lebanese army, the object of a struggle for influence between Syria and the Lebanese Front, was confined to its barracks and not used to enforce the authority of the central government. Efforts by President Sarkis to transcend partisan and sectarian divisions were obstructed during the first years of his presidency by too close an affiliation with Syria. He later distanced himself from Syria and drew closer to the Lebanese Front, but in so doing he forfeited the confidence of Syria and its Lebanese allies.

In the absence of any progress toward national reunification and political normalization, Lebanon's domestic politics were conducted within and among the major political camps and factions.

These internal conflicts were carried on simultaneously with the national political process, and most of the time they overshadowed it.[9]

The development of the Lebanese Front was unquestionably dictated by the Phalangist drive, under Bashir Jumayyil's leadership, for undisputed hegemony.[10] Jumayyil, who was unknown and twenty-eight years old at the end of the civil war, became during the next few years the virtual leader of the party in the broad sense of the term, usurping the position that his father was still formally holding and that his older brother, Amin, might have expected to inherit. It is difficult to separate the personal dimension from questions of policy and orientation in the unfolding of this process. Bashir Jumayyil was unusually ambitious, determined, and gifted. He was also a consistent advocate of a close relationship with Israel and unambiguously hostile to Syria and the PLO, more like Camille Chamoun in this respect than like the traditional Phalangist thinkers. His closeness to the Israelis and the growing gap between the Maronites and the Syrians played into his hands and accelerated his progress to the party's leadership. The corresponding decline in the position of his elder brother and of part of the party's hierarchy must have produced tensions in its ranks, but except for occasional references in (mostly hostile) press reports, such tensions were well disguised by a show of party solidarity.[11]

Bashir Jumayyil's formal position was not in the party's hierarchy—he became commander of the Lebanese Forces after William Hawi was killed in Tel Za'atar in August 1976. This arrangement not only helped relations within the Jumayyil family but also enabled the Lebanese Front to attract Christian supporters who had not been identified with the Phalange in the past and who might have found a direct affiliation with the party awkward. Bashir Jumayyil's position also reflected the Phalangist belief in military power as the basis of political power and in the need to unify Maronite military forces. The Phalanges maintained that fragmented and divided forces, a characteristic of Maronite politics, was a luxury that a beleaguered community, fighting for its future against numerical and political odds, could not afford. Maronite political pluralism ought perhaps to be tolerated, but the community's military power had to be under one authority, and that authority had to be theirs.

97

On that premise, the Phalanges sought to break the independent power bases of their two principal partners. The conflict with the Faranjiyya family occurred first, in the spring of 1978, and was expedited by profound political disagreements over the Maronite community's relations with Syria. The Phalanges dispatched political and labor organizers, who agitated against the Faranjiyya family. Matters came to a head when the Phalanges sought to expand their party organization into northern Lebanon and to undermine the Faranjiyya family's economic base. In the social reality of Maronite northern Lebanon, political power could hardly be separated from the paramilitary organization and its economic underpinning. The Faranjiyyas responded to the challenge by killing the chief Phalangist organizer, Jud Bayeh. Bayeh's humble origins added a social dimension to the incident, showing the conflict between the traditional patriarchal family of northern Lebanon and the leveling influence of the Phalangist mobilization of Maronite society. The Phalanges retaliated by shelling Tony Faranjiyya's home in the village of Ehden, killing him and his immediate family in June 1978. Whether or not his assassination had been planned, it is obvious that excessive brutality turned the incident into much more than a settling of scores or the weakening of a rival faction. Syria's proximity and protection helped the Faranjiyya family keep its regional position and assert its independence, now as sworn enemies of the Phalanges and the Jumayyil family.[12]

Two years later, in July 1980, Bashir Jumayyil's militia destroyed the military infrastructure of the Tigers, the National Liberal Party's militia in the Beirut area. Camille Chamoun accepted the new reality, but his son Dany chose to oppose his former ally by joining other Lebanese expatriates in Paris. Camille Chamoun's acceptance of the Phalangist victory, essential for the continued existence of the Lebanese Front, was more than just another symptom of his pragmatism. It reflected his complex attitude to Bashir Jumayyil, the son of his colleague and competitor, whose role on the national stage seemed to be that of Chamoun's political successor.[13]

In the same vein, the Phalanges sought to expand their mandate and their demographic and territorial bases by becoming the representative authority for all Lebanese Christians, not just the Maronites. This search was most notably embodied in the establishment of a Phalangist military and political presence in the predominantly Greek Catholic town of Zahle in eastern Lebanon in December 1980. Later, an attempt was made to build a road linking Zahle to Mount Lebanon and to Jounieh, the territorial nucleus of Christian Lebanon.

In complete contrast to that of the Lebanese Front, the post– civil-war history of its chief Lebanese rival, the National Front, was characterized by decline and disintegration. The National Front, already seriously weakened by its conflict with Syria in 1976, lost its one national leader when Junblatt was assassinated in 1977. His son, Walid, inherited his father's command and political position but lacked the experience, stature, and charisma that could have made him into a real leader of a political camp.

Syria further weakened the National Front by basing its Lebanon policy not on its leftist clients and sympathizers but on a broad spectrum, which included traditional Lebanese politicians like Suleiman Faranjiyya and Rashid Karami as well as the Palestinians and the revisionist militias—a strategy that was another obstacle along the way to national reconciliation in Lebanon. The Lebanese Front continued to argue categorically that the Palestinians were an alien presence in Lebanon and that their problem should be solved by the Arabs collectively and not at Lebanon's expense. The PLO (and its Syrian and Lebanese allies) naturally objected to this position as well as to any settlement in Lebanon that did not meet its requirements. And while incapable of imposing their own settlement, it was powerful enough to veto any settlement accepted by the Lebanese Front.

Syria's Quest for Hegemony

From Syria's vantage point, the settlement in October 1976 was a partial success. The Arab consensus endorsed Syria's preeminence in Lebanon, and the prospects of consolidating Syrian hegemony appeared excellent. Clearly, Syria was not seeking to annex Lebanon: that was an unrealistic and indeed not an advantageous policy goal. But Syrian influence might be ensured, without the burden of maintaining a large expeditionary force in Lebanon, by continuing

99

to cultivate a Lebanese political clientele, by shaping a subservient central government, and by formalizing Syrian hegemony through a treaty relationship. The patient pursuit of these goals was likely to meet with success; but it exacted an immediate price that the Ba'thi regime, especially when in the midst of a severe domestic crisis, was hard put to pay.

And then there were other immediate difficulties. The alliance with the Lebanese Front was artificial, but another about-face would provoke a conflict with the most important domestic Lebanese force. That force, the Syrians knew very well, maintained close ties with Israel, whose interests and involvement in Lebanon had already curtailed Syria's freedom of action. The Palestinian-Israeli conflict in Lebanon presented Syria with yet another dilemma. The Syrian regime had no desire to prevent the PLO from launching raids against Israel from southern Lebanon but found it increasingly difficult not to react to Israel's preemptive and punitive strikes, aerial reconnaissance, and raids into Lebanon. Still, despite the apparent radicalization and ideological nature of the regime and the chronic state of Syrian-Israeli relations, Syria conducted its contest with Israel in Lebanon with remarkable pragmatism. Syria's and Israel's long-term goals in Lebanon were conflicting. For a brief period in 1976, they both supported the same party, but as a rule they backed rival protagonists in the struggle for Lebanon's future. In this struggle, Syria carefully calculated Israel's interests, sensitivities, and capabilities and sought to minimize direct contact. The first clash between Syria and Israel in Lebanon occurred in the spring of 1979, when the Syrian air force challenged its Israeli counterpart and lost. For the next two years, direct Syrian-Israeli conflict in Lebanon was confined to a series of similarly unsuccessful Syrian attempts.

Most significant, though, were the domestic repercussions of Syria's involvement in Lebanon. The regime headed by Hafiz al-Asad, which from 1970 to 1976 had enjoyed domestic and external successes, encountered difficulties in 1977 which developed into a serious crisis that the regime has not yet been able to overcome. Its eruption was to a large extent a side-effect of Syria's 1976 intervention in Lebanon, which fanned Syria's communal tensions, caused friction in the regime's upper echelons, compounded economic difficulties, and embittered the public. It was against this background that radical elements in the Syrian Muslim brotherhood decided to follow Iranian tactics in a renewed attempt to topple the regime. Their successive challenges—a campaign of personal terror in 1977, the massacre of the Alawi artillery cadets in 1979, the revolt in Syria's northern cities later that year, and the attempt on Asad's life in 1980—nearly brought down the regime.[14]

The protracted domestic crisis imposed, in turn, serious constraints on Syria's policy in Lebanon. In 1979 and 1980, the Ba'thi leadership found it increasingly difficult to attend to Lebanon and was sometimes even hard-pressed to spare the necessary troops when it was using large military formations to suppress the opposition in northern Syria. Furthermore, Syrian public opinion was less likely to tolerate Syrian casualties over the Lebanese crisis than over the conflict with Israel. And when Saudi Arabia and its client states changed their attitude toward Syria's role in Lebanon and reduced their financial support for Syria's military presence there, the cost of keeping a large military contingent in Lebanon became more burdensome. Finally, although in the long run control over Lebanon would enhance Syria's defensive and offensive posture vis-à-vis Israel, for the time being the maintenance of some thirty thousand troops in Lebanon without the necessary military infrastructure weakened Syria's position, which had already been undermined by the Egyptian-Israeli negotiations and subsequent peace treaty.

Early in 1980, these considerations persuaded Asad to announce a partial withdrawal and a redeployment of Syrian forces in Lebanon. The announcement produced one of the telling ironies in the Lebanese crisis, because even some of the harshest Lebanese critics of Syria's role in Lebanon expressed their dismay at the prospect of an early Syrian withdrawal. With the fundamental issues of the crisis still unresolved, a withdrawal was likely to result in a recrudescence of an all-out crisis, for which the Lebanese Front, for instance, was not ready.

The Palestine Liberation Organization

The Lebanese civil war had a paradoxical effect on the PLO and on its standing in Lebanon. In the war's immediate aftermath, its consequences from the PLO's vantage point appeared negative. For the second time within six years, Palestinians clashed with an Arab state and were defeated politically and militarily. Syria stopped short of consummating her victory but continued trying to subdue and harness the PLO in more subtle ways during the final months of 1976 and early 1977. The organization's only autonomous territorial base and only direct access to Israel's borders were in danger of being lost.

But a few months later, the situation began to change. The opening of the Israeli-Egyptian peace process led Syria and the Palestinians to mend fences. Tension and conflict between them remained, but the PLO's virtual freedom of operation in Lebanon was restored. This enabled the PLO to take full advantage of the disintegration of the Lebanese state to expand and develop the territory of Palestinian autonomy. In the early 1970s, it had practically expropriated the refugee camps and Lebanon's southeastern corner (Fatahland). By the end of the decade, the organization was the actual government in a continuous area stretching from West Beirut to the Litani River. The paraphernalia of government and statehood offended the Lebanese, who referred to it angrily as al-watan al-badil (the alternative homeland). It was limited to the western sector of Lebanon's southern half. In the eastern sector, PLO units were under Syrian control, and in the central sector they were kept at arm's length by the Druze population, a tenacious defender of its own territory and autonomy. Most of the area south of the Litani was held by the United Nations Interim Force in Lebanon (UNIFIL), which was dispatched to the south in 1978, and Major Haddad's militias.

A number of social and political processes were generated by the establishment of PLO dominion over a sizable territory and a sizable population. Among the Palestinian population of southern Lebanon the patterns established between 1948 and 1970 were disrupted by the changes of the early 1970s. During the 1950s and 1960s the Palestinians seem to have become an intermediate class between the traditional elite and the mostly Shi'i peasantry. But the influx of Palestinian refugees from the Jordanian civil war of 1970 created a new Palestinian elite, affluent and armed. As the area became a battleground between the PLO and Israel, with the imposition of greater PLO control, the organization's authority over the Palestinian population became complete.

Built into this process was a conflict with the local Lebanese political forces in the south. The development of the PLO's political power and territorial base was part of the wave of change that in the late 1960s and early 1970s undermined the position of the traditional Lebanese leadership. Later, the development of the PLO's position proceeded at the expense of its local allies, the Lebanese opponents of the beleaguered or ousted traditional elite. The PLO's predominance over most of its Lebanese partners in the revisionist coalition was felt still more acutely in southern Lebanon, where much of its physical presence and attention were concentrated. The most significant aspect of the antagonism between the Palestinians and their erstwhile allies there was their conflict with al-Amal, the organization that had displaced the Shiʿi Zuʿama of the south. Thus the Palestinians were pitted against the single largest group in southern Lebanon, the Shiʿis—which also had an important representation in Beirut.[15]

For the PLO in the late 1970s and early 1980s, the autonomous territorial base stretching from West Beirut to the vicinity of the Lebanese Israeli border had a number of important functions. It provided the organization with a comparatively firm foundation for developing its power and standing as an actor in Palestinian, Arab, and Lebanese politics. The Palestinian leadership was aware, on the basis of experience, of the difference between an organization depending on the support and good will of one or several Arab countries and one that enjoyed many of the advantages inherent in virtual statehood without some of the limitations that normally entailed.

At its northern edge, in Beirut, the PLO's territorial base put it on the scene in an important center of regional and international politics and communications. Its presence in Lebanon's political center was, and was perceived as, essential for maintaining its influence on Lebanese politics. At the other end, proximity to Israel's northern border was vital for a continuation of the "armed struggle" against Israel. Having formally renounced terrorist activities in 1974, the PLO came to depend almost exclusively on operations launched through Lebanon to preserve its character as a fighting movement.

But its leadership was also aware of the price exacted by the creation and maintenance of a large territorial base. Conflict with former allies was but one aspect of the transformation undergone by a movement which came to exercise power over population and territory. Other repercussions affected the PLO's posture vis-à-vis Israel, which became increasingly a stance based on regular or semi-regular formations deployed in southern Lebanon. The organization's doctrine was developed to accommodate the new reality: Israel remained the target but a large-scale conflict in southern Lebanon was depicted as an interim phase. In the summer of 1981 such a clash appeared inevitable and imminent. The PLO's preparations for it are described in chapter 5.[16]

Israeli Policies

The outbreak and evolution of the Lebanese civil war ended the third phase of Israel's relationship with the Lebanese state.

During the first few years of Israeli independence, Israel's outlook on Lebanon was still influenced by the close relationship between Palestine's Jewish community and several Maronite religious and political leaders of the 1930s and 1940s. Such Maronite leaders as the Patriarch Antun Arida, archbishops Ignatius Mubarak and Abdallah al-Khuri, and President Emile Eddé, seeing a community of fate between Maronites and Jews against the pressure of Islam and Pan-Arab nationalism, supported the establishment of a Jewish state in Palestine.[17] The political department of the Jewish Agency cultivated relations with non-Maronite politicians as well, but its most significant achievements were among Maronites. This suited and reinforced a concept dominant among Zionist—and subsequently Israeli—leaders, of an alliance of minorities, a belief that the Yishuv (the Jewish community in mandatory Palestine) and, later on, Israel could break out of isolation by joining forces with other foes and victims of Pan-Arab nationalism.[18] In 1946, the relationship with the Maronite community in Lebanon was formalized by an agreement between the Jewish Agency and the Maronite church, but the agreement's limited value was reflected in the latter's insistence that the treaty be kept secret, and the ensuing controversy between Patriarch Arida and his emissary, Tawfiq Awwad, who both sought to disassociate themselves from it.[19] Indeed, when the other Arab states decided to participate in the first Arab-Israeli war, the Lebanese government bowed to domestic and external pressure and joined the war effort. The Lebanese army in fact fought well in the Galilee.[20]

David Ben-Gurion's 1948–49 diaries and the recently opened files of the Israeli Foreign Ministry shed light on the extent of Israel's relationship with various Lebanese politicians in the late 1940s as well as on Israeli contacts with a Phalangist emissary in the war's immediate aftermath. The Israelis were not averse to a Phalangist (or another variety of "Christian") takeover in Lebanon; they were, however, dubious as to its prospects. As late as 1954–55, Israeli leaders like Ben-Gurion and Moshe Dayan believed that Israel could take advantage of separatist Maronite sentiments (which had become marginal in the 1940s), to bring about a pro-Israeli change in Lebanon. Other Israelis, most notably Moshe Sharett, understood that most Maronites had accepted the post-1943 pluralistic Lebanese system and that Israel, too, ought to accept it as an established fact.[21]

This, indeed, was done for the next twenty years, during which Israel's relations with Lebanon were a marginal aspect of its Middle Eastern policies. Lebanon was perceived as Israel's one harmless Arab neighbor, a state that since 1949 had not taken part in Arab-Israeli wars and would perhaps improve relations and even make peace if it were up to the Christians. But the Maronite community's standing was being eroded and Israel, as a supporter of the status quo, could only offer discreet aid to its friends.

It became increasingly difficult, however, for Israel to tread softly in a country that after 1970 was the PLO's principal base. Israel was, in fact, in a harsh dilemma. In establishing itself in Lebanon and in expanding its autonomy and activity, the PLO took advantage of the Lebanese state's weakness and contributed to its disintegration. Israel, by staging preemptive and punitive raids, reduced PLO pressure on its own border but played into the hands of those who sought to weaken the Lebanese state further and transform it into an entity far less acceptable to Israel.

In the winter of 1975–76 such a transformation appeared imminent. The collapse of the Lebanese state and political system, the ascendancy of the PLO and its Lebanese allies, and the specter of Syrian intervention persuaded the Israeli government that the status quo in Lebanon could be preserved no longer. It considered three possible policy lines. First, Israel could decide to intervene in the crisis and was in fact invited to do so by the Maronite leaders with whom it was now dealing directly. But Prime Minister Rabin declined. His regional policy was focused on Egypt and predicated on Israel's coordination with the United States. In September 1975, the interim agreement on the Sinai was signed, and in January 1976, Rabin returned from Washington with an agreement in principle on the next stage of the Israeli-Egyptian settlement process. He believed that a massive Israeli intervention on behalf of the status-quo militias was bound to lead to war with Syria and disrupt the fragile peace process. Rabin's attitude toward the status-quo militias was skeptical. He was willing to help them but not to commit Israeli troops to fight on their behalf.

Second, if Israel did not intervene and the traditional Lebanese entity was doomed, then a Syrian takeover was preferable to domination by the PLO and its allies. Syria's standing in the region and vis-à-vis Israel would be enhanced, but Israeli deterrence of Syria would then have to include not only the Golan front, but Lebanon as well. The third policy line was an intermediate one, accepting Syrian intervention but with limitations (the red line) arranged through the United States. Syria would not dispatch forces south of the Litani River, would not use its air force, and would not deploy ground-to-air missiles on Lebanon's territory. Israel would continue its relationship with the status-quo militias. This is the policy Israel adopted.[22]

The ground for a radical change in Israel's policy toward Lebanon was prepared by the 1977 Israeli elections and the rise to power of Menachem Begin and the Likud bloc. Begin's foreign policy was bolder and more activist than Rabin's; he reduced the level of coordination with the Carter administration, and he sympathized with Lebanon's Christian communities. They fitted into his world view, which emphasized the similar course of their history with that of the Jewish people and assigned Israel a role as protector of Western and Christian interests more enthusiastic and committed than the Christian and Western powers themselves. But these factors did not come into play immediately. During Begin's first two years in power his regional policy, like Rabin's, was predicated on Egypt and governed by the negotiations that culminated with the Israeli-Egyptian peace treaty in 1979.

In 1977 and 1978, Israel's preoccupation with the Palestinians in southern Lebanon overshadowed interest in the Lebanese crisis as a whole. Syria's relations with the PLO gradually improved, easing PLO operations in southern Lebanon. Israel built an elaborate defense system along the Lebanese border, supported three enclaves of Major Sa'd Haddad's militias, and struck Palestinian targets in Lebanon. It was a generally effective strategy, but the occasional Palestinian penetration of the defensive system was dramatic, even traumatic. In March 1978, a Palestinian squad originating in Lebanon infiltrated Israel's naval patrols, landed near the coastal highway south of Haifa, took over a bus full of passengers, and was only stopped near Tel Aviv. The heavy casualties and Israel's obvious vulnerability persuaded the Israeli government to launch the massive Litani operation later that month.

The operation was based on the assumption that the problem of southern Lebanon could be solved, or at least neutralized, by destroying the PLO's military strength south of the Litani without attempting to resolve the larger Lebanese crisis. It caused numerous casualties and much destruction and failed to solve the problem. But it did have several important consequences: Haddad's territory became a continuous strip along the Israeli border; a large Shi'i element was added to Haddad's militias and to the population they controlled; and UNIFIL was introduced to the region.

But although Israel conducted an operation of such magnitude, it resisted the temptation to become involved in the conflict that developed in 1978 between Syria and the Lebanese Front in Beirut. Israel supported the Front with arms and military training, and the Israeli air force flew warning missions above Beirut, but the Begin government was determined not to be drawn into war with Syria over Lebanon's future.

Only late in 1980 did a change in that policy become detectable. Israel's new attitude to the Lebanese crisis manifested itself in a closer alliance with Bashir Jumayyil, now the unquestioned leader of the Lebanese Front, in Israel's greater commitment to the Front, and in its determination to bring about Syria's departure from Lebanon. When and precisely how the change occurred is difficult to determine, but it is clear that many of the reservations about Israel's relationship with the Lebanese Front that had been held by the Rabin government, and by the Begin government itself during its first two years in power, disappeared during its third year.

Several developments combined to bring about the new direction and set Begin on a policy course in Lebanon that suited his own predilections. Both Moshe Dayan and Ezer Weizman, the foreign and defense ministers who as a rule had exerted a moderating influence, resigned from Begin's first cabinet. Begin became his own defense minister and the chief of staff, General Rafael Eytan, an advocate of a forceful Israeli policy in Lebanon, gained influence in the formulation and conduct of Israel's national security policies. A number of regional developments had a similar impact.

By the end of 1979, Israel's regional and foreign policies were no longer governed, as they had been in the previous two years, by the negotiations with Egypt and the transformation of the settlement process into a peace process. The new relationship with Egypt had followed its course, and its limitations had become fully apparent; other aspects of Israel's regional policy now took on greater prominence. The weakening of Asad's regime in Syria and its apparent difficulties in maintaining Syria's position in Lebanon, plus the new set of attitudes displayed by the Reagan administration, induced the Israeli government to believe that the time might have come to seek Syria's eviction from Lebanon.

But perhaps most important were the development of Bashir Jumayyil's personality and leadership, the build-up of his party's and militia's power, and the dynamics of the relationship between him and his Israeli allies. By 1980, Bashir Jumayyil had developed, at least in some Israeli eyes, from the charming and volatile younger son of a veteran political leader into the mature head of the single most powerful political and military force in Lebanon, a real ally of Israel, and a man with the capacity to change the paradigms of both the Lebanese crisis and the Lebanese polity.

The Crisis, 1977–82

The evolution of the Lebanese crisis from the end of the civil war to the war of June 1982 can be conveniently divided into seven phases:

From Riyad to Shtura, October 1976 to July 1977

In this transitional period, patterns were fixed that characterized the Lebanese crisis until its transformation in 1982. Syria invested considerable efforts consolidating its position. Its relations with the Maronite leaders were no longer intimate, but they were still good. Junblatt's assassination blunted the left's opposition to Syria and facilitated its subordination to Syrian authority. Elyas Sarkis began his term as president in September, and in December, Salim al-Huss, his confidant and economic adviser, formed a "technocrats'" cabinet. Syrian influence and aims were apparent in the first measure taken by the Huss cabinet, the censorship of the Lebanese press. As a result, several leading publishers and journalists (along with anti-Syrian politicians) moved to Europe, where, in a freer atmosphere, they published their magazines and newspapers for the large Arab communities which had formed there after 1973. One publisher, Salim al-Lawzi of *Al-Hawadith*, made the mistake of returning to Lebanon where he was kidnaped, killed, and mutilated, apparently by Syria's emissaries.[23]

Less sinister was Syria's success, in cooperation with the Sarkis–Huss administration, in restoring a measure of public order in Lebanon and launching a process of rebuilding and economic rehabilitation. They were not so successful, however, in devising a formula for national reconciliation and in disarming the militias of the Lebanese Front and of the PLO and its Lebanese allies. The Lebanese Front refused to disarm as long as the PLO remained an armed presence in Lebanon. A compromise formula applying the principles of the Cairo Agreement was finally arrived at. But all attempts to implement it failed, and the various militias retained their weapons and their high political profiles.

During the same months, southern Lebanon, which had enjoyed the benefits of benign neglect when the civil war was being fought in the center and the north, became again a focus of tension, not only because of renewed Palestinian-Israeli conflict, but also because the PLO's drift southward and conflicts between Lebanese factions reversed the earlier trend. The level of violence in the south escalated while the center and the north passed through a period of relative calm. Israel's policy of giving humanitarian aid to the civilian population on the one hand and building up Major Haddad's militia on the other, which began spontaneously, hardened into a coherent strategy.

Syria, except for one attempt to dispatch its forces to the town of Nabatiyya, respected the terms of the indirect understanding with Israel and stayed north of the Litani. The regime was perturbed by Israel's presence in southern Lebanon but sought to contest it by proxy—through the PLO and its Lebanese allies.[24]

Syria and the Lebanese Front, September 1977 to October 1978

Politically, the next phase of the Lebanese crisis was governed by the second *renversement des alliances*—Syria's rapprochement with the PLO and the Lebanese left and its estrangement from the dominant groups in the Lebanese Front. As has already been noted, Syria tried to distance itself from the embarrassment of its alliance with the conservative and essentially Maronite militias and from November 1977 drew closer to the PLO.

For their part, the Phalanges and the National Liberals changed their attitude toward Syria. As the civil war became more remote, Syria appeared less as their savior and more as a foreign occupier. Junblatt's disappearance from the scene and Syria's renewed cooperation with the Palestinians strengthened that perception. Some of the Front's leaders, Camille Chamoun in particular, felt that a showdown with Syria was inevitable. Syria, they argued, was determined to stay in Lebanon and to dominate it, and if the Front were to resist it, it should do so soon, before Syria's presence eroded the Front's position. From this point of view, a closer alliance with Israel was desirable and efforts to draw the new Israeli government nearer and to elicit an even greater commitment followed naturally. Faranjiyya's estrangement from the Lebanese Front and his former partners was closely related to the deterioration in their relations with Syria. The Faranjiyya family's alliance with Syria made the Phalanges more determined to destroy the family's power. The brutal fashion in which they pursued this aim—the killing of Tony Faranjiyya and his immediate family, in particular—turned the rivalry into a vendetta and increased Faranjiyya's dependence on Syria.

Syrian troops in Lebanon first clashed with the National Liberals in February 1978. The fighting took place in the Fayadiyya barracks in Beirut and was occasioned by a conflict over appointments in the Lebanese army. It was renewed in April and again in June and July and continued in some fashion until October, when international political pressure and Israeli threats brought it to an end. Most of the fighting took place in Beirut, but Syrian forces also fought in Mount Lebanon, where they succeeded in eroding the boundaries of the Front's territorial base.[25]

The course of this conflict revealed that a large portion of the Lebanese army's officer corps supported the Lebanese Front and that President Sarkis was distancing himself from Syria and drawing closer to the Front. Caught in the cross-pressures and seeking to improve his position, Sarkis tendered his resignation in July, knowing full well that he was irreplaceable and therefore indispensable. These developments turned Prime Minister Huss into Syria's main ally and prop in the Lebanese government. The decline of Syria's standing in Lebanon was somewhat redressed by a renewal of the Arab world's mandate when the Bayt al-Din conference reaffirmed the principles laid down at the Cairo and Riyad conferences.

The other important development during this phase was Israel's Litani operation, which introduced new patterns in southern Lebanon, but failed to transform the situation. Southern Lebanon remained the object of rival bids for control and the scene and victim of the Palestinian-Israeli violence. It was significant that Syria did not intervene on behalf of its Palestinian and Lebanese allies, despite the proximity of Syrian troops and the scope and duration of the operation. This failure was indeed criticized by rivals of the Ba'thi regime, but it was determined not to be drawn into war with Israel when the latter had a decisive military advantage. In the terminology of the Ba'thi regime, Egypt's decision to negotiate directly with Israel created a "strategic gap," which left Syria in a position of weakness vis-à-vis Israel. Cooperation among Arab states, a military buildup, and Soviet support would enable Syria and the eastern front states to stand up to Israel; but as long as these were not yet realities, an extensive Syrian-Israeli conflict should be avoided.[26]

"Free Lebanon," Summer 1978 to April 1979

In 1977, when "the problem of southern Lebanon," as shaped by the outcome of the civil war, became apparent, it was suggested that it could best be solved by placing Lebanese army units in that part of the country. It was a scheme fully congruent with efforts to rebuild the authority and institutions of the Lebanese state and to extend its de facto sovereignty over the entire territory of Lebanon. Syria, its allies in the Lebanese government, and the United States were the chief advocates of this approach.

Israel and Sa'd Haddad objected to the scheme. They argued that the Lebanese army was too weak to police an area that, in the late 1960s and early 1970s, a stronger Lebanese army had failed to maintain, and that in any case the units designated for the south were not proper Lebanese units but rather formations under Syrian control. Ironically, their opposition was augmented by that of the PLO and the Lebanese left, wary of central government and Syrian authority in their area. Their formal argument was that the Lebanese army was "confessional." They wanted to see a "balanced" Lebanese army and to have it positioned in the area under Haddad's control before they would agree to admit it to their domain. In the summer of 1978, with American pressure, a Lebanese army battalion was sent to southern Lebanon. But continued opposition and the Lebanese army's own weakness aborted the effort. The Lebanese battalion reached the village of Kaukaba and then dispersed.

In April 1979, yet another Lebanese battalion was dispatched to the central sector of southern Lebanon. This time, Major Haddad responded sharply and announced the formation of "Free Lebanon" in the small territory under his control. His extraordinary reaction was also induced by the central government's earlier effort to delegitimize his position. Until early 1979, despite his close cooperation with Israel, Haddad had retained his military rank and position, apparently because the government had seen that as a way of asserting its authority in the disputed area. In February, however, Haddad was stripped of his rank and his Lebanese army salary stopped. The episode had no practical consequences, but it added a theatrical element to the sad story of southern Lebanon. It also highlighted the problems Israel had in controlling its Lebanese protege—as the leaders of a small state experienced in the subtleties of patron-client relations (from the other side), the Israeli authorities could appreciate the difficulties of controlling the actions of a seemingly fully dependent client.[27]

A New Syrian Posture, October 1978 to July 1980

Syria's pressure on the Lebanese Front, which had been interrupted in October 1978 largely owing to external intervention, was
lifted a few months later because of the Ba'thi regime's domestic
weakness. The crisis, which had become apparent in 1977, reached
its peak between the summer of 1979 (the massacre of the Alawi
artillery cadets) and the summer of 1980 (the attempt on Asad's life
and the execution of over four hundred Muslim Brothers at the
Palmyra prison). The other protagonists in the struggle over Lebanon's future were fully aware of the extent to which the regime's
weakness and preoccupation with other matters limited its ability to
pursue its objectives in Lebanon.

The most significant early symptom of the change in Syria's position appeared in the autumn of 1979 when, on the eve of the Tunis
Arab summit conference, President Sarkis indicated that he
intended to raise the issues of southern Lebanon and Palestinian
activity in Lebanon at the meetings. His plan was thwarted, but
Syria was displeased not only with the policy itself, which resembled that of the Lebanese Front, but also with the show of
independence.

In January 1980, Syria announced first the withdrawal and then
the redeployment of its troops in Lebanon. Politically the reactions
to the announcement improved Syria's standing in the Lebanese
crisis but not to a degree that could significantly offset its decline in
power. Syria recalled some of its units from Beirut and the coastal
areas and handed over their positions to the PLO, but kept some
troops in Beirut and along the Beirut-Damascus road, and concentrated the bulk of its forces in the Beqa valley in the east.

This new deployment was a statement of priorities. However
weakened, the Ba'thi regime was determined to uphold its influence
in Beirut, the political center, and to preserve a strong defensive
position in the Beqa valley. The Beqa, which Syria had administered
directly since 1976, was not only contested but was strategically
crucial. If Israel ever sought to outflank Syria's main defense line, it
could do so either through northern Jordan or through the Beqa
valley. The latter option was the more likely, and a strong Syrian
defensive line there seemed vital to Syria's military and political

planners. Later, if and when the tide changed, this base could be used for an offensive rather than a defensive Syrian deployment.

Yet another manifestation of the new circumstances in Lebanon was the renewal, in the spring of 1980, of Syria's dialogue with the Lebanese Front, the Phalange in particular. Syria once again sought a reconciliation that would facilitate its own goals. Phalangist leaders, aware of Syria's weak bargaining position, tried to extract concessions that Syria had refused to make in the past. The Syrian regime refused to make such concessions even in its hour of weakness, and the attempted dialogue collapsed in the summer of 1980.

The Phalangist Challenge, Summer 1980 to Spring 1981

In the summer of 1980, the Phalanges completed the campaign begun two years earlier to take control of the Lebanese Front. On July 7, they destroyed the military power of the National Liberals' militia. Despite the bloodshed, most of the Chamounists accepted the new reality, continued to cooperate with the Phalanges, and accepted Bashir Jumayyil's supreme authority. Initially, Chamoun tried to save face by transferring his military strongholds in Ayn al-Rumani to the Lebanese army and not to the Phalange. But Jumayyil's determination to impose his authority—he was ready to fight the Lebanese army if necessary—persuaded both Chamoun and the army's command to accept his position. The Phalangist drive was more than the pursuit of power and domination; it was rooted in a concept in which the unification of the Maronite and Christian communities' resources was a crucial interim strategic goal in the struggle over Lebanon's future. There was no need to make, indeed no point in making, a decision on the Front's ultimate aims in that struggle. If a unified Lebanon could be maintained, which would preserve the ethos and power structure of the traditional Lebanese entity, then the Front should strive for it. If that were not to be the case, the "smaller Lebanon" strategy should be resorted to, whether in the form of partition or cantonization. In either case, the independent power base of the Front should be enlarged and reinforced.

The Lebanese Front's official line was articulated in a document published in December 1980 under the title *The Lebanon We Want to Build*. Essentially, the manifesto addressed the cardinal question asked by the Maronite community since the outbreak of the civil war: how to reconcile the desire to maintain a predominantly Christian entity with the demographic realities of Lebanon, given the opposition of a powerful domestic and external coalition to both the perpetuation of the traditional Lebanese system, and to the creation of a "smaller Lebanon."

The Front argued that the formula of the 1943 National Pact no longer applied. It demanded on behalf of all Lebanese Christians that they should have a special position in Lebanon (regardless of population figures). Lebanon's Christians had played a special role in shaping its history and in any case needed the protection of their own entity. Curiously, the English-language version of the document described the Middle East, of which Lebanon was an integral part, as a pluralistic region composed of other non-Arab states such as Turkey, Israel, and Iran. The Arabic version, however, omitted this reference to Israel, another indication of the Front's ambivalent relationship with that country.

At the same time, the development of the infrastructure for an embryonic Christian state in the mountains and coastal area north of Beirut proceeded vigorously. It comprised a small army (trained and supplied mainly by Israel), governmental and administrative apparatus, and an intellectual center at Kaslik, the University of the Holy Spirit. Christian autonomy offered security, economic prosperity, and a new style of government—immediate and demanding, quite different from the customary weak Lebanese state. (Service in the Maronite militias, once a matter of choice or social pressure, became mandatory for students in 1981.)[28]

The growing power and confidence of the Lebanese Front, the continued weakness of the Syrian Ba'thi regime, and greater Israeli support induced the Front's leadership to take a bold step at the end of 1980 and extend its military and political presence to Zahle. The move to Zahle and the effort to link it to the Maronite heartland by a direct road beyond Syria's control were interpreted by Syria as an attempt to change the status quo and to undermine Syria's position in the part of Lebanon most vital to its interests. Syrian spokesmen suggested that the Front's initiative had been coordinated with Israel and was part of a scheme to enable the two allies to join forces after an Israeli thrust toward Zahle from southern Lebanon. This interpretation has not been confirmed, but the possibility of Israeli troops or their Lebanese allies in the Beqa valley was most unsettling for Syria's leaders.[29]

During the winter of 1980–81, Syria and the Front were in subtle conflict over Zahle and the road from Zahle to Mount Lebanon. They each sought to capture Mount Sanin, at the eastern edge of Mount Lebanon, a position dominating Zahle on one side and affording access toward Jounieh on the other. But in March 1981, the conflict assumed entirely different and ominous dimensions. A Phalangist unit, trying to take control of a strategically located bridge in Zahle, trapped a Syrian unit and inflicted heavy casualties. Syria responded with massive, sustained shelling of the Phalangist militia as well as Zahle's civilian population. The severity and ferocity of the Syrian response was undoubtedly a reflection of the gravity of the challenge as perceived in Damascus: apparently not only Zahle and eastern Lebanon but Syria's position and investment throughout Lebanon were at stake. The various protagonists in Lebanon were already positioning themselves for the 1982 presidential elections, and an extension of the Lebanese Front's area of influence could have far-reaching ramifications for its own and Syria's position.

Hafiz al-Asad is a man who calculates his moves carefully, and he must have known that his fierce counterattack in Zahle and his subsequent attack on the Lebanese Front's positions on the eastern slopes of Mount Lebanon were likely to bring an Israeli reaction. It seems he was ready for a confrontation with Israel, and possibly even relished it. For one thing by the spring of 1981, the Syrian Ba'thi regime felt that it had weathered the crisis of 1979–80. Armed with a new treaty with the Soviet Union and in command of a large and well-equipped army, Asad had displayed a renewed sense of confidence since the end of 1980. Syria was able to disrupt the Arab summit conference in Amman and to threaten war with Jordan. Phalangist and Israeli challenges, countenanced in time of weakness, were no longer to be tolerated. Furthermore, in March 1981 Secretary of State Haig toured the Middle East on behalf of the new American administration. His mission was to bring Washington's

diverse friends together into some pattern of cooperation and formulate a U.S. policy for the next phase of the Arab-Israeli peace
process. Syria was excluded from Secretary Haig's itinerary, and
references to Syria in his statements were couched in negative
terms. It suited Asad's purpose to demonstrate to the Reagan administration that it could not afford to snub Syria.

Syria's actions, primarily helicopter landing of commando units
on Mount Sanin, demonstrated how thin was the line separating
success from failure and the offensive from the defensive throughout the Lebanese crisis. Syria was no longer the beleaguered defender of its most vital area of interests in Lebanon but rather was
posing a threat to the heart of the Lebanese Front's territorial base.
The Israeli government, which had probably been aware of its ally's
plans in Zahle, was suddenly presented with an odious choice.
Should it intervene in a crisis initiated by the Front, one that might
not be acceptable to the Israeli public? Syria's use of helicopters
against the Phalanges was an infringement of the 1976 agreement.
Could Israel ignore the infraction? And what could it do, short of
fighting the Syrian army, to enforce the rules established in 1976?

The crisis and the debate it generated, three months before the
crucial Israeli parliamentary elections in June 1981, served to un-
cover many details about the Israeli alliance with the Lebanese Front
and to turn a semiclandestine relationship into a matter for public
scrutiny and discussion. The deputy minister of defense, Mor-
dechai Tzipori, made no secret of his opposition to close cooperation
with the Lebanese Front and alluded publicly to his fear that the
Front was dragging Israel into an ever greater involvement in the
Lebanese crisis. Moshe Dayan, the former foreign minister, criticized the whole drift of Israel's policy in Lebanon. Prime Minister
Begin, in its defense, made two significant revelations: that Israel
had promised the Front that it would not allow the Syrian air force to
operate against it and that Begin had dispatched an emissary to "the
Christians" to tell them that Israel would not be drawn into war on
their behalf.[30]

With regard to Syria, the Israeli government finally decided to
escape its dilemma by ordering the Israeli air force to shoot down
two Syrian helicopters carrying supplies to its newly established
positions on Mount Sanin, signaling that neither the use of the air

force nor the advance toward Mount Lebanon would be tolerated. Implicit in the signal was the message that Israel was willing to accept Syrian hegemony in Zahle. In terms of the "rules of the game" for the Lebanese crisis, Israel was acknowledging that its allies (and indirectly Israel, too) had overplayed their hand in Zahle and was proposing a return to the status quo.

The Missile Crisis, Spring 1981

Syria, which had made technical preparations in advance, responded to Israel's shooting down of its helicopters by introducing ground-to-air missiles to the Zahle area and by deploying additional long-range missiles in Syrian territory along the Lebanese border.

These measures were taken partly in the context of the conflict over the Zahle area. Israel had aerial superiority, which Syria countered with the weapon system proven effective in 1973. But some of Syria's new missiles, particularly those positioned on the Syrian side of the border, covered Lebanon's airspace well to the west and south of the Zahle area. Their positioning could be interpreted as a Syrian decision to take part in future conflicts between Israel and the Palestinians elsewhere in Lebanon. And in any case, while the use of helicopters in Mount Sanin could possibly be explained away, the introduction of ground-to-air missiles to Lebanon's territory was an unequivocal violation of the 1976 agreements.

Once again the Israeli government faced a confounding array of contradictory considerations. The challenge and its implications were clear, and a response was called for. Israel had developed, in response to the lessons of 1973, the technology and the techniques to neutralize the Syrian missiles. But was it worthwhile to expose the new development in a crisis that fell far short of a real war? And as the elections drew closer, it was difficult to separate crisis management from domestic politics. The United States did not relish the prospect of a Syrian-Israeli war, and from that point of view, if military action were to be taken, it had to be taken immediately.

And indeed, as Prime Minister Begin later revealed, an Israeli military action was planned for April 30. (It was postponed owing to weather conditions.) A few days later, the Reagan administration dispatched Philip Habib, a retired senior State Department official, to mediate between Syria and Israel. Ambassador Habib's mediation did not resolve the missile crisis, but it enabled the Begin government to proceed through the June elections without resorting to military action and encouraged the Syrian Ba'thi regime to hope for a renewed dialogue with the United States under relatively favorable circumstances. Habib tried to negotiate, with Saudi Arabia's help, a broader settlement for the Lebanese crisis. He failed, but his long mission provided him with the experience and personal knowledge that made him so effective a year later.

The missile crisis also provided the first test for the October 1980 Soviet-Syrian treaty. The treaty undoubtedly emboldened Syria, and the Soviet Union might have been interested in a controlled crisis that would obstruct the Reagan administration's initiatives against Soviet policies in the Middle East. But the escalation of the situation brought Moscow's dilemma to the surface: it did not wish to be pulled by Syria to the brink of a crisis and potential embarrassment. It chose to act ambiguously: while the helicopter carrier *Moscow* was brought closer to the Lebanese coast, the Soviet ambassador to Beirut stated that the Soviet-Syrian treaty did not necessarily apply to Lebanon. This was taken to mean that the Soviet Union would not respond to a Syrian defeat in Lebanon but was likely to intervene if Syria itself, and certainly Damascus, were threatened. As tension slackened and Syrian-Israeli fighting seemed less likely, statements by Soviet spokesmen became bolder.

Egypt under Sadat was far less ambiguous. Various Egyptian spokesmen criticized Israeli policy in Lebanon and took exception to the isolationist trends of the Lebanese Front; but they also demanded the withdrawal of Syrian forces from Lebanon. Furthermore, at the height of the crisis, Sadat visited Begin in Israel, which on the eve of the June elections was an unmistakable sign of support. Sadat's actions were governed by one consideration: nothing was to interfere with Israeli withdrawal from the Sinai by April 25, 1982. Once Egypt had the whole of the Sinai, a new strategic equation would come into being, and such regional problems as the Lebanese crisis could be confronted from a different vantage point.

Israeli-Palestinian Fighting, July 1981

While the Syrian-Israeli missile crisis remained unresolved, another related crisis erupted in July. Israel's defense establishment was worried by the buildup of the PLO's military infrastructure in southern Lebanon, which they feared could enable the Palestinians to launch a war of attrition along the Lebanese-Israeli border. The "umbrella" provided by the Syrian missiles reinforced these fears. In July, the Israeli cabinet authorized the Israeli army to try to destroy that military infrastructure, particularly the artillery, from the air.

Eventually, the Israeli operation brought about the very thing that had motivated it: The PLO shelled northern Galilee, inflicted heavy damage, and kept the population in air-raid shelters for days. Israel's artillery and air force were incapable of stopping it. The Israeli cabinet authorized an extensive air raid on Palestinian headquarters in Beirut, which resulted in massive loss of life and damage to neighboring areas. The Reagan administration then intervened, and with the help of Ambassador Habib and Saudi Arabia, arranged for a cease-fire.

The July crisis was an important event in the transition from the earlier phases of the Lebanese crisis to the war of 1982. It demonstrated the PLO's capacity to paralyze the northern part of Israel at will from its territorial base in southern Lebanon. The July cease-fire did not solve, or even alleviate the problem; it merely froze it. All parties to the crisis realized that when a Palestinian-Israeli conflict reerupted along the Lebanese-Israeli border it would not be limited. The PLO was capable of shelling northern Israel, and the Israeli government was determined to put an end to its capacity to do so.

By suspending the issue, the cease-fire served also to place it in the context of the broader political developments that shaped the course of the Arab-Israeli conflict during the following year, a year during which the nature and scope of the war which broke out in Lebanon in June 1982 were determined.

CHAPTER 5

War, June–September 1982

THE FIFTH ARAB-ISRAELI WAR, which began on June 6, 1982, departed radically from the patterns of the previous thirty-four years of conflict. The war was fought in Lebanon, to some extent for Lebanon, but primarily by Israel and the PLO and to a lesser extent by Syria. It was the first Arab-Israeli war fought during a period of partial Arab-Israeli peace. Paradoxically, its outbreak was affected by the dynamics of the Egyptian-Israeli peace process of the previous five years. The war was unusually long, lasting just over three months, if mid-September is taken as its end point, and its military dimension was often overshadowed by its political aspects—the goals it sought, the controversies it generated, and the impact it has had on the Lebanese political system, on the Palestinian issue, and on Israeli and Arab politics. If one wants to understand the war's novel elements and the paradoxes it produced the making of the war and its unfolding should be examined first.

The Making of the War

On June 6, 1982, the Israeli cabinet issued a statement explaining the goals of the military operations launched by the Israeli Defense Forces (IDF). The cabinet had decided:

(1) To instruct the IDF to place all the civilian population of the Galilee beyond the range of the terrorists' fire from Lebanon where they, their bases, and their headquarters are concentrated.

(2) The name of the operation is Peace for Galilee.

(3) During the operation the Syrian army will not be attacked unless it attacks our forces.

(4) Israel continues to aspire to the signing of a peace treaty with independent Lebanon, its territorial integrity preserved.[1]

Various government spokesmen argued on June 6 and in the following few days that "Israel's sole purpose is to destroy the PLO's infrastructure in southern Lebanon."[2] But as the cabinet's original statement implied, operation Peace for Galilee had far more ambitious goals. Defense Minister Sharon and other spokesmen became increasingly explicit during the summer of 1982 about the purposes of the Israeli operation.[3] Over the next few months, the growing controversy in Israel and within the cabinet resulted in a deluge of revelations concerning the war's goals. These goals can be summed up under four headings: (a) destroying the PLO military infrastructure in southern Lebanon and the creating of a security zone of some forty kilometers, the effective range of the PLO's artillery and rocket launchers; (b) destroying the PLO's position in the rest of Lebanon, particularly in Beirut, to eliminate its hold on the Lebanese political system and to diminish its role in the Arab-Israeli conflict; (c) defeating the Syrian army in Lebanon to effect its full or partial withdrawal from that country and to preempt the possibility of a Syrian-Israeli war; (d) thereby facilitating the reconstruction of the Lebanese state and political system under the hegemony of Israel's allies—Bashir Jumayyil and the Lebanese Front.[4]

The definition of the objectives and the planners' belief that they could be implemented resulted from several developments that in the second half of 1981 and in the early months of 1982 affected the Lebanese crisis, the Arab-Israeli conflict, and the Israeli political system.

The Syrian "missile crisis" of 1981 and the Palestinian-Israeli fighting in July of that year moved the Lebanese crisis to a new phase, in which the preservation of a delicately balanced status quo became untenable. For Israel the presence of the Syrian missiles in the Beqa valley was not only a violation of the 1976 "red line" agreement, but a serious threat and a step toward an increasingly offensive Syrian posture in Lebanon. But a more immediate challenge was the PLO military capability, demonstrated in the ex-changes in July 1981, when its artillery and rocket launchers sent the population of northern Galilee to (inadequate) shelters, and Israel's artillery and air force were unable to neutralize them. The cease-fire that Philip Habib negotiated at the end of July provided a relatively calm year along the Lebanese-Israeli border but not a fundamental solution. During the next ten months the actual scope of the cease-fire agreement was much debated. Israel argued that it applied to all anti-Israeli activities originating in Lebanon whether they occurred in Sa'd Haddad's territory, along the Jordanian-Israeli frontier, or in Western Europe; the PLO insisted that the agreement was limited to actions directed at Israel proper from across the Lebanese border.

But this controversy served to disguise the issue—that the PLO had the capacity to create havoc in northern Israel at will and that the only way for Israel to eliminate that threat, given the nature of its relationship with the PLO, was through a large-scale operation on the ground. The Israeli leadership felt, furthermore, that the PLO was using the cease-fire and the cessation of Israel's preemptive raids to expand and improve its military position in southern Lebanon against the inevitable collapse of the cease-fire.[5]

Whether a large-scale ground operation could solve the problem was the subject of an unusually open debate in Israel during the spring of 1982. The minister of defense, Ariel Sharon, took no part in the public debate, however, leaving it to the chief of staff, General Eytan, to argue that there was a military solution to the problem of the PLO in southern Lebanon.[6] Two of the Labor party's chief spokesmen on national security affairs, Yitzhak Rabin and Mor-dechai Gur (both former chiefs of staff), argued that a large-scale operation could not solve the problem and that it was better to keep the cease-fire, unsatisfactory as it might be.[7] Two debates were in fact conducted simultaneously though they were not clearly dis-tinguished. The Labor opposition was primarily opposed to a large-scale operation; it was not as strongly opposed to a limited one, designed to create a "security zone" in southern Lebanon. The government's position was that a limited operation was meaning-less, another Litani; as long as the PLO remained entrenched in Beirut, any operation in southern Lebanon was bound to be merely a temporary remedy.

In Lebanese politics the approaching end of President Sarkis's term of office (September 23, 1982) and the need to elect a successor between May and September provided a sense of urgency. Three major candidates emerged: the Lebanese Front's (Bashir Jumayyil); Syria's (Suleiman Faranjiyya); Raymond Eddé (who as an independent Lebanese nationalist, anti-Syrian and anti-Phalangist politician was in a category by himself). A fourth possibility was a compromise (either the extension of Sarkis's term or the nomination of a respectable neutral Maronite politician such as Jean Aziz).

In early 1982, Bashir Jumayyil, Suleiman Faranjiyya, and Raymond Eddé were building up support and alliances for their campaigns. The election of any one of them would represent a victory for a distinct policy orientation. Bashir Jumayyil had showed himself to be the most explicit of the three when, on November 21, 1981, in a forceful speech broadcast on the Phalange radio station, he presented a platform, a timetable, and a characterization of the desirable candidate. Jumayyil's move ended a brief period during which he had given Saudi Arabia an opportunity to pursue a political settlement of the Lebanese crisis. It will be recalled that in the aftermath of the missile crisis, he had formally severed his relationship with Israel, at once a reflection of his disappointment with Israel's position and an acceptance of Saudi Arabia's precondition. But by November the Saudi effort produced no results, and at the Arab summit in Fez, Saudi Arabia was defeated and humiliated by Syria. It became evident that other avenues had to be explored.

It was at about that time that the idea of linking Bashir Jumayyil's quest for the presidency with a large-scale Israeli operation reaching as far as Beirut's international airport was born. The plan was apparently discussed during Sharon's visit to Beirut in January.[8] It was one of several options being considered by Jumayyil, and it had serious drawbacks: if an electoral victory were grafted onto an Israeli military campaign, the new president's legitimacy would be affected; and there was no certainty that Israel would launch an operation or do so successfully. So Jumayyil and his followers explored other options, most notably an attempt in April and May to renew a dialogue with Syria. An understanding was not reached, but the propaganda warfare was toned down.

Developments among the Lebanese Front's rivals gave additional signs that a fundamental change in the paradigms of Lebanon's domestic politics was becoming more feasible. There was open rivalry and actual fighting between the PLO and both Shi'i militias in Beirut and southern Lebanon and the Nasserites in Sidon, unrest in West Beirut, and fighting between pro-Syrian and anti-Syrian groups in Tripoli. In response to the violence in Tripoli Walid Junblatt, the titular leader of the National Front, called for "a Lebanese solution" to Lebanon's problems. These developments should not be blown out of proportion by telescoping the events of 1982 into a chain of causes and effects, but they did provide the essential background for the bold plans Israel's government made in the spring.[9]

Less notice was taken at the time of the change in Washington's outlook on the Lebanese crisis. The nominal continuation of Philip Habib's mediation mission created the impression that Secretary Haig's denunciations of Syria's role in Lebanon in the spring of 1981 were a passing episode. But the Reagan administration had to contend with the ever-present danger of deterioration of the Lebanese crisis; in November 1981 it was also made aware of Israel's determination to effect a radical change in the status quo in Lebanon.[10] In February 1982, the Israeli director of military intelligence, General Sagi, was dispatched to Washington with a similar message. On both occasions the United States acted to prevent an attack on Lebanon, arguing that Israel's charges of cease-fire violation were no justification for such action and that the anticipated repercussions were too dangerous.[11] The U.S. government's principal concern was that a war in Lebanon might jeopardize the completion of Israel's withdrawal from the Sinai and consequently the stability of Husni Mubarak's regime.

By May the mood of the Reagan administration, as articulated by the secretary of state, had changed. The risks inherent in an Israeli operation seemed to be outweighed by the opportunities it might produce. The cease-fire was bound to collapse sometime, and Israel was then expected to launch a large-scale operation. It was preferable to avert a war in Lebanon altogether, but if it was bound to happen, the opportunity should be seized for bringing about a comprehensive solution to the Lebanese crisis, perhaps even for seeking a new breakthrough in the Arab-Israeli peace process.

This was by no means the only perspective within the Reagan administration on a large-scale Israeli operation in Lebanon. Secretary of Defense Caspar Weinberger and Special Assistant to the National Security Council William Clark in particular advocated a different view: such an operation would generate anti-American feeling in the Arab world, endanger the stability of conservative pro-American regimes in the Persian Gulf and give the Soviet Union the opportunity to reestablish its influence in the region. And as for the Arab-Israeli settlement process, it would be obstructed by the opening of a new front in Lebanon.

Yet this body of opinion was not taken sufficiently into account by Sharon and the Israeli cabinet when they evaluated the significance of Secretary Haig's meeting with the Israeli minister of defense in Washington in May; rather, the secretary's response was interpreted as a tacit endorsement of their intentions. The Israelis were impressed by the change in the secretary's position since April as well as by the fact that his support was more explicit than any of his predecessors' in comparable circumstances.[12] But they overlooked some of the nuances of his statements as well as the fact that Haig did not represent the whole gamut of administration opinion. The result was an ambiguous understanding, which undergirded the Israeli decision to launch a large-scale operation in Lebanon in June but which contributed to subsequent misunderstandings between the Reagan administration and the Begin government.

Haig's belief, in the spring of 1982, in a swift, thorough solution to the Lebanese crisis was also expressed in public, when he appeared before the Chicago Council on Foreign Relations on May 26, 1982. Such occasions are conducive to bland statements, but the secretary was unusually explicit: "Lebanon today is a focal point of danger . . . and the stability of the region hangs in the balance. . . . The Arab deterrent force, now consisting entirely of Syrian troops . . . has not stabilized the situation. . . . The time has come to take concerted action in support of both Lebanon's territorial integrity within its internationally recognized borders and a strong central government capable of promoting a free, open, democratic, and traditionally pluralistic society."[13]

Secretary Haig's remarks referred to the anticipated collapse of the cease-fire in southern Lebanon with which the United States,

Israel, and the Arabs were preoccupied in the final months of 1981 and the first half of 1982. But ominous as the Palestinian-Israeli conflict in Lebanon had become, it was only one of several concerns endowing Israel's Middle East policy with the frenzied quality that characterized it that year.

It was a policy formulated and conducted by the reelected Likud government, which operated in the atmosphere of incongruity produced by the combination of an ideological commitment, a sense of power, and an equally acute sense of impending disaster. The electoral victory in June 1981 returned to power a different Likud government. Menachem Begin's first government had been affected by inexperience and lack of confidence. Its four years in office might have proved no more than a passing episode in the history of a polity dominated by its political opponents. People alien to the Herut movement—Moshe Dayan, Ezer Weizman, and others shaped by an earlier era—went against the grain of the Herut movement's policies and diluted its message. But the second electoral victory and the belief that it reflected the underlying currents of Israeli society instilled in Begin, his party, and his government a new sense of confidence and a determination to implement their ideas. This was particularly true of the commitment to Eretz Israel (the idea of the ancestral homeland), the determination to hold on to the West Bank and the Gaza Strip, and to ensure that while these might not be annexed to Israel, they would not come under any other sovereignty, least of all that of a Palestinian state.

The second dominant figure in the new government was the new minister of defense, Ariel Sharon. He had matured in the tradition represented by David Ben-Gurion, Moshe Dayan, and the defense establishment of the 1950s and 1960s, but he had been instrumental in the formation of the Likud bloc and, since 1977, in developing Jewish settlements and an infrastructure tied to Israel in the West Bank. Formerly a renowned general and field commander, he enjoyed an unusual authority in his determination to control the large apparatus composed of the IDF, the defense bureaucracy, and the defense industry. He had a comprehensive view of Israel's national security problems and needs, a fresh set of concepts and policies which he was determined to put into practice, and the capacity to launch them simultaneously. Less than six months after becoming

minister of defense, Sharon had come to dominate, nearly to monopolize, Israel's defense (and, to a large extent, its foreign) policy.
He had begun to reorganize the ministry of defense and the defense
industries, to institute a new policy in the West Bank and Gaza
Strip, to couch the Israeli-American relationship in terms of "a strategic understanding," to deal with Israeli-Egyptian relations and
the evacuation of the northern Sinai settlements, and to seek a
diplomatic breakthrough in Africa. He formulated his comprehensive view of Israel's national security in a strategy position paper
that was made public in December 1981. But it barely mentioned a
subject to which he had devoted much thinking—the Lebanese
crisis.

The sense of power and confidence that was instilled in the new
government by its electoral victory was bolstered by the unusual
state of the Arab-Israeli military and political balance. Egypt was
ostracized by the Arab states, and Sadat's policy toward Israel was
governed by the expectation of receiving the rest of the Sinai by
April 25, 1982, and a determination not to jeopardize that
eventuality by a forceful response to Israeli actions, resented as they
might be. With Iraq bogged down in the campaign against Iran and
Syrian-Jordanian relations in a state of active hostility, the likelihood
of an active eastern front seemed remote. Israel enjoyed a clear
military superiority and could act with apparent impunity. A political price would have to be paid for settling the West Bank and for the
destruction of the Iraqi nuclear reactor, but as long as the fundamental support of the United States was guaranteed, such other reactions as international condemnation and increasing world support
for the PLO appeared, or were depicted as, inconsequential.

However, this sense of power should not be confused with com-
placency or a sense of security. The same Israel that appeared so
awesome to the Arabs and the rest of the world was genuinely
troubled by dark visions of soon expected radical change in the
Arab-Israeli balance of power. An incongruous blend of confidence
and anxiety had become a familiar element in Israel's frame of mind
and national security policies, but in 1981-82 the anxieties were
particularly acute.

For one thing it appeared then that the most important aspect of
Begin's foreign policy, his strategy in the Israeli-Egyptian peace

process, was in danger of collapsing. Begin's interpretation of the Camp David accords was that he had given up all of the Sinai, a concession well beyond the Israeli consensus, in return for full peace with Egypt and for a vague and a limited autonomy for the West Bank and the Gaza Strip. According to that interpretation Israel, too, was entitled to lay a claim to these territories at the end of the transitional period envisaged by the Camp David accords.[14] This was not an interpretation shared by the other two participants at the Camp David conference. During the next three years all sought to advance their respective interpretations (the American and Egyptian versions were rather similar), and this difference of opinion was an important factor contributing to the collapse of the autonomy negotiations in 1980.

The failure of the autonomy negotiations added yet another difficulty to those besetting the precarious Egyptian-Israeli relationship, but it did not produce an acute crisis. By 1981 the completion of Israel's withdrawal seemed close enough to warrant some more Egyptian patience. Egyptians felt—and said—that with the whole of the Sinai in their possession they would be in a much better position to assert pressure to settle the Palestinian issue.

In the summer of 1981, the Israeli government became increasingly perturbed by the very same thought. April 1982 was some eight months away, an Egyptian-Israeli agreement on the autonomy plan had not been reached, and the roles were reversed. Egypt became interested in a continuation of the peace process (implementing Israel's withdrawal from the Sinai and maintaining the current level of normalization) while Israel, before its bargaining power was seriously crippled by the final withdrawal, began to insist that an agreement on the autonomy plan had to be reached. The Israeli government's anxieties were soon compounded by other developments. The publication of the Fahd plan, in August 1981, was seen as an adumbration of trends expected to take full shape after April 1982. In the plan Saudi Arabia presented an alternative to the Camp David framework, an attempt to put the Arab-Israeli settlement process back on the course from which, according to the Saudis, it had deviated in November 1977. The United States and Egypt, while not endorsing the Saudi plan, were careful not to reject it. Was Israel, then, to complete its withdrawal from the Sinai only to begin the struggle for the West Bank under adverse circumstances? The impact of these developments was increased by the conflict between the Reagan administration and the Begin government over the AWACS sale to Saudi Arabia, which not only was anticipated to alter the Arab-Israeli military balance, but also demonstrated the extent of Saudi influence in Washington. Saudi Arabia's desire to return to the idea of comprehensive settlement was likely to be equally effective.

The policies devised by the Begin government to counter these trends did not prove very successful. The assassination of Anwar Sadat in October 1981 was in itself a grave blow. Israel may have had doubts about Sadat's ultimate intentions, but there was no doubting the centrality of the new relationship with Israel in his policies. Nothing so certain could be said about his successor, whose political prospects and commitment to a peaceful relationship with Israel had yet to be ascertained. In more immediate terms Sadat's assassination meant that Israel lost whatever leverage it had possessed vis-à-vis Egypt. In September, the Begin government could still suggest that failure to reach an agreement on autonomy might jeopardize the completion of withdrawal from the Sinai; in October such implied threats ceased to be credible. The stability of Mubarak's regime became a matter of great concern to Washington, and Egyptians and Israelis alike knew that the United States would go to great lengths to ensure Israel's withdrawal. President Mubarak was determined that the autonomy negotiations would not be resumed before that event, and indeed they were not.

In the West Bank, Israel's efforts fell into two categories. Construction of new settlements and development of a physical infrastructure linked to Israel could be largely controlled and proceeded at a swift pace. But efforts to cultivate a new local political leadership that would participate in implementing the limited autonomy envisaged by the Begin government met with little success. It was the government's view that as long as the PLO retained its hold over the population in the West Bank and the Gaza Strip, its autonomy plan could not be put into effect, a state of affairs for which the policies pursued by the military government during the previous fourteen years were largely responsible. The second Likud government thus set out to change the concepts and style of governance in the West Bank and the Gaza Strip and, in a radical departure from the patterns of Moshe Dayan, began to intervene in all aspects of daily life, to assail and undermine the political influence of the PLO and its supporters and to nurture a new leadership. The new policy was put into full swing with the launching of the so-called civilian administration in November 1981.[15] By late winter 1982, it had run into enormous difficulties. An effective local leadership ready to cooperate with the Israeli government would evidently not be available for quite some time.

Yet another measure taken by the Begin government, which should be placed in the same context, was the extension of Israeli law to (or virtual Israeli annexation of) the Golan Heights in December 1981. The step probably had a number of motives, some of them domestic, but the primary one seems to have been a desire to demonstrate that Israel still had options available, and would resort to these if others attempted to jettison the Camp David accords and to deny the legitimacy of Israel's claims to the West Bank and the Gaza Strip.[16] But there was a further aspect to the Israeli decision: it was based on a sober calculation of the Arab-Israeli and Syrian-Israeli balance of power at the time. Israel's military superiority and Syria's political isolation and weakness were such that Syria was seen as unlikely to respond to the challenge, severe as it was. And, indeed, it did not. But a significant grievance was added to the relationship, and when Syria was militarily ready, it was deemed certain to retaliate. That prospect did not seem remote; in fact, Syrian military build-up, it was argued, might in a relatively short time prove a factor in altering the Arab-Israeli military balance.

The Syrian armed forces were already impressive, with three armored divisions, two mechanized divisions, six independent armored or mechanized brigades, over 400 combat airplanes, two missile regiments, and several independent commando and paratrooper regiments. If their build-up continued at the same pace, Syrian leaders might within two or three years, perhaps sooner, decide that they had the capacity to challenge Israel. By that time the Egyptian-Israeli relationship might have deteriorated, and Egypt would have absorbed the new American-made weapons systems. Other currently favorable circumstances, the Iraqi preoccupation with Iran and the Syrian-Jordanian hostility, might also change,

Israelis reasoned. The Arab world, unable to contend with Israel's might in 1981 and 1982, might well be able to threaten it in 1983 and 1984.[17]

Within the Begin government, the most ambitious and comprehensive effort to deal with these possibilities was made by the minister of defense. On two occasions at the end of 1981, Sharon publicly discussed his perception of the security challenges facing Israel in the 1980s and some of the solutions he advocated. In October 1981, he defined Israel's "red lines," his view of what constituted a *casus belli:* Arab development or acquisition of nuclear weapons, Arab troop concentration along Israel's borders, violation of demilitarization agreements, and such belligerent acts as interference with naval or aerial communications.[18] In December a statement concerning his conceptual outlook on Israel's strategic problems and policies was published in Israeli newspapers. Like his quest for a strategic understanding with the United States, his conceptualization reflected his view that Israel's impressive military power and potential was the basis for a solid American-Israeli relationship. Accordingly, the Soviet challenge in the region was depicted as the most crucial problem for the 1980s and Israel's security interests were defined in sweeping terms. Sharon's other central point was that Israel would not continue to participate in a quantitative arms race, for which it possessed neither the financial nor the human resources. Instead, it would seek to maintain a "qualitative advantage" (whether this was a reference to a nuclear option is moot).[19] In contrast to the specific references to "red lines" and "security valves" the Lebanese crisis was mentioned only in passing. Clearly this was not a potential "red line," but one that had been crossed. In fact, according to his own testimony, the minister of defense was developing his "big plan"—the plan to remove the challenge to Israel in southern Lebanon with a master stroke that would at the same time solve several other problems and reap numerous other benefits.

The Concept of the War

The "plan" was predicated on a number of premises—that a large-scale operation in southern Lebanon was unavoidable, that

Israel could afford to act only once on a large scale, that the problem in the south could not be solved without solving the wider Lebanese crisis, that a solution to that crisis was possible, and that it could be the key to a significant change in the politics of the whole region.[20] There was no sense in an operation seeking to create just a security zone of some forty kilometers, the range of the PLO artillery north of the Israeli border. By advancing a few more kilometers, by reaching the environs of Beirut and the Beirut-Damascus road, Israel would create a new strategic situation. The PLO base in Lebanon would be destroyed, Syria would have either to withdraw or be defeated and the Lebanese Front, Israel's ally, would take over the whole of Beirut and become the dominant local political force. Bashir Jumayyil could be elected president, and the Lebanese political system reconstructed under a pro-Israeli head of state.

The reconstruction of the Lebanese state would remove the host of problems caused by its disintegration, while the legitimacy of the new government in Beirut and its friendship would endow the security arrangements made in the south with permanence and effectiveness. The destruction of the PLO autonomous territorial base would eliminate one of the foundations of its influence, and weaken the threat it posed, particularly in the West Bank and the Gaza Strip, improving Israel's prospects of implementing an autonomy plan and upholding its interpretation of the Camp David accords. Syria's loss of position in Lebanon would postpone, perhaps even remove, the danger of Israeli-Syrian war later in the decade. Finally, if a new Lebanese government were to sign a peace treaty with Israel or at least have normal open relations with it, the Egyptian-Israeli relationship would be buttressed because it would cease to be a separate peace.[21]

Several of Sharon's cabinet colleagues, as well as the leaders of the opposition, were not persuaded by the plan and refused to condone it. He himself referred to the comprehensiveness of his planning and consultation processes in an interview published in the Israeli newspaper *Maariv* on September 17, 1982: "Many months before the (January) war I traveled to Beirut. I studied and investigated the problem from all possible sides, aspects and directions and in the most thorough fashion. Upon returning I presented to the cabinet, together with the General Staff, a comprehensive plan for the solution of the problem of terror in Lebanon. I can now say that this is the plan that was finally carried out and the results of which we are witnessing today. This plan was discussed a number of times, in cabinet meetings as well as with the leaders of the opposition."

After thorough discussion, the cabinet opted for a more limited plan, and accordingly the IDF launched the operation. But on Saturday, June 5, at a discussion held at the prime minister's home a day before the war began, one of the ministers asked, "What happens when we reach the security zone, beyond the terrorists' artillery range, and the fighting continues?" The prime minister responded, "For that reason the cabinet will meet daily and make decisions according to the evolving situation."[22] The June 5 meeting became one of the principal points of contention during the following year between Ariel Sharon and his critics in the cabinet, who complained they had been misled into endorsing measures well beyond the limits they had in mind. Sharon himself has argued repeatedly that every single step taken in the course of the war was approved by the cabinet. In retrospect, it seems that a suspicious cabinet closely monitored the defense minister's mood and thwarted some of his ideas and initiatives, but not the thrust of his and the chief of staff's plan. The broad lines of the internal debate in Israel can be reconstructed on the basis of the existing evidence, but a more specific description of the deliberations that preceded the launching of the war and subsequently affected its conduct will have to wait until more authoritative documentation becomes available.

The process of consultation was one way Sharon's plans leaked to the Israeli, Arab, and international media, where they were discussed during the six months which preceded the war.[23] Several times during that period PLO violations of Israel's interpretation of the July 1981 cease-fire generated expectation of an imminent Israeli invasion. The war finally broke out in circumstances that seemed to have the inevitability of a Greek tragedy. A Palestinian terrorist squad sent by the organization of Abu Nidal (who at various times was associated with the PLO, Syria, and Iraq) attempted to assassinate the Israeli ambassador to London. Israel retaliated by bombing Palestinian targets in Beirut, and the PLO shelled northern Galilee. On July 5 the Israeli cabinet approved the launching of "Operation Peace for Galilee."

The Five Phases of the War

The course of the war in Lebanon was rather different from the scenarios envisaged by the planners, both the limited version approved by the Israeli cabinet and the broader one that the minister of defense ultimately implemented. The interplay between the anticipated and the unexpected emerges clearly from a look at the five phases through which the war unfolded.

The Initial Thrust

During the first three days of the war, Israel's major effort was invested in the western and central sectors of southern Lebanon. (See Map 4.) In the west ground troops, joined by troops landed from the sea, made a rapid advance toward Damour, a Christian town just south of Beirut, which had been taken over by the PLO in 1976. Fighting in the west was almost purely against the PLO. The larger towns of Tyre and Sidon were passed, besieged, and taken over later—a strategy influenced by the contradictory quests for swift advance and limited casualties. The PLO put up only limited resistance to the Israeli troops, preferring to withdraw to the north. This strategy had two important consequences: it brought the Israeli army to the outskirts of Beirut within three days of the war's outbreak, but it also preserved most PLO combatants and concentrated them in the city's western and southern sections.

In the central sector, an Israeli column advanced through difficult mountainous terrain, fighting against both Syrians and Palestinians and seeking a way to the Beirut-Damascus highway. In the east, only a limited military effort was made, in keeping with the stated policy that Israel would not attack Syria's forces unless attacked by them first.

During these first three days, the war was still believed by most observers to have the limited goal implied by its name—the creation of a security zone in southern Lebanon. It was endorsed by the Israeli Labor opposition and encountered virtually no criticism in Israel and only mild opposition abroad. Despite its reservations about the campaign, the Reagan administration was clearly determined to enable Israel to complete it and defeated efforts made at

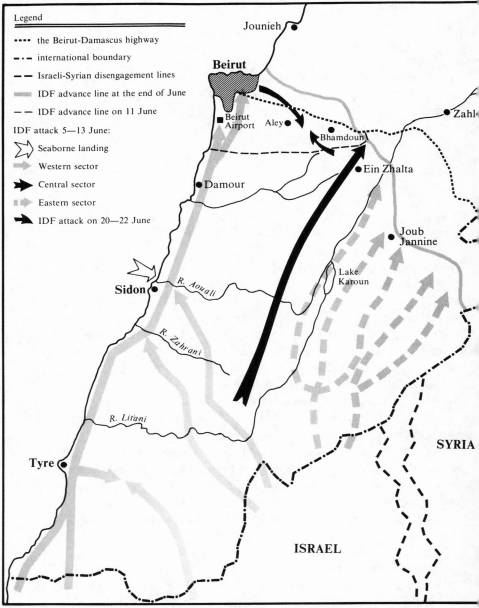

Map 4. Israel's Lebanese campaign of June 1982, major routes of advance.

Legend

• • • • the Beirut-Damascus highway

• — • — international boundary

— — Israeli-Syrian disengagement lines

▨▨▨ IDF advance line at the end of June

— — IDF advance line on 11 June

IDF attack 5—13 June:

▷ Seaborne landing

⇨ Western sector

➤ Central sector

⇨ Eastern sector

➤ IDF attack on 20—22 June

Jounieh

Beirut

Zahl

Beirut Airport

Aley

Bhamdoun

Ein Zhalta

Damour

Joub Jannine

Lake Karoun

R. Aouali

Sidon

R. Zahrani

R. Litani

Tyre

SYRIA

ISRAEL

the UN to impose an early cease-fire. The protests of the Soviet Union and the Arab states were remarkably mild.

A Limited War with Syria

By June 9, a limited war had developed between Israel and Syria. Syria was clearly reluctant to join the war in Lebanon—it had so signaled to Israel in the winter, and during the war's first three days Syrian forces tried not to cross the fine line that separated limited support of the PLO from the level of fighting likely to provoke an Israeli response.[24]

The effort failed. The Israeli government accused the Syrian government of bad faith during Ambassador Habib's efforts to prevent Syrian-Israeli fighting, but two other factors should also be taken into account. One was the minister of defense's feeling that a limited military victory over Syria in Lebanon was preferable for the advancement of the war's aims. The other was a contradiction inherent in the very definition of the limited war plan. Israel could move twenty-five miles northward into Lebanon without colliding with Syrian troops in the western sector but not in the central and certainly not in the eastern sector, where Syrian troops and PLO units under a Syrian umbrella were stationed close to the Israeli border. Consequently as long as the Palestinians were not ousted from the southern Beqa Valley or at least put under strict Syrian control, the principal stated aim of Operation Peace for Galilee could not be achieved.

The Israeli forces then began to exert pressure on the southern flank of the Syrian forces in the Beqa Valley in eastern Lebanon, taking full advantage of the fact that, by the third day, the Israeli column in the central sector had outflanked the Syrian forces in the Beqa Valley. At the same time the Israeli airforce destroyed the Syrian ground-to-air missile system in Lebanon and shot down several dozen Syrian fighter planes.[25]

On June 10, the war's fifth day, Syrian forces were held in a pincer. A large Israeli army was stationed in the Golan Heights, deterring the main body of the Syrian army from expanding the war, while in the Beqa Valley a beleaguered Syrian force, shorn of air support, was trying to check the IDF's advance in an area alarmingly close to Damascus. And no real support was forthcoming from the Soviet Union or any Arab nation. Syria exerted heavy pressure on Moscow, Moscow did the same in Washington, and Washington, for reasons of its own, pressed the Israeli government to agree to a cease-fire. The cease-fire went into effect on June 11, before the Israeli forces in the center reached the Beirut-Damascus road and before a more satisfactory line could be secured in the east.

In the western sector, the Israeli army had reached the southern outskirts of Beirut, and Sidon and Tyre were captured, except for small pockets of resistance. These two developments fed the political controversy that developed during this phase of the war. The IDF's progress toward Beirut as well as a change of tone in the public and private statements of Israeli officials suggested that the war's aims had been far more ambitious than originally declared—which aroused criticism from the political opposition, from the Israeli media, and from abroad. The government's domestic critics argued against the expansion of the war, its conduct by the prime minister and the minister of defense, and the civilian casualties and physical destruction in Tyre and Sidon.[26]

Transition to the Siege of Beirut

The cease-fire of June 11 ended a significant phase of the war. The IDF had succeeded both in defeating the Syrian army in Lebanon and in limiting the scope of the encounter—the war did not spread to the Golan Heights and the Soviet Union did not intervene on Syria's behalf. The IDF demonstrated that it could contend with two weapons that had previously caused concern—the Soviet-made ground-to-air missile systems and the T-72 tank. Equally significant, Syria, by seeking an early cease-fire left Israel free to focus on Beirut. In the days following the cease-fire, Israeli forces continued their advance toward southern and eastern Beirut and established a territorial link with the forces of the Lebanese Front.

Evidence regarding the events of those days is still fragmented and controversial, but it seems that Israel expected the forces of the Lebanese Front to capture West Beirut and complete the PLO's rout.[27] But whatever the understanding between Ariel Sharon and Bashir Jumayyil on this issue, the leader of the Lebanese Front had no intention of storming West Beirut, and his forces' military activity remained negligible. With thousands of PLO combatants in West Beirut, any attempt to take that part of the city by force was not likely to succeed and most likely to be very costly, an important consideration for the leader of a small force representing a community haunted by a sense of steady demographic retrenchment. Equally important was the feeling that by sending his men to storm West Beirut under an Israeli umbrella and in circumstances bound to lead to massive destruction and bloodshed, Bashir Jumayyil would ruin his prospects of becoming the legitimate president of Lebanon. Beyond these two considerations, there was a crucial difference in Israel's and the Front's perceptions of their cooperation. From the Israeli government's vantage point, the Front was to help liberate its country and pave its own road to power. From Jumayyil's point of view, if Israel wanted to act as a regional power and bring about political changes through a military campaign, it ought to pay the price that the capture of West Beirut was bound to exact.[28]

This turn of events presented the Israeli government with a painful dilemma. As Jumayyil may have shrewdly calculated, Israel could not afford to let the PLO stay in West Beirut. The course of the war had created an entirely new situation, and Israel had already defined its purposes in terms much more ambitious than those announced originally. Israel's impressive achievements during the first week had already been dwarfed by promises and expectations of "a new order in Lebanon." Thus, failure to evict the PLO from West Beirut would constitute a self-defined political defeat and, conversely, a distinct victory for the Palestinians. The majority of the cabinet, as well as the IDF high command, objected to an Israeli attack, arguing that the toll in Israeli and civilian casualties and the political price of storming an Arab capital city were prohibitive. But after a few days of confusion and equivocation, Israel did begin to besiege Beirut, trying to move the PLO out with "unlimited military and political pressure." This resulted in a new wave of fighting with Syrian army units which controlled dominant positions in the hills east of Beirut and near the Beirut-Damascus highway.

But the position of the Israeli cabinet and the Reagan administration toward moving the Israeli army into West Beirut was unclear. Nor was it clear under what terms Washington expected to achieve the PLO evacuation from Beirut. As both the Israelis and Haig argued, however, if a swift evacuation was to be obtained the threat of an imminent Israeli thrust into West Beirut had to remain credible even if such a thrust was actually unacceptable to the United States or Israel. This credibility was undermined by contradictory signals sent by the Reagan administration, which, Haig complained, undermined his policy and efforts. Sources inspired by Haig cited several examples. One was a statement by Larry Speakes, the White House press secretary, that "assurances were given by PM Begin to President Reagan that the IDF would not enter Beirut." More difficult to verify are charges that Vice-President George Bush and Defense Secretary Weinberger (at King Khalid's funeral in Saudi Arabia) and William Clark (in a meeting with the Saudi ambassador in Washington) conveyed the impression that a partial Israeli withdrawal in the Beirut area and American good will toward the PLO could be obtained in exchange for the evacuation.[29]

These signals had a dual effect. They must have reinforced Yasir 'Arafat's conviction that he ought to hold on as long as possible in Beirut. They also exacerbated the tension between Haig and his rivals in the Reagan administration, expediting his resignation and thus magnifying the effect of the administration's discomfort with Israel's policies. Haig was publicly identified with U.S. support of the Israeli operation, and his departure and replacement by George Shultz were taken to signify a change of priorities.

Israeli and American ambivalence as well as the passage of time altered the PLO's outlook. In the third week of June, the PLO leadership was persuaded that the Israelis were about to enter West Beirut and in a *sauve qui peut* state of mind. Thus a British newspaper described on June 18 how "Lebanese government ministers for whom the PLO has shown scant respect in the past have suddenly found themselves being courted by the PLO leader, who has come to seek their advice about a ceasefire in West Beirut." And the UN spokesman in Beirut, the object of 'Arafat's scorn a week earlier, was "welcomed by the PLO leader as one of several men who just might be able to save the Palestinian resistance movement from physical extinction."[30]

But by the end of June the PLO leadership had become persuaded that an Israeli invasion was not imminent, that time was not necessarily running out and that it had an opportunity to improve, perhaps even to transform, the organization's bargaining position. And so the stage was set for the lengthy siege of Beirut.

The Siege of Beirut

When the Israeli government launched its military operation on June 6, 1982 it clearly did not envisage that the IDF would be engaged in a ten-week siege of Beirut; and at several points between the middle of June and the end of October the government and many others were hard put to believe that the protracted and complex negotiations conducted by Philip Habib would end in a peaceful PLO evacuation of Beirut. That outcome, as well as the preceding siege and negotiations, was determined primarily by the conduct of three actors—Israel, the PLO, and the United States.

The interests, outlooks, and positions of Israel and the Palestinians were, as they have so often been, diametrically opposed. Israel wanted the PLO to leave Beirut, and possibly Lebanon, without political concessions and sweeteners, so as to enable the reconstruction of the Lebanese state. To achieve that, it had to sustain a credible threat of an imminent invasion of West Beirut. This it did by shellings, air raids, and limited ground operations directed mainly (but not exclusively) at Palestinian targets, and by a tightening of the siege in an effort to turn the civilian population against the PLO and its allied Lebanese militias. These were harsh measures, conducted under the critical scrutiny of the international community, and even as means to advance a political solution they generated opposition primarily in the two countries where it mattered most—Israel and the United States. The political price increased with the passage of time, as the siege and its conduct became more controversial and the prospects of a successful diplomatic solution seemed dim.

The PLO, in turn, tried to preserve its position in Beirut and Lebanon and to obtain the highest political price for the concessions it was asked to make in the course of the negotiations. It is easy to understand the organization's desire to stay; the autonomous territorial base in Beirut and Lebanon was unique and irreplaceable; furthermore, by preserving it, or part of it, the Palestinians could claim an impressive achievement against Israel. Given the accumulating pressure on the Israeli government, the PLO had grounds for believing that the longer the siege continued, the more likely it was to gain a partial victory or at least to improve the terms of settlement. But beyond Israel was the United States—the power that defined certain limits of Israel's freedom of action, that conducted the negotiations, and that was capable of extending to the PLO the recognition it had been trying so long to obtain. Could Washington's growing nervousness and ambivalence, its natural desire for diplomatic success, and its impatience with the lingering siege be translated into recognition as the price of withdrawal? And if not, could a measure of recognition be obtained in the course of the negotiations?

The Reagan administration oscillated between the conviction that the Palestinians ought to leave Beirut if the Lebanese state were to be restored and impatience and irritation with the stalemate in Beirut. The administration was determined to tie a solution of the Lebanese crisis to the next phase of the Arab-Israeli peace process. But the chief role on the Arab side was to be assigned to Jordan and not to the Palestinians; and even if they were to be brought into these negotiations, why should one of Washington's main bargaining assets, its capacity to extend or deny recognition, be spent at such an early stage? Nor were the advocates of recognition helped by the rigidity of 'Arafat's position and formulations. The vague formula given by 'Arafat to U.S. Congressman Michael McClosky and 'Arafat's subsequent retraction are an excellent illustration of the results he could achieve through flexible diplomacy and of his inability to pursue it to his own advantage: on July 25, 'Arafat apparently signed a statement written by McClosky, according to which "Chairman 'Arafat accepts all UN resolutions relevant to the Palestinian question." For a while it was unclear whether or not this implied acceptance of Security Council Resolution 242 and what the ramifications of such an acceptance would be; but PLO spokesmen settled the debate by denying any acceptance of that resolution.

That development may have prompted the Israeli government to escalate its air and ground assaults in August. The fierce attacks,

particularly those on August 4 and 12, were among the most controversial measures of the war and resulted in added friction within the
Israeli cabinet and between the Reagan administration and Israel.
But they also served to persuade the PLO that a full-blown Israeli
attack was imminent, which enabled Habib to negotiate an agreement for the PLO's evacuation of Beirut by the end of the month.

From the PLO Evacuation to Amin Jumayyil's Presidency

In contrast to the long weeks of stalemate that characterized the
siege of Beirut, late August and September were marked by a rapid
succession of important developments—the evacuation agreement,
the arrival of the international force, Bashir Jumayyil's election to
the presidency, the gradual evacuation of the PLO from West
Beirut, the publication of President Reagan's Middle East plan,
Bashir Jumayyil's assassination, Israel's entry into West Beirut, the
massacre at Sabra and Shatila, Israel's withdrawal from Beirut, and
Amin Jumayyil's election to the presidency.

The PLO's departure from Beirut and Bashir Jumayyil's election
to the presidency seemed to suggest that the ambitious goals of the
war in Lebanon were within reach. Lebanon's political center had
been freed from the hold of Syria and the PLO, and the central
government's authority was to be rebuilt in an unorthodox fashion
under Israel's close ally. A demand by the new Lebanese government that Syria evacuate the rest of its troops from eastern and
northern Lebanon, bolstered by Israel's clear military superiority,
would be the next logical step.

But the sense of achievement was marred by other developments.
The publication of Reagan's plan served as a reminder that the
Lebanese war had been fought in a broader context and that within
that context the United States had a policy regarding the West Bank
and the Palestinian issue that was markedly different from the Israeli government's. If the war in Lebanon served to weaken the positions of Syria and the PLO, it was Washington's view that advantage should be taken of this fact to bring Jordan back into the
negotiations on the future of the West Bank.

Nor did the Reagan administration favor the idea of an authoritarian central government in Lebanon that relied on Maronite militancy and Israeli support. It would be better for Bashir Jumayyil to keep his relationship with Israel discreet and to seek ways of broadening the base of his following in Lebanon and the region. Washington's views reinforced ideas that had been on Bashir Jumayyil's mind, as his conduct since June implied. Consequently, while the Israeli government insisted on a full and open relationship with the new Lebanese government, culminating in a peace treaty, the president-elect preferred that his alliance with Israel be informal and practical. This was but one of the differences of opinion that surfaced during the meeting held between Menachem Begin and Bashir Jumayyil in Nahariyya, in northern Israel, in early September. Jumayyil's concept of a "strong central government" included the extension of its authority over southern Lebanon at the expense of Israel's reliable local ally, Sa'd Haddad. Israel, in turn, on grounds of principle as well as for practical considerations (Haddad had demonstrated his reliability and effectiveness in maintaining a *cordon sanitaire*, the Phalange had not), refused to jettison its ally.

A far more serious short-coming of the Israeli alliance with the Lebanese Front was revealed by Bashir Jumayyil's assassination on September 15. No other Maronite leader combined the ability to govern Lebanon in these difficult circumstances with a political orientation acceptable to Israel, let alone pro-Israeli. Furthermore, Syria and the PLO still controlled a large part of Lebanon; the Israelis believed some two thousand PLO combatants had stayed behind in West Beirut in violation of the evacuation agreement where, together with the militias of the National Movement, they could contribute to a reversal of earlier political trends, and perhaps force the election of an undesirable candidate.

Under these circumstances the Israeli leadership hastily dispatched the Israeli army into West Beirut, justifying its decision by the need to maintain order and security after the assassination of the president-elect. It was an apparently valid argument, but its very use served to undermine Israel's political standing when, under the umbrella of Israel's military presence, Christian militiamen massacred Palestinian civilians in the camps (or rather, neighborhoods) of Sabra and Shatila.

Based on the report of the Kahan Commission of Inquiry, which was appointed to investigate Israel's possible responsibility, the following chain of events can be reconstructed. While Bashir Jumayyil was still alive, it was agreed that cooperative Lebanese army units would locate and remove the PLO combatants still in Beirut. But following Jumayyil's assassination, the government of Shafiq al-Wazzan ordered the army to discontinue this operation. Israel and the Phalange leadership decided that the need to go ahead was crucial, but the Israeli government refused to employ its own army for this purpose, fearing casualties and determined that the Phalanges should "do something to free their homeland." Israel would facilitate the militia's entry into Sabra and Shatila, but its men would have to fight on their own.

The grim facts of the massacre, the circumstances in which they came to light, and the initial response of the Israeli government were in the first place a blow to Israel's influence in Beirut. It was forced to agree to a withdrawal of Israeli forces from Beirut, where they were replaced by an international force. Amin Jumayyil, representing a different political orientation and enjoying at least the superficial support of a broader segment of the Lebanese political spectrum, was elected to replace his brother as president. The significance of the massacre and of his election is discussed at greater length in chapter 6.

Actors and Policies

Thus far, the 1982 war in Lebanon has been considered primarily in terms of the plans and conduct of the principal actor, the Israeli government. But before an evaluation of the war's significance is attempted, the roles and policies of the other principal actors should be addressed more systematically.

The Reagan administration's ambivalent attitude toward a large-scale Israeli operation in Lebanon and the disagreements on this issue within its ranks that surfaced in the winter and spring of 1982 persisted as elements of the administration's policy after the war began. Criticisms of Israel's action were fanned by its scope and duration as well as by trivial factors, such as its alleged interference with the success of President Reagan's European trip. But during most of the war they were overshadowed by the conviction that Israel's actions could be made to serve the ends of American policy. Washington was aware of the risks inherent in launching a war as well as of the divergence of Israel's goals and its own, but these difficulties seemed surmountable and the opportunities opened by the Israeli operation in Lebanon and in the region promising.[31]

Consequently, the United States, despite verbal protestations and other gestures and occasional genuine irritation, lent Israel the political support that enabled it to proceed with the war for an unusually long time. After the Sabra and Shatila massacre, the United States exerted powerful and effective pressure on Israel to withdraw from Beirut but continued to condone the Israeli presence south and east of the city as one condition for achieving a comprehensive settlement of the Lebanese crisis. This policy was facilitated during the war's early part by the swift advance of the Israeli forces, the limited nature of the Syrian-Israeli war, the passive Soviet stance, and the meek reaction in the Arab world. Furthermore, some immediate gains become apparent—the Iranian threat to Iraq and to the conservative oil-producing states in the Gulf was weakened, Soviet clients, Soviet weapons systems, and Soviet prestige were adversely affected, and despite sharp Arab criticism of American support for Israel, American influence increased as Syria and other Arab states realized that the United States alone could check Israel in Lebanon and undo some of its gains in the war.

Yet it became increasingly difficult to maintain that policy against accumulating criticism, particularly in the murky situation in Beirut in the latter part of June. These difficulties hastened the resignation of Secretary of State Haig and induced the administration to distance itself demonstrably from Israel, but did not change the essence of its policy. Although the United States wanted the PLO to leave Beirut and realized that U.S. policy would be seen to suffer a defeat if evacuation did not take place, it was a less crucial matter for American policy than for Israel's, and details of the negotiations that seemed so important from Israel's perspective appeared petty from a superpower's vantage point.

The successful conclusion of the negotiations brought the latent divergence of American and Israeli outlooks on the Lebanese crisis and its broader Middle East context to the surface. The announcement of Reagan's Middle East peace initiative was made at the end of the PLO's evacuation from Beirut—a clear attempt to sweeten the bitter pill for the Arab world (regardless of each government's partisan calculations) and yet another measure to distinguish American policy from Israel's. Substantively, the plan offered the first official American interpretation of the Camp David accords: it designated Jordan as the intended recipient of the bulk of the West Bank. In other words, Syria's and the PLO's defeat in the war was not to provide Israel with opportunity or incentive to proceed with its creeping virtual annexation of the West Bank. It should rather be used to undo the Rabat resolutions of October 1974, which recognized the PLO as "the sole legitimate representative of the Palestinian people," and to restore Jordan's previous position regarding the West Bank and the Palestinian issue.

In a subtler way the Reagan administration also opposed Israel's plans for Lebanon and, as we saw, encouraged Bashir Jumayyil's refusal to sign a peace treaty. His assassination was a blow to American policy, but although Amin Jumayyil may not be as effective a ruler as his brother, his political orientation was much closer to the traditional American outlook on the reform in Lebanon.

The Soviet Union's conduct in the Lebanese crisis calls to mind the mirror-image metaphor sometimes (often incorrectly) used to describe Soviet-American rivalry in the Middle East.[32] The Soviet Union acted with remarkable passivity and caution as two of its clients and some of its weapons systems were defeated during the war's first week. The vague wording of Soviet warnings to Israel gave way to more explicit threats only on June 14, when the Syrian-Israeli cease-fire had been secured (partly as a result of Soviet pressure on the United States). Passivity and caution were again notable during the siege of Beirut, even when the Soviet embassy was damaged by Israeli troops.

It has been suggested that Soviet restraint was "calculated," that the Soviet Union believed that neither superpower could advance its interests through an assertive policy toward the Arab-Israeli conflict. But while one might argue cogently that the Soviets can profit by concentrating their efforts in the outlying areas of the Middle East (notably the Persian Gulf), the available evidence does not quite warrant an interpretation of their policy during the war in Lebanon as a case of sagacious resignation.

The Soviet Union had in fact treated its relationship with Syria and the prospect of a Syrian-Israeli war in Lebanon with considerable trepidation well before the summer of 1982. Its reluctance to sign a treaty of friendship and cooperation with Syria in 1980 and its conduct during the 1981 missile crisis after the treaty had been signed clearly indicated that it did not relish a war in which Syria would be fighting outside her national borders against an American ally with a decisive military superiority. Furthermore, as was clearly demonstrated during the missile crisis, Syria was keenly interested in resuming the dialogue with the United States that had been interrupted in 1977: there was little sense in supporting Syria through a confrontation that might ultimately play into the hands of the United States. The same was true of the PLO, whose leadership patently sought American recognition as one of its main political goals.

Soviet passivity was reinforced by the meekness of the Arab response to the Israeli operation, by the limited scope of the Syrian-Israeli fighting, and by the Soviet leadership's preoccupation with other problems—Leonid Brezhnev's impending death, Poland, and Afghanistan. In the early months of 1983, however, the effects of a new Soviet posture toward Syria and Lebanon began to be felt. On the eve of Brezhnev's death, preparations were begun for sending new Soviet ground-to-air missiles and Soviet personnel to Syria. With their appearance there, after Yuri Andropov's accession to power, a new element was introduced in the Lebanese crisis and in Soviet-American rivalry.

Like their Soviet patrons, Syria's leaders had anticipated an Israeli operation in Lebanon with a full realization of the dilemmas with which it was bound to confront them. Unlike their Palestinian clients, they even tried to signal Israel that if it decided to ignore their warnings and stage the operation, it should at least limit its scope and enable Syria to minimize its own participation. Thus on February 13, 1982, Louis Fares, Radio Monte Carlo's correspondent in Damascus through whom the Ba'thi regime often conveyed its views unofficially, quoted "a high-ranking diplomat" who ex-plained that one had to distinguish between two situations.

> If the Israeli intervention takes the form of strikes against Palestinian positions and camps in Lebanon, Syria's intervention will remain lim-ited . . . but if it is a matter of occupation, Syria will certainly give the Palestinians and the Lebanese patriotic forces all the means necessary for checking the occupation and turning the occupier's life into an unbearable hell, and this in addition to conducting the battles that will be called for in a time of need. It is no secret that Israel's military force is now larger than Syria's; therefore, the possibility of Syria's turning to a full-scale war at a time and a place determined by Israel should be excluded. . . . The activity will be limited to resistance to the occupa-tion and to the attrition of the occupying forces . . . but might develop into all-out war if circumstances so determine.

During the war's first three days, the Syrian regime probably thought that Israel was responding to its warning; when on the fourth day it seemed Israel was determined either to fight Syria in Lebanon or to extract considerable concessions, Syrian forces in Lebanon had already been outmaneuvered and defeated. Damascus then sought and obtained a cease-fire, which saved Syria from a greater military defeat but which facilitated Israel's further movement into Beirut.

As a new phase opened in the war Syria faced new challenges. It was vitally important to prevent an Israeli-Phalangist victory in Beirut and to appease Palestinians and other Arabs who accused Syria of deserting its Palestinian proteges when they most needed help. The still sizable Syrian forces in and near Beirut fought fiercely against the Israelis and made a considerable contribution to the creation of the stalemate in that area in mid-June. The elaborate and apologetic argument that was developed in Damascus to justify the acceptance of the June 11 cease-fire was rendered much more credi-ble by the continuing Syrian-Israeli fighting near Beirut.[33]

When the confusion of mid- and late June was replaced by the reality of a full-fledged Israeli siege of the city, Syria shaped its policy to affect the unfolding conflicts over the PLO's departure from Beirut and over the broader settlement in Lebanon. The two were closely related. Once the PLO left Beirut, Bashir Jumayyil was

expected to form a new Lebanese government, and Israel and Lebanon could then join to press Syria to evacuate the sizable territories it
still held in eastern and northern Lebanon. Syria initially refused to
accept Palestinian evacuees from Beirut. But when a settlement
seemed imminent the Ba'thi regime changed its mind and agreed to
accept a large number of evacuees, partly in the hope of gaining
assets for the more serious struggle that lay ahead: American in-
debtedness for helping Philip Habib's mission and yet another
source of influence over the PLO. But despite their ill-disguised
dissatisfaction with Moscow's performance in June,[34] the Ba'thi
leaders continued to treat the Soviet Union as their major ally. They
sought to renew a dialogue with Washington, but Washington was
not to be fully trusted, and the Soviet Union was still the chief source
of international support, the main deterrent against an Israeli offensive in the Beqa Valley and the source of weapons to replace the
equipment lost in June.

Bashir Jumayyal's election to the presidency was a dark moment
for Syria, signifying as it did the probability of a strong Lebanese
government allied with Israel and hostile to Syria. Jumayyil's assassination changed much of that, but Syria's public reaction was
cautious—a note of relief and vindication coupled with an attempt
to shift suspicions for sponsorship of the assassination from Syria to
Israel. The massacre in Beirut, Amin Jumayyil's election to the presidency, and the new Soviet posture further improved Syria's
position.

As we saw earlier, the PLO's strategy of light resistance during
the war's first three days had a far-reaching influence on subsequent
developments. This strategy, it seems, reflected the PLO anticipation of somewhat different Israeli moves.

During the first half of 1982 the PLO leaders, like many others,
expected a large-scale Israeli invasion, which they could conceivably anticipate by changing their deployment or strategy. But such
alteration was never considered seriously; the autonomous territorial base in southern Lebanon was much too valuable and the
maintenance of a resolute stance against Israel too crucial. Israel, it
was argued, was determined to attack the PLO in Lebanon and seek
to eliminate it, and would find a pretext no matter what the PLO

did. The July 1981 cease-fire, as interpreted by the PLO, should be kept, so as not to provide Israel with too convenient a pretext and so as not to alienate the United States. The struggle should be pursued in other ways, and when the Israeli attack did occur, it might deal a physical blow to the organization but would ultimately provide it with another political victory.[35]

This optimistic view seems to have been more than a rationalization of the inevitable. It was, rather, based on an interpretation of the previous rounds of fighting in southern Lebanon and on a specific scenario of the anticipated Israeli attack. The PLO leadership viewed the previous six years of armed conflict with Israel as an ever-expanding circle of violence in which its advantages as a guerrilla organization fighting a regular army operating under severe political limitations were bound to increase with time.

As for the impending invasion, although, it seems, the PLO leadership was aware of Sharon's meeting with Bashir Jumayyil in January and considered the possibility that "Phalangist forces might join in the fray by attacking Palestinian camps in the southern outskirts of Beirut," its main concern was apparently Israel's anticipated attempt at "boxing the P.L.O. forces into a fairly small area and then grinding them down piecemeal." It expected "seaborne landings along Lebanon's coast road and helicopter landings in the Jezzine area" and "landings as far north as the Palestinian base in Damour . . . to prevent reinforcements from reaching the embattled Palestinians in the south."[36]

Accordingly, when the war broke out, the PLO strategy was to conduct an orderly withdrawal to the north, seeking to inflict casualties on Israeli troops rather than to defend territory. This spoiled Israel's own objectives at that phase by facilitating a too-rapid advance toward Beirut and the Beirut-Damascus road. Later, when Israel's further advance was halted, the influx of several thousand additional PLO combatants to Beirut served to reinforce the organization's position during the siege.

The PLO performed quite well in the limited fighting that took place during the siege and displayed a remarkable degree of internal unity in difficult circumstances. But efforts to maintain that unity reinforced the rigidity of the organization's political and diplomatic position in the face of Israeli military pressure. Without international and Arab support and with most Lebanese political factions, including its own allies, seeking its departure, the PLO's only hope was a change in American policy. An effort to effect such a change might not have been successful in any case, but the telling point is that it was not seriously undertaken.

It is ironic that the Lebanese state and political system for whose sake the 1982 war in Lebanon was fought, at least in part, remained passive almost to the war's end. To some extent this was a consequence of the preceding ten years of crisis. The Lebanese state had been emasculated, particularly in the areas under Syrian and Palestinian control where most of the fighting took place. Then the various political forces in the country had their own reasons for reticence or passivity. Israel's allies, as we saw, expected Israel to bear the brunt of the fighting. Some PLO allies among the militias participated in the fighting but most of the organization's political allies in the National Movement, tired of its domination, expected it to leave, and even said so.

The effort made at the end of June to revive the Lebanese political system by convening a National Salvation Council representing the major political forces in the country failed because it was premature. It was by then clear that the war's first two weeks had shifted the balance of power in Lebanon, but as long as the war was not over, those who had lost power were unwilling to acknowledge the change. Also, with PLO and Syrian forces still in Beirut and Israeli troops closing in, circumstances were not conducive to Lebanese national reconciliation. Beyond these considerations, there was an unarticulated sense that the foreign invaders and occupiers should be allowed to complete their war before a fresh start in Lebanese politics was attempted.

CHAPTER 6

An Interim Assessment

BETWEEN AMIN JUMAYYIL'S ELECTION and the end of 1982, much had happened but not much had changed in the Lebanese dilemma. The new president assumed power in deceptively auspicious circumstances—he was elected by an unusually large majority of the parliament, he was greeted by Lebanese Christian leaders, Syria, and the PLO, who saw him as a vast improvement over his late brother, and he enjoyed U.S. support. At the behest of his Sunni allies, he retained as prime minister Shafiq al-Wazzan, who formed a "technocratic cabinet," clearly a transitional arrangement, which, when a measure of stability and normalization had been secured, would be replaced by a "political cabinet" reflecting the new realities of Lebanese politics.

But during the following months normalization seemed remote because of the war's immediate and paradoxical outcome. The war did have a profound impact on Lebanon, but it did not break the deadlock that had characterized the Lebanese crisis during the previous four years, and seemed, in fact, to have in some ways compounded it.

To a considerable extent the new ramifications of deadlock derived from the turn of events in mid-September. Bashir Jumayyil had had a clear-cut strategy—to assume office, to demand the evacuation of Syrian forces, and to rely on Israel's help to secure their withdrawal. Following that, an Israeli withdrawal was to be obtained through negotiations, and the authority of the Lebanese state was to be extended over much of Lebanon's territory. Many Lebanese Muslims feared and distrusted the president-elect but their reservations would be mitigated by their relief that the war and their domination by Syria, the PLO, and the Muslim militias had ended. It would not have been an easy strategy to implement and it might very well have failed, but it was never tested.[1]

Bashir Jumayyil's assassination and the subsequent massacre in Sabra and Shatila had far-reaching consequences for the two chief agents of change in Lebanon. His supporters in the Lebanese Front and Lebanese Forces lost their leader and moving spirit. The original plan had called for their integration into the Lebanese system and armed forces, endowing these with new power and vigor. Now they formally accepted the new president as their head of state and party leader, but he, his entourage, and his policies had to be watched, and tested.

Israel's plans for Lebanon were based to a large degree on Bashir Jumayyil personally. In Israeli eyes his brother represented a markedly different outlook on Lebanon's future, and relationship with Israel, and could not be relied upon to cooperate in securing even some of the goals for which the war had been launched. In addition, the massacres in Sabra and Shatila and the appointment of a commission of inquiry to look into possible Israeli responsibility for them cast a shadow over the Begin government. As long as the commission's work had not been completed, the government's future was uncertain and its power curtailed. (In February 1983, the Kahan Commission's report was published; it found fault with the conduct of several cabinet members and army officers. The government as a whole survived its publication, but Ariel Sharon was forced to resign as minister of defense.)

In this uncertain state of affairs, the evacuation of Israelis, Syrians, and the PLO from Lebanon could not be set in motion. Israel, the Lebanese government, and the Reagan administration were interested in an early agreement, but their divergent aims and Syrian and PLO opposition militated against one. Israel wanted an agreement that would embody its achievement and allow it to bring Israeli troops back from Lebanon. But it insisted on Syrian and Palestinian withdrawal, as well as on a substantial agreement with the Lebanese government providing both for security arrangements in the south and for a measure of normalization in the relationship of the two states.

These conditions were difficult to meet. The PLO held on to whatever territory it had in Lebanon under a Syrian umbrella and in fact fought to expand it. Syria wanted to keep its troops in Lebanon to protect its investment and to influence the course of events still taking shape. The other Israeli aims—security in the south and some normalization of relations with the government in Beirut—were also unacceptable to Syria, as, by and large, was Washington's policy in Lebanon and in the region. Syria viewed Lebanon as its own sphere of influence, and an American policy seeking a Syrian withdrawal and a Lebanese government independent of Damascus had to be obstructed. The same applied to the Reagan plan and the effort to bring about a Jordanian-Israeli settlement on the West Bank, which was a policy bound to isolate Syria, weaken its claim to custodianship of the Palestinian issue, and to leave it as the only Arab state that had failed to retrieve the territory lost in 1967. In September, the two issues had become linked, leading the Syrian leadership to perceive that by opposing American policy in Lebanon it was also obstructing the Reagan plan.

Syria's hand was dramatically strengthened by the Soviet Union's decision in the fall of 1982 to dispatch new ground-to-air missiles and Soviet personnel to Syria. There were two ways by which the United States and Israel might possibly induce Syria to take its forces out of Lebanon. One was Israeli force or the threat of it. In the circumstances obtaining after mid-September, this possibility was not seen as very likely, and the Soviet Union's reappearance in the area made it even less so. The other approach was an American effort to create political inducements for Syria to leave. But with the larger regional policy proposed in the Reagan plan and the new Soviet-Syrian cooperation, this was not a practical option.

For his part, Amin Jumayyil was both reluctant and hard put to respond to Israel's demands, and was opposed to a close relationship with Israel.[2] His administration in some respects was a return to a more traditional pattern of Lebanese politics—an alliance between a Maronite president and the Sunni Zu'ama of Beirut. Sa'ib Salam and his colleagues, who had been eclipsed by the PLO and the militias in the 1970s, were cast once again in the roles of spokesmen for Arabism and Islam and representatives inside Lebanon of the Saudi and other Arab points of view.[3] The Lebanese government dealt also directly with Syria and was subjected to its pressures regarding both the bilateral Syrian-Lebanese relationship and Lebanon's relations with the United States and Israel.

As Syria, Israel, and the PLO continued to occupy the bulk of Lebanon's territory, the writ of Amin Jumayyil's government was limited to an area not much larger than that of his predecessor. True, Beirut itself was free of the presence of Syria, the PLO, and the Muslim militias, but tension was growing between the new president and those in his military forces and, to a lesser extent, in the party, who remained loyal to his brother. This group's insistence on the need for the Israeli alliance was but one of the bones of contention between them and those who came to occupy chief positions in the new administration: the group of traditional politicians, personal confidants and technocrats surrounding Amin Jumayyil.

The outbreaks of violence in two different parts of Lebanon, the city of Tripoli in the north and the Shuf mountains just east and south of Beirut, illustrated both the intricacies of the Lebanese crisis at the end of 1982 and the helplessness of the new central government.[4] The fighting in Tripoli reflected the rivalries between Syria and Iraq, Sunnis and Alawis, local militias and the PLO. Like much of northern Lebanon, the area lay outside the actual jurisdiction of the central government, which had hardly any effect on the conflict. Some aspects of the disputes were traditional and familiar—the Faranjiyyas' hostility to the Jumayyils, and Rashid Karami's rivalry with the Sunni politicians of Beirut. But there were novel questions as well: was the PLO trying to substitute Tripoli for Beirut, and was Syria drawing the lines of a virtual partition of Lebanon?

A similar mixture of old and new elements characterized the fighting between Druze villagers and Maronite militia in the Shuf mountains. The struggle between the two communities for control of the region dates back to the eighteenth century, when the Maronites migrated southward and the Maronite Emir Bashir II tried to break the power of the rebellious Junblatts. In 1976, when he criticized Kamal Junblatt's attitude toward the Maronites, Hafiz al-Asad charged that what was involved was a vendetta with roots extending a hundred-and-forty years into the past. In 1977, as has already been mentioned, the Druzes vented their anger at Kamal Junblatt's assassination on their Maronite neighbors in the Shuf, and Maronites fled. In the summer of 1982, taking advantage of the heyday of the Phalangist-Israeli alliance, they returned to the Shuf, accompanied by men of the Lebanese Forces. They were seeking more than a restoration of the 1977 status quo: they wanted to guarantee the central government control over Mount Lebanon, particularly that part of it that was so close to Beirut. But what the Phalanges saw as an extension of the state's authority, the Druzes perceived as a threat to dispossess them. As they have done on similar occasions in the past, the Druzes closed ranks and prepared to display their military skill.

After a wave of fighting in the vicinity of the capital, the Lebanese Forces were defeated, and Israel in turn faced a dilemma. Though the Druzes were a loyal minority in Israel, the Junblatts, who were seen as the dominant force in the Lebanese Druze community, were considered anti-Israeli. As long as Bashir Jumayyil was alive, the Israeli government tended to side with the Phalanges. But with Amin Jumayyil distancing himself from Israel, the Israelis wondered why they should confront the Druze community in Lebanon, alienating their own Druze community, for an increasingly questionable alliance with Maronite groups. But Israel's decision to take a neutral attitude between Druzes and Maronites in the Shuf was soon resented by both parties.

The Lebanese Druze community played a dual role in these events: undoubtedly motivated by anxiety that the Phalange's power would be extended at its expense, it was also seeking a larger place on the national political scene. Though the Druzes constitute but 6 percent of Lebanon's population, their location, social organization, and military ability have endowed them with an influence well beyond their numerical strength, as the events of 1982 demonstrated. Furthermore, as the Lebanese state's jurisdiction shrank, the Druze population's relative weight increased.

In an effort to end the stalemate, the Lebanese government adopted a two-pronged strategy. A format and venue for formal negotiations with Israel under American auspices and with American participation were agreed upon. At the same time members of Amin Jumayyil's entourage conducted secret negotiations with the

Israeli minister of defense in which the principles of a Lebanese-Israeli agreement were apparently arrived at. This agreement was to underwrite the success of the formal negotiations, in the wake of which withdrawal of Israeli, Syrian, and Palestinian forces and the ensuing reconstruction of the Lebanese state would follow. But when Sharon disclosed that the agreement had been reached—apparently seeking to force the Lebanese government's hand and to strengthen his own government's position—the Lebanese government denied its existence, and the formal negotiations began at the end of December with a wide gap separating the positions of the two parties. An end to the stalemate seemed a distant and uncertain prospect. The war of 1982, which sought to solve the Lebanese crisis, fitted instead into its pattern—sustained domestic conflict, punctuated by outbursts of violence that change the balance of power within the Lebanese equation but not the equation's contours, and intertwined with foreign intervention and occupation.

That pattern and the subsequent reformulation of the Lebanese political order are familiar phenomena in Lebanon's modern history. The periods 1840–61, 1914–20, 1940–46, and the year 1958 fit the same mold. In the twentieth century, conflict over Lebanon has revolved around four rival concepts of the Lebanese state: a small Christian Lebanon, a greater Christian Lebanon, a greater pluralistic Lebanon, and an Arab Lebanon. A small Christian Lebanon existed during the period of the autonomous Mutasarifiyya at the sufferance of the Ottoman Empire and with the support of the European powers. Emile Eddé was the most prominent of the Maronite politicians who during the twenties, thirties, and forties advocated a return to the notion of a smaller, predominantly Christian Lebanon primarily in the conviction that, because of demographic reality, a greater Lebanon was bound to lose its Christian character.

That character was maintained as long as France had the will and the power to support it. When France lost its position in Lebanon during World War II, the Lebanese devised a formula for a pluralistic Lebanon. For some thirty years, until it collapsed in 1975, there existed a Christian-Muslim partnership under Christian hegemony. The main pressure on that system came from the advocates of an Arab Lebanon (in its Syrian and Pan-Arab versions). During the next seven years the Lebanese, Syrian, and Palestinian champions of this concept controlled most of Lebanon's territory, and seemed increasingly able to contend for the domination of the Lebanese state and political system.

At first there was no uniform Maronite response to this challenge, but in time the Phalange—and the Lebanese Front and Lebanese Forces, which it dominated—came to speak for the Maronite community. Their position developed through a number of phases. At the outset the Phalange fought to preserve the Lebanese system of 1943–75. By the end of 1975, persuaded that this could not be done, it opted reluctantly for a smaller Christian Lebanon. The change was manifested in military strategy as well as in ideological formulations. Then in the late 1970s came a phase devoid of clear-cut strategy—the Phalange cooperated with both Syria and Israel and then contended with the ambiguities of the transition from the civil war of 1975–76 to the lingering crisis. It entertained a vague notion of cantonization, which was a rationalization of the status quo as much as a plan for the future.

A profound change came in 1980, when the establishment of a Christian Lebanon embracing the territory of greater Lebanon, or most of it, appeared feasible. Israel would play the role of France and neutralize the PLO and Syria, and the mobilized Maronite community could easily dominate the rest of Lebanon. It was an attitude remarkably similar to that of the 1918–20 Maronite nationalists, who had exerted pressure on French policymakers to create a Greater Lebanon. As we saw, there emerged another school of thought, first in the 1930s and more clearly during the 1975–76 civil war, which argued that the creation of Greater Lebanon was a mistake and a tragedy, that Christian Lebanon should be a self-sustaining entity. But the quest for larger Lebanon and the tendency to rely on external support—French, British, American, Syrian, or Israeli—ephemeral as it may be, remained important elements of the Maronite political tradition.

It would be erroneous to assume that a concrete plan was formulated by Bashir Jumayyil in 1980 and carried out in 1982. But the commander of the Lebanese Forces did have a set of ideas on the nature of the Lebanese entity and state and on their future relationship with their constituent communities and external environment that he set out to implement by whatever methods were feasible.

As his party's new programs and his speeches indicated, Bashir Jumayyil and his circle believed that Christian hegemony in Lebanon was not a function of numbers but of historic tradition. That hegemony should be based on the military and political power of the Maronite community and its allies in Lebanon, and that power in turn should, at least for the time being, be based on an alliance with Israel and on a new approach to domestic politics. The weak Lebanese state should be replaced by a powerful state, commanding a strong military force and the direct allegiance of the citizens. And yet, most of the institutions of the Lebanese state—the "Lebanese legitimacy"—should be maintained. A strong Lebanese state and a strong Maronite community would find the necessary domestic political allies for the functioning of the parliamentary system. And if played correctly, the Israeli card would ensure the maintenance of Lebanon's relations with the rest of the Arab world, important not only to the Muslim communities, but also to the economic interests of Maronite businessmen. It would be wrong to view the Phalanges as strictly mountain vigilantes fighting to preserve their traditions and political privileges against the cosmopolitanism and Arabism of the coastal towns.[5] Such considerations were undoubtedly important, especially among the Phalangist armed militias and the north Lebanese clans, but their influence was reduced by others, some of them in Bashir Jumayyil's own entourage, who urged the development of the Maronites' relationship with other Lebanese communities and with Lebanon's Arab environment.

Bashir Jumayyil's one public pronouncement in the summer of 1982 that came close to presenting a comprehensive program for the future was delivered on June 18 over the Voice of Lebanon. He told his listeners that: "the new Lebanon would be built on bases completely different from the hegemony, vituperations, indifference, and irresponsibility on which Lebanon has been built since 1943. . . . We must not return to the past; we must forget the old establishments. . . . From now on we must not have a Chamber of Deputies which includes middlemen and profiteers. . . . We must not have weak presidents who appease everybody." He said nothing, naturally, about Christian-Maronite hegemony. "Lebanon for which we have gambled for eight years, will be for everybody, without any sectarian or religious discrimination. . . . We must create a new Lebanon and build it together with the Lebanese Muslims, our partners in destiny, particularly since many of them have begun to understand us." But allusions to the profound changes that lay ahead were carefully planted in the speech: "we will build a new Lebanon and a new national charter," and "now that our military organizations with their artillery and vehicles have performed their mission," they would have to be integrated into the state system. It was premature and impolitic to elaborate this point, and the would-be president merely stated, "it is our duty immediately to study the future of our state in the light of urgent developments."

The conciliatory elements discernible in Bashir Jumayyil's attitude to Lebanon's Muslim population and Arab hinterland were far more prominent in the outlook of Amin Jumayyil and his entourage. It is difficult to separate the personal from the political and ideological dimensions in a political family, but in the late 1970s and early 1980s Amin Jumayyil and his wing of the Phalange appeared as loyal opposition and corrective to the policies of his brother. If Bashir Jumayyil sought to recreate a Christian greater Lebanon, Amin Jumayyil was, both before and after his election to the presidency, an advocate of the restoration of the pluralistic Lebanon of 1943–75. Reality, moreover, reinforced the new president's preferences. The Maronite community and the Lebanese Front had lost the cohesive leadership of the previous few years, the Lebanese state was weak, and Lebanese politics was a network of over lapping alliances and rivalries.

The Israeli government's decision in 1982 to launch a military operation that sought among other things to help Israel's Maronite ally gain power in Lebanon and to generate broad regional changes can be seen in the context of both Israel's specific relationship with Lebanon and the evolution of its policies in the Arab-Israeli conflict.

The previous occasion when an Israeli action in Lebanon was viewed as a key to a change in Israel's regional position was in 1954. The idea had come up in a small way in 1950–51, when the Israeli government considered investing money in trying to help the Phalange win several seats in Parliament. Several Israeli emissaries met with a Phalangist politician, Elyas Rababi, who was trying to solicit financial and political support. Some of the Israelis dealing with the issue argued that it would be useful to encourage pro-Israeli ele-

ments in order to have a friendly Christian Lebanon, but the dominant view was that the efforts would be futile, so the result was that
a symbolic sum of money was spent.[6] But an entirely different
situation obtained in 1954. David Ben-Gurion, who had resigned
the premiership and retreated to Sdeh Boker, remained preoccupied with Israel's national security problems and particularly
with the combined effects of regional and international isolation. He
came to the conclusion that Lebanon, "the weakest link in the
[Arab] League's chain," was the place in which a breakthrough
could be effected that would lead to a qualitative change in Israel's
regional position.[7] His plan called for the establishment of a smaller
"Maronite state" that would be allied to Israel. Ben-Gurion had
given thought to Israel's relationship with the Lebanese Christians
in the past. In July 1937, after analyzing the recommendations of the
Peel commission, he determined that one of its most important
contributions was "the allotment of the whole Galilee to the Jews
and the extension of our border in the north to the Lebanese frontier. This contiguity has huge political value because both Lebanon
and the Jews are interested in it. The Christians in Lebanon would
hardly be able to survive without a neighboring Jewish state, and we
too are interested in an alliance with Christian Lebanon."[8] He was
clearly familiar with the ideas held in the 1930s and 1940s by Emile
Eddé and his followers. "It was France's gravest error," he wrote to
his successor, Moshe Sharett, "to have expanded Lebanon's borders," and he knew that there were those in Lebanon who had "no
need for expanded borders and a large Muslim community." Ben-
Gurion argued that "the establishment of a Christian state here is a
natural matter; it has historic roots and will be supported by great
forces in the Christian world." He realized that the Lebanese Maronites themselves had come to accept the status quo, but argued
that "in a time of confusion, commotion and revolution or civil war
things change and the meek person feels like a hero." Israel should
seize the opportunity and bring about "the formation of a neighboring Christian state." This seemed to him to be "the central task or at
least one of the central tasks of our foreign policy."

The idea was revived a year later, when Ben-Gurion returned to
Sharett's government as minister of defense, and the prospect of an
Iraqi takeover in Syria raised fresh anxieties in Israel. Ben-Gurion's

plan was supported by Moshe Dayan, then chief of staff, who, according to Sharett's sardonic description, believed that "all that is needed is to find an officer, even at the rank of captain, to win him over or buy his co-operation so as to declare himself the savior of the Maronite population. Then the IDF will enter Lebanon, occupy the relevant territory and form a Christian government in alliance with Israel. The territory south of the Litani will be annexed to Israel and everything will fall into place."[9]

David Ben-Gurion and Moshe Dayan were the leading figures of the school in Israeli public life which saw the solution to Israel's national security problems in bold, activist policies. Foreign policy, particularly relations with the great powers, was a crucial aspect of national security policy, but against the wall of Arab hostility, diplomacy and political gestures could be fatuous, and the state's military might was the key to its survival. In the early and mid-1950s their school defeated the rival one of which Moshe Sharett was the most notable representative and which believed that diplomacy and the political act should play a greater role in Israel's national security policies. During Sharett's premiership (when his school enjoyed a brief moment of limited supremacy), he ruled out any bold Israeli initiative in Lebanon. His considerable familiarity with Lebanese politics (which his exchange of letters with Ben-Gurion amply reflects) persuaded him that the agitation for a Maronite state had not developed into a serious movement in previous decades; "and with the course of time these voices disappeared as well." Sharett marshaled impressive arguments against Ben-Gurion's plan. But the brunt of them (though not phrased in these terms) was that the Maronites had come to accept the pluralistic formula of the first 1943 Lebanese republic: "As for the Maronites, the great majority among them have for years given their support to those practical political leaders of the community who had long relinquished the dream of restoring past glories and have staked their future on a Christian Muslim coalition inside Lebanon."[10]

Sharett's line typified the Foreign Ministry's traditional skepticism regarding an Israeli alliance with Lebanese Christians. Thus, in December 1950, cautioning against pinning high hopes on the Phalange and on an Israeli nexus with them, Gidion Rafael wrote to the director general of the Foreign Ministry: "In the present circum-

stances in the Middle East, I cannot imagine that a Christian movement, when it reaches power in Lebanon, will dare enter into a
conflict with the Moslem world by maintaining friendly ties with
Israel. On the contrary, my opinion is that so long as the other Arab
states persevere in their stubborn policy towards Israel, Lebanon
will not be able, even under a friendly Christian government, to give
concrete expression to friendly proclivities."[11]

It is tempting to interpret Ben-Gurion's and Dayan's statements
as early manifestations of an Israeli grand design on Lebanon, finally attempted some twenty-five years later. But such a direct line
cannot be drawn. The 1954–55 debate is not entirely irrelevant, as
we shall see, to Israel's policies in 1982, but its real importance lies
elsewhere: the Ben-Gurion-Sharett exchange of letters illuminates
Israel's outlook on its role in the region at that time and its specific
view of Lebanon both as a neighbor and as a possible key to over-
coming Israel's regional isolation. Ben-Gurion and most other Israelis saw Pan-Arab nationalism as the most hostile force in the region. As long as that doctrine held sway, Israel would remain
isolated from its neighbors and would have to survive by the sword.
Any change in the balance of power (as a result, for example, of
Britain's withdrawal from the Suez, an Iraqi takeover in Syria, or the
Czech arms deal with Egypt) would jeopardize Israel's existence. As
well as a deterrent military force and international support, Israel
needed to look for any crack in the wall of Arab hostility. The best
place to find such cracks would be among the other opponents of
Pan-Arab nationalism, particularly the non-Sunni Muslim communities in the Arab world. As early as the 1930s and 1940s, members
of the political department of the Jewish Agency, an embryonic
foreign office, developed working relationships with political leaders in several Arab countries, particularly in Lebanon. The lingering
effects of this period are evident in the text of Ben-Gurion's letter to
Sharett, and its sequels can be found in Israel's aid to the Kurds in
Iraq and other minorities in conflict with Arab nationalist regimes. A
similar aim motivated Ben-Gurion to develop in the late 1950s,
when it became feasible, "the policy of the periphery"—the alliance
with Turkey, Iran, and Ethiopia against Pan-Arab nationalism in its
Nasserite embodiment.

This alliance, one of the important manifestations of Israel's ability to break out of the isolation of the early 1950s, made Israelis more secure and confident, but in the core area of the Middle East, Israel's immediate environment, the Arab-Israeli conflict remained intractable even after the Six Day War. In that context, Israel's relations with Lebanon from 1955 to 1975 remained a marginal aspect of its Middle East policies.

We considered in the previous chapter the process that led Israel, between the summer of 1981 and the summer of 1982, to launch a military operation designed to accomplish a remarkably ambitious set of goals. But to understand the Israeli decision, we must examine how the connection between Israel and a number of Maronite groups developed into an intimate alliance with Bashir Jumayyil and the Lebanese Front.

The relationship had been complex from the start. Israel and the Maronite militias had some common enemies and overlapping interests in Lebanon, but not identical ones, a situation that became apparent during Pierre Jumayyil's first meeting with the Israeli leadership in 1976. Jumayyil wisely refrained from trying to explain away the anti-Israeli statements and actions of his and his party's long career. "Fortress Lebanon," a small Christian-Maronite Lebanon in conflict with Muslims and Arabs, was for Jumayyil a last resort. If a version of the pluralistic Lebanon of 1943 was to be revived, the relationship with Israel had to remain limited, surreptitious, and temporary. Lebanon was part of the Arab world and could thrive only as such. Furthermore, although the PLO was a dangerous enemy, it was the establishment of Israel that had brought the Palestinian refugees to Lebanon; Israel thus bore at least some responsibility for the collapse of a system that, as the Phalange saw it, would have prevailed had the matter been left to the Lebanese. Finally, Israel could not be fully trusted as the Maronites' guarantor and savior. The Maronite leaders had tried since 1976 to draw from Israel a firm commitment, but Israel refused to go to war on their behalf then and was likely to refuse to do so in the future.

Pierre Jumayyil's reservations were held even more vigorously by the wing of the party identified with his older son, Amin. Bashir Jumayyil had different views but he and his circle occasionally displayed similar reservations.

Israel's concerns, as the senior partner in the alliance, were of a different nature. Could the Phalanges be trusted not to turn around and conclude a deal with Syria and the other Arab states with whom they maintained contact? Would they really fight for their own cause or would they expect Israel to fight on their behalf? And would they draw Israel into an ever-greater commitment beyond its control and against its better judgment?

These questions were underlined by the fighting in Zahle in 1980–81 and the missile crisis in 1981. Some Israelis, the deputy minister of defense in particular, argued the Lebanese Front provoked the fighting and was drawing Israel into the confrontation. During the crisis it came to light that Israel had made a commitment to the Lebanese not to let Syria use its air force against Lebanese forces, and it honored this commitment by shooting down two Syrian helicopters. But Israel was forced to state the limits of the commitment in explicit terms. Prime Minister Begin's oral message to Bashir Jumayyil, the text of which he read in the Knesset, affords an unusual insight into the evolution of the Israeli relationship with the Lebanese Front:

> An emissary of ours communicated to them, in the name of the cabinet committee for Defense affairs the following—hold on, we will continue to help you directly and indirectly. Directly with effective weapons and indirectly by putting all the diplomatic factors to work. . . . Second, we repeat our promise that should the Christians be attacked by the Syrian air force we will help you with our air force. Thirdly, we will continue to hit the [Palestinian] saboteurs. I further told them—our emissary reported to us—that the decision had been reached after a lengthy, thorough, and profound series of discussions in the framework of the war cabinet. I emphasized . . . the sense of heavy responsibility which all shared in view of the grave situation portrayed by the Christians. I pointed out that the Israeli government saw no reason for changing its earlier decision not to be drawn into war with Syria except on the basis of its own considerations. This does not contradict the statement that the security and survival of the Christians and the preservation of a non-hostile Lebanon are vital to Israel's security. I added that this repeated decision, despite the severity of the situation was perhaps easier than the one made in October 1978. When the men, namely the Christian emissary from Lebanon and his friends and someone else as well, argued that they could not bear the loss of Zahle, which had actually not been lost, I said that the State of Israel in her wars, which are not over yet, knew how to lose territories and

regain them and much more. One needs patience and the right perspective.[12]

The events of 1981 led to a period of reassessment on both sides. Bashir Jumayyil and the Lebanese Front entered an "Arab phase"; they announced the cessation of their relationship with Israel and their willingness to let Saudi Arabia seek a solution to the Lebanese crisis through the "traditional" patterns of Lebanese and Arab politics. By the end of November, particularly after the Fez Arab summit, it was evident that the attempt had failed. Bashir Jumayyil's sentiments were clearly reflected in the powerful speech he delivered on November 29. The Israeli connection, which had never been fully severed, was fully resumed.

From the Israeli point of view, another important change had taken place during the same period. As the Kahan report of 1983 and other sources have shown, Israel's relationship with the Phalange and Bashir Jumayyil, a relationship maintained by the Mossad, had been controversial. How the Mossad presented the value of the relationship is not known, but we are told that Military Intelligence (which was entrusted in practice with preparing the national intelligence estimate) had a low opinion of Phalangist political and military reliability.[13] By the end of 1981, however, such differences of opinion were completely overshadowed by the fact that the relationship had become largely a personal one between Ariel Sharon and Bashir Jumayyil, and was fitted into Israel's "big plan."

But as the events of the war and its aftermath clearly showed, it was a relationship too ambiguous and too slight for the baggage it had to carry. The Lebanese Front, whose cooperation in the war was essential for the successful implementation of the original Israeli plan, determined to limit its participation to a minimum, obstructing that plan and causing confusion and complications by the end of June. But if Israel was furious with Bashir Jumayyil and the Front it could hardly afford a display of anger since their cooperation remained indispensable. Israel's Lebanese allies were in turn bewildered by the fluctuations in planning produced by the give and take between the Israeli cabinet, minister of defense, and military leadership. The relationship was further altered when Bashir

Jumayyil was elected president and began to act as the head of a sovereign state, a man with additional options and obligations, rather than as a dependent junior partner.

Israel's pondering the significance of this change was cut short by Bashir Jumayyil's assassination. His brother did not want an Israeli alliance as such. He had to accept Israel's massive presence in Lebanon and realized that it could also be used to counterbalance Syria and the PLO. But often as his emissaries explained that his public conduct and pronouncements, affected by objective constraints, differed from his real outlook, their Israeli counterparts remained suspicious. In the final months of 1982, conflict over the future of the Phalange, the Lebanese Front, and the Maronite community continued and with it the debate over the community's ability, through its control of the central government, to dominate the Lebanese state. Between June and December 1982, Israel discovered that Bashir Jumayyil did not fully represent the Phalange, that the Phalange did not represent the whole Maronite community, that the Maronite community did not speak for all Lebanese Christians, and that Lebanon's Christians were no longer assured of their ascendancy.

But the evolution of the Israeli-Maronite and the broader Israeli-Lebanese relationship should not be seen in purely political terms. For six years the connection had been clandestine, limited to a small number of participants on each side. The war of 1982 brought a large number of Lebanese and Israelis into contact. The enthusiasm with which many Maronites, and other Lebanese, received the Israeli troops dissipated; the liberators of June became a force of occupation before December. But in other ways the encounter between Lebanese and Israelis was different from the previous two encounters between Israel and Arab societies: the West Bank and Gaza since 1967 and Egypt since 1980. Israel clearly had no territorial ambitions, and cooperation among various political leaders and groups has been open. Economic and commercial cooperation has also developed well beyond the exigencies of occupation as, on a more limited scale, have social and cultural relations. Israeli and Lebanese societies have acquired a more nuanced view of each other's complexities and weaknesses, even though these were tenuous developments, overshadowed by political issues and events.

But absorbing as the intricacies of the Israeli-Lebanese relationship are, they should not overshadow the significance of the war of 1982 for the attitudes and policies of both sides in the Arab-Israeli conflict. The conduct of the war and the public debate it generated reflected the two societies' responses to the settlement and peace process after the profound changes of the 1970s.

In Israel the rift between government and opposition was in some respects a reincarnation of the national security debate in the 1950s. The Labor party, or the mainstream of opposition to the Likud government, inherited Moshe Sharett's position. Its large nationalist wing and its sensitivity to the voters' reaction prevented the Labor party from adopting a consistent position, but one can be distilled from the total of its actions and statements.

The opening of the settlement process, its development into the peace process, and other subsequent events persuaded the advocates of this line that a qualitative change had taken place in Arab-Israeli relations and that the process should go ahead. True, negotiations were bound to be difficult, and the Arab position on the Palestinian issue and the international support for it were dissonant with the position of Israel, to whom the same issue was crucially important. But this was a shortsighted view. Israel's greater power should be translated into advantages through negotiations rather than into a consolidation of its hold on the West Bank.

The Likud's leadership, in turn, made a conscious effort to cast itself in the role of Ben-Gurion, a leader of political and military daring and also a chief architect of Zionism's material basis. Israel was powerful, and the Arab world was not interested in genuine peace. This government made peace with Egypt, conceded and sacrificed, and received a hollow peace in return. If real peace could not be negotiated with Egypt, it could certainly not be negotiated with Syria and Jordan, let alone the PLO. Egypt maintained a formal peace with Israel because of Israel's power; that power should be used to consolidate the territorial basis of Israel's existence and security and to create a regional role for Israel, which other states of the region would respect. Upon such a sound material foundation, political and diplomatic activities could be predicated later. It would be premature and hazardous to depend on them now.

The Likud's position was coherent, activist, and assertive, free of the uncertainties and ambiguities of the opposition's. Its attraction was grudgingly acknowledged by a perceptive Israeli writer to the left of the Labor party, who saw the second electoral victory of the Likud and the war in Lebanon as different manifestations of the same process:

> The major problem of the Labor alignment's fall has to do with the sense of impotence it radiated in the 1970s. A certain paralysis prevailed. . . . A lot can be said against the present government, but not that it is not creative. It is sometimes a dangerous creativity, one that may lead us to destruction, but it is not willing to let the problems sink and stay as they are. . . . [The War in Lebanon] is the distinctive illustration [of this creativity]. And by creativity I mean effervescence, the will to keep addressing problems can be solved which may be derived also from the feeling that ambiguities cannot be tolerated over time. Labor's flag, the more essential flag, is territorial compromise. It is not just a political matter. It is a broader psychological matter, something lukewarm in the middle.[14]

But the war of 1982 offered little reward to the advocates of assertive action. Instead, it threatened to become yet another manifestation of the "cunning of history." The military campaign, which began with the support of a broad segment of Israeli opinion, turned into Israel's most controversial and divisive war. Its initiators were subjected to the scrutiny of a commission of inquiry whose findings had a profound impact on their political futures and possibly on the broader course of Israeli politics. The war, furthermore, produced results well beyond the expectations of its planners—the Reagan plan of September 1982 and the PLO's growing dependence on Syria. Like the Middle East war of 1973, the Lebanese war of 1982 could propel the Arab-Israeli settlement process, but the direction and pace of that process seemed to be beyond any one actor's control.

For the Arabs, the war of 1982 closed a decade that began with the momentous events of 1973.[15] It is difficult, even in retrospect, to impose a pattern on developments in the Arab world during that decade. The military achievements of the first part of the October war, the effective use of the "oil weapon," and the accumulation of unprecedented wealth in parts of the Arab world generated a new sense of power, an expectation of a status and role in the world that the Arabs had been denied in modern times.

The disintegration of inter-Arab relations, which had begun in the 1960s, was expedited by the rise of new foci of power and influence, the decline of Egypt's relative weight and its own partial disengagement, and the rise of particularist concerns at the expense of Pan-Arab commitments. The Arab regimes that had been in power when the 1970s began were all able to hold on for the rest of the decade, but this formal continuity reflected no underlying stability. The 1975 Lebanese civil war and its brutality were seen by Arabs at the time as the true consequence of the dislocations that failed to shake the more vigorous authoritarian regimes of other Arab states. The Iranian revolution at the close of the decade was another indicator of accumulating revolutionary potential. By the end of the 1970s, most Arab regimes were confronted with powerful domestic oppositions, some of them violent, and most taking the form of Islamic movements.

The "Islamic resurgence" of the 1970s derived from the intrinsic development of a religious community, but it also reflected reactions to events—too rapid a change, loss of ideological and political bearings, and the realization, by the decade's end, that the new Arab sense of power was illusory. The Arab world had acquired new wealth and influence but could still not contend with the power of the Soviets, the Iranians, and the Israelis.

The developments of the 1970s had contradictory effects on the Arab states' outlook on the Arab-Israeli conflict. The war of 1973 led to the opening of the Arab-Israeli settlement process; Egypt, and to a lesser extent other Arab states, took the path of settlement. The new wealth and the new relationship with the West encouraged pragmatism among some toward Israel as well. Others saw the new Arab wealth and influence and the anticipated acquisition of power as the key to an eventual victory over Israel. Why settle now, when more, perhaps all, could be obtained later? The settlement process and subsequently the peace process became a cardinal issue in inter-Arab relations, and the ephemeral blocs and coalitions of the 1970s were affected and occasionally governed by attitudes to it.

It was a measure of the Arabs' collective weakness that, despite the almost universal denunciation of the Camp David accords, they could not prevent Egypt from proceeding with their implementation. Arab reaction to the Egyptian-Israeli peace process was ambivalent. Israel was living up to its commitments and returned the Sinai to Egypt despite domestic convulsions in Israel. A process of normalization was taking place, albeit awkwardly, between Egypt and Israel, and Israelis were being de-demonized. But at the same time, Israel continued the war against the PLO in the West Bank and in Lebanon. And as the Arabs seemed to grow weaker, Israel seemed to grow more powerful. The slow steady pace of settlement in the West Bank was humiliating in one way, the spectacular destruction of Ossirak, a symbol of power and technological advancement, humiliating in another.

The Arab world's failure to respond effectively during the war in Lebanon can be explained in terms of both the Arab collective and the separate Arab nations. The Arab collective was caught at a time of division and weakness, accentuated by the Iranian-Iraqi war, the trend of the international oil market, and the inability to reintegrate Egypt into the Arab system. Various Arab states—Saudi Arabia, Iraq, and Jordan to name three—saw advantages in a weakening of Syria and the PLO, and had no intention of jeopardizing these advantages to help them.

When the war was over, no clear-cut conclusions appeared. The process of de-demonization was arrested, and Israel again appeared a dangerous enemy. But the fury and humiliation were mitigated by realism—Israel was powerful and other Arabs could not be counted on. If peace should not be made with Israel, war should, perhaps, be averted as well. More penetrating questions, however, were being asked about the state of the Arab world itself. Is there something fundamentally wrong with Arab society and political institutions that handicaps the Arab world, prevents it from coping with the Israeli challenge, and makes it watch passively with morbid fascination through ten weeks of an Israeli siege of an Arab capital?

For two Arab parties, the war's ramifications were immediate and direct. The PLO lost its autonomous base and the advantages offered by territorial concentration. The two bases close to Israel, Tripoli and the Beqa, in northern and eastern Lebanon, were under Syrian control. Yasir 'Arafat and his colleagues could operate with considerable freedom from Tunisia, but this would make them largely irrelevant. To retain a measure of influence on Palestinian politics, the PLO had to choose between submissiveness to Syria and a mending of fences with the Hashemite regime in Jordan. Black September of 1970 had not been forgotten, nor were the PLO leaders unaware of the irreconcilability of Hashemite interests with theirs. But in September 1982, Jordan was designated as the beneficiary of the Reagan plan, and a dialogue with Jordan, it appeared to the PLO, might provide the organization with some leverage vis-à-vis Syria.

But would it? When ʿArafat went to Amman to negotiate with King Hussein he, like many others, viewed Syria as one of war's losers and Jordan as one of the winners, a view reinforced by the resolutions of the second Fez summit in September 1982. At the first Fez summit, ten months earlier, Syria succeeded in scuttling the Saudi Fahd Plan, at meetings clearly dominated by the Syrian foreign minister, as a reading of the minutes reveals. At the second Fez summit, the Fahd Plan was accepted.

But the tide in Lebanon was turning during that very month: Syria's position, weakened in June had not been destroyed, and the assassination of Bashir Jumayyil and the massacre in Sabra and Shatila made possible its rebuilding. At the end of 1982, six years after drawing the original "red lines," Syria and Israel again confronted one another in Lebanon.

CHAPTER 7

The Lebanese Crisis, 1983–85

THE WAR FOR LEBANON ended in September 1982, but the struggle over Lebanon's character and future has continued, reshaped by the war, for nearly three years now with remarkable intensity and ferocity. The Lebanese crisis has also remained a focal point of Middle Eastern politics, with occasional repercussions in the larger international arena.

In the busy chronology of this period several events stand out as marking particularly important developments or turning points. They also provide a convenient framework for the ensuing examination of the principal actors in the Lebanese crisis.

In December 1982 negotiations began for a Lebanese-Israeli agreement that would bring about an Israeli withdrawal from Lebanon. With American help and participation, an agreement was finally reached on May 17, 1983. Almost at once it was vehemently denounced by Syria, which organized Amin Jumayyil's various Lebanese rivals into a National Salvation Front (July 1983). The Front's first major success was achieved by its Druze component when Walid Junblatt's militia defeated the Lebanese Forces (and indirectly the president) in the battle for the Shuf Mountains that followed the Israeli withdrawal from that area (September 1983).

President Jumayyil won an apparent victory over the Shi'i community when his troops took control of West Beirut in August. But the suicide attacks against the U.S. Marines, the French contingent of the Multi-National Force, and the Israeli military headquarters in Tyre (September–October) were effective demonstrations of the revolutionary and fanatic potential stored in the community.

The pressure of the opposition forced Amin Jumayyil and the other reluctant Maronite leaders to agree to a national reconciliation conference, which met in Geneva in October and November. The effort to devise a formula for transferring part of the political power held by the Maronites to the other communities failed. Druze military pressure on Beirut from the east continued but it was the Shiʻa takeover of West Beirut (February 1984) which prompted a radical change in Lebanese politics. The Reagan administration decided to withdraw its Marines from Beirut. Shorn of that external support, Amin Jumayyil was forced to come to terms with his rivals closer to home. He traveled to Damascus, where on February 29 he capitulated to most of Syria's demands and together with other Christian leaders made concessions to his Lebanese opponents in the second national reconciliation conference, held in Lausanne in March. A new cabinet headed by Rashid Karami was formed on April 30. Among its other members were Camille Chamoun, Pierre Jumayyil, Walid Junblatt, and Nabih Beri.

Amin Jumayyil's Syrian and Lebanese critics were gratified by the abrogation of the May 17 agreement (March 5, 1984) and the closing of the Israeli mission in Dbaya, just north of Beirut, on July 25. But efforts to continue with redistribution of political power, as well as to extend the state's and government's authority and to normalize public life—the other major issues discussed in Damascus and Lausanne—met with little success.

During the first half of 1985 the course of the Lebanese crisis was dominated by the conflict in southern Lebanon. The new Israeli government formed in September 1984 decided in January 1985 to withdraw the IDF to the international border in three phases. The implementation of the first phase, withdrawal from the Sidon area, on February 16, was followed by an escalation of Shiʻi attacks on Israeli troops and by the adoption of what came to be known as Israel's "iron fist" policy. The result was an unprecedented cycle of Shiʻi-Israeli violence over the next two months. The level of violence decreased considerably by the end of April, however, when the second phase of the withdrawal was completed, with the IDF evacuating both the town of Tyre on the coast and its strategic positions in eastern Lebanon, where it had faced the Syrian army.

The Jumayyil Administration and the Major Communities

In the brief history of Amin Jumayyil's administration, February 1984 was a decisive turning point. During the previous year and a half, the president pursued a complex strategy aimed to sustain and gradually consolidate his weak government, primarily by mobilizing American support and by playing his numerous rivals and competitors one against the other.

Domestically the new president relied on the vital importance of his role in perpetuating the legitimacy of a Lebanese state, on the support (often grudging) of the Maronite community, whose leaders realized that it would be very difficult to have another Maronite president elected in the parliament, on the Phalanges, on the limited power that was still vested in the Lebanese presidency and, initially, on his alliance with the Sunni establishment in Beirut.[1]

During Jumayyil's first year or so in office the Reagan administration's support was the cornerstone of his political strategy. Armed with that support, he could hope to neutralize both Syria's and Israel's efforts to shape and influence his government and obtain the withdrawal of their respective armies without making undue concessions to either. If exploited correctly, the conflicting interests and ambitions of his two powerful neighbors could create a stalemate of which the new Lebanese central government would be the principal beneficiary. Domestically reinforced by American military presence and subsequently by the new army the United States was equipping and training, the president could eschew the concessions that his Lebanese adversaries demanded.

Since Jumayyil's foreign and domestic policies were different facets of the same strategy, it is hardly surprising that the campaign against his administration temporarily united a diversified coalition of domestic and external adversaries. Syria played the principal role in organizing the National Salvation Front, which served as a convenient framework for the administration's foes and critics. The first communique published by the Front was, indeed, principally a denunciation of the May 17 agreement. It charged that the agreement was in fact an abandonment of the 1943 convention, that it violated Lebanon's sovereignty, and that the government's conduct in this matter amounted to "the cancellation of every democratic process" and "deprived" the Lebanese people of a participation in decision-making that was instead given to Israel. From the government's perspective, the communique continued, these "are only the first practical steps to cede parts of Lebanon in order to carry out structural changes that will further the establishment of a little Lebanon."[2]

Reality was more complex than the apparent cohesion suggested by the Front's formation. Syria and the PLO were primarily concerned by the general thrust of Amin Jumayyil's government and his foreign policy. A government relying on the United States, seeking to eliminate or minimize the influence of Syria and the PLO, and willing to negotiate, sign, and then implement an agreement with Israel was unacceptable to them. To his Lebanese rivals —the Druzes, the Shi'is, Suleiman Faranjiyya, and Rashid Karami —Jumayyil was a Phalangist president seeking to perpetuate his community's privileged position, working to further his family's and party's interests, and laboring to resist changes that should have come about before—and were unquestionably necessary after—the summer of 1982. Behind this common opposition there lay particular grievances and interests: the Druze-Maronite conflict in the Shuf Mountains, the Faranjiyya clan's vendetta against the Jumayyils, and Karami's resentment of the new prominence enjoyed by his Sunni competitors from Beirut.

The demand that the May 17 agreement be undone was central to the opposition's political platform, and the main drama of the Lebanese crisis during the next ten months can be defined as a conflict between that agreement's defenders and its foes.

It soon developed that the uneasy coalition clustered around the agreement—the United States, Israel, the Jumayyil administration and the Lebanese Forces—was hampered by serious contradictions of aims. American support and American military presence

177

were crucial for Jumayyil's success. In view of the continued violence, however, the Reagan administration, which had no intention of engaging its troops in actual fighting on Jumayyil's behalf,
came to the conclusion that he must make concessions in order
to accommodate at least some of his Lebanese rivals. But Jumayyil
was relying on the Americans precisely in order to avoid such
concessions, and Washington's pressure was to no avail. Moreover, the president's relationship with the Lebanese Forces, commanded by his niece's husband, Fadi Frem, was at best ambivalent. Protestations to the contrary notwithstanding, Jumayyil was
also his community's senior leader. As such he knew that the
Lebanese Forces together with part of the Lebanese army were
the community's military arm—and yet, as the president of the
state he had to keep his distance from a partisan militia. Furthermore, the Lebanese Forces were Israel's close ally, the keepers of
his brother's flame, and watchdogs of the radical Maronite line.[3]
Israel, with whom the president's relationship had long been
awkward, held the key to potentially important developments. It
agreed on May 17, at a price, to withdraw from Lebanon. The
regions it held, a sizable portion of Lebanon, could in principle
be added to the small area ruled by the central government, thus
endowing the Lebanese state with one of the essential characteristics of statehood—actual authority over (at least part of) its territory. Israel's withdrawal, if effected at the right time and in the
proper fashion, could be used as a lever to induce a Syrian withdrawal as well. But could the Israelis be trusted or were they,
in fact, conniving and scheming with Jumayyil's competitors and
enemies?

The next round of events ended with defeat for the president
and the awkward partnership supporting the May 17 agreement.
When Israel withdrew from the outskirts of Beirut and the Shuf
Mountains, the plan to hand this territory to the Lebanese army
failed abysmally. In the Shuf Walid Junblatt's Druze militia (with
Syrian backing and some Palestinian participation) defeated the
Lebanese Forces commanded by Samir Ja'ja and established con-
trol. Fighting to defend the eastern approach to the city, the Leba-
nese army was finally able to hold a line at Suq al-Gharb. Other
Lebanese army units took charge in West Beirut and apparently

consolidated the president's hold over his capital, but this ephemeral achievement was completely overshadowed by the dominant position that Walid Junblatt and his militia had acquired in the mountains just east and south of the capital.[4] The suicide attacks committed by Lebanese Shi'is, probably with Iranian and Syrian help, against the American Marines, the French contingent of the MNF, and the Israeli headquarters near Tyre were significant in two important respects—they weakened the American and Israeli will to stay in Lebanon and foreshadowed the impact that the Shi'i community was about to have on the Lebanese political scene.[5]

The cumulative effect of these developments sufficed to send the president and the other senior political leaders of the Maronite community to Geneva to negotiate political reform and national reconciliation with the major opposition leaders. But it did not suffice to effect a breakthrough to any workable compromise. It was the collapse of the Lebanese army before the sheer numerical weight of the Shi'i community in West Beirut that signaled the final failure of the president's strategy. Having been deserted by the United States and lacking an Israeli option (he seems to have toyed briefly with the idea of drawing Israel in again), Amin Jumayyil capitulated to the Syrians.[6]

The capitulation had three immediate results: the replacement of the Wazzan cabinet by the Karami cabinet, the concessions made at the Lausanne conference, and the abrogation of the May 17 agreement. But other significant developments occurred soon thereafter. By capitulating to Syria, the president transformed his standing in Lebanon. Using its influence through the president and the central government and establishing a working relationship with at least part of the Maronite community had been important elements in Syria's policy in Lebanon. Therefore, once he was willing to capitulate and reverse some of his policies, Amin Jumayyil, who had previously been reviled in the strongest of terms, was viewed as acceptable by the Ba'thi regime and became a principal tool of Syrian policy in Lebanon. His government now enjoyed a measure of Syrian backing and support while Syria's partners in the National Salvation Front were embarrassed by the *volte-face*. The radical Maronites, in turn, argued that in return for short-term and short-sighted gains the president was undermining the community's security and its future.

In the ensuing months no progress was made along two of the paths that were charted in Lausanne to reach some measure of normalization: a more thorough constitutional and political reform and the implementation of the "security plan" designed to minimize fighting and to extend the authority of the state. In other areas advances were more apparent than real; thus the growth of the Lebanese army continued but it did so along communal lines. Army brigades and battalions in most cases represented communal or political interests rather than being an instrument of a revitalized state machinery. In the absence of serious progress in the national political arena, the course of the Lebanese crisis in the year between the spring of 1984 and that of 1985 was dominated by the Shi'a-Israeli conflict in southern Lebanon and by developments within the major communities.

In the Maronite community the tension between the president and the Lebanese Forces came to a head in March 1985. During the previous eighteen months the president had been adroitly taking advantage of his state and party positions and of the Forces' defeat in the Shuf in order to corrode their power and standing. Pierre Jumayyil's death in August 1984 removed his restraining influence, and in October Amin Jumayyil could finally remove Fadi Frem from his position. Frem was replaced by Fu'ad Abi Nader, the president's nephew, who was considered more likely to be a pliable tool in his uncle's hands. But several months later two of the Forces' radical leaders, Samir Ja'ja and Eli Hubeika, rebelled. In March 1985 they deposed Abi Nader, and Ja'ja became commander of the Lebanese Forces, only to be himself replaced by Hubeika in May, following his humiliating failure in the conflict over the future of the Christian community in the Sidon-Jizzin area.

In the Druze community the struggle for the Shuf in 1982–83 resulted in the affirmation of Walid Junblatt's position as unquestioned leader. Between 1977 and 1982 he had failed to become his father's full successor as leader of the National Movement and the Druzes. But in a fashion reminiscent of Sultan al-Atrash's rise during the 1925 revolt, his conduct of the military and political campaigns in the Shuf established his personal and political dominance. During this period the rival Arslan clan was completely overshadowed and the differences between Junblatt's Progressive Socialist Party, the armed militia, and the religious establishment lost much of their significance. In 1984 and 1985 Walid Junblatt's role in the larger Lebanese arena and his ability to maneuver between Syria and Israel diminished, but his standing within his community was not seriously affected.

Perhaps the sharpest decline in standing and power was undergone by Lebanon's Sunni community. During Amin Jumayyil's first months in office his partnership with Beirut's Sunni establishment, the PLO's evacuation from West Beirut, and Saudi Arabia's role in Washington's Middle Eastern policies endowed Sa'ib Salam and his school with renewed prominence. But this resurgence was short-lived. The developments described above shifted political influence elsewhere. In their three major cities, Beirut, Sidon, and Tripoli, the Sunnis were overwhelmed—by the Shi'is in the first two and by Syria's direct presence in the third. The Sunnis' decline was expedited by their lack of militia power. In the absence of state authority, autonomous military power was indispensable for any group seeking political influence, and though before the 1982 war, the PLO had dispossessed the Sunni establishment, it acted as a militia of sorts for the community as a whole. When it departed, the Murabitun of West Beirut were the Sunni community's only organized force, and they too were defeated in April 1985 in a combined attack by al-Amal and the Druze militia. Syria, it seems, gave its blessing to this attack since it viewed the Murabitun as Yasir 'Arafat's allies. Likewise, the Syrians made no serious effort to stop the Shi'is' attack on the PLO stronghold in Sabra and Shatila in May and June.

The Shi'i community emerged from the war of 1982 divided physically and still far from achieving political power and standing commensurate with its numerical strength. One part of the community lived in southern Lebanon under Israeli rule, another part in the Beqa under Syrian rule, and a third group in the southern part of West Beirut. The Beqa remained, as it had been since 1976, under uncontested Syrian control. Syria has also allowed, as part of its cooperation with the Islamic Republic of Iran, some 1,500 Iranian Revolutionary Guards to operate in that part of Lebanon.

The Shi'is of the Beqa thus became important transmitters of Syrian and Iranian political influence and of a radical revolutionary version of Shi'ism to the rest of their community as well as to Lebanon's larger political stage. In the western and southern parts of Beirut the Shi'i population provided the human mass which exerted a growing pressure on the center of national politics. Also housed there were the political organizations (Amal and Hizb Allah) and the institution (Supreme Shi'i Islamic Council) within which the conflict over the community's future orientation has been conducted. The conflict has been shaped by several factors, but its most important aspect can be defined as a struggle between an essentially secular political orientation and a theocratic one. The first, represented primarily by Nabih Beri, accepts the legitimacy of the Lebanese state and seeks to obtain for the Shi'i community the status, power, and role in Lebanon warranted by its demographic strength. The theocratic outlook is expounded chiefly by Husein Fadlallah, who seeks to establish an "Islamic Republic" in Lebanon. Others, such as Husein Musavi and Mahdi Shams al-Din, occupy positions along the spectrum. Husein Huseini, the present speaker of the Lebanese parliament, is a secular politician like Beri but, unlike him, is very close to Syria.[7]

From both perspectives southern Lebanon and its large Shi'i population assumed during this period an ever-increasing importance. This was the area in which, once Israel withdrew, an autonomous Shi'i region, comparable to the areas of Christian and Druze autonomy, could be established. The large Shi'i population of the south would be linked to that of Beirut, and their combined impact could be brought to bear on the capital. Clearly, ascendancy in the south was a crucial key to ascendancy in the Shi'i community and possibly, later on, in Lebanon. It soon became apparent that after the waning of the traditional leadership no new indigenous leadership was developing in the south, and Israel did not try to cultivate a cooperative local leadership. Instead, realizing that the local population was looking to Beirut for direction, the Israelis tried in vain to open a dialogue with Amal. Amal's leadership, in turn, was determined to avoid any contact with Israel. Rather than risk delegitimization through negotiations with Israel which, it became increasingly clear, was disengaging,

Amal's leadership sought to underline its militant posture and augment its prestige by orchestrating the attacks against Israel's troops and local collaborators. Before long, and even more clearly so in 1985, the contest for leadership of the anti-Israeli campaign and eventually preeminence in the south became the principal channel through which the intracommunal Shi'i conflict came to be conducted.[8]

American Policy

The main contours of the Reagan administration's policy in Lebanon in the period September 1982–February 1984 will have emerged from the preceding analysis of Amin Jumayyil's strategy and failure. It is a curious and telling fact that, at least from the present day's limited perspective, a glaring failure in an important arena involving several regional and international issues should have had such minor consequences for the United States and for the Reagan administration.

In the confused circumstances of 1982 an American policy toward Lebanon was formulated that was predicated on the anticipated gradual consolidation of Amin Jumayyil's administration and the state's authority: Unlike his brother, Amin Jumayyil was to base his government on dialogue with the Maronites' traditional partners, as well as, it was hoped, with new ones. Israel would evacuate its troops in return for an agreement, negotiated under American auspices, and the prospect of that withdrawal would be used in order to obtain a comparable (though not necessarily a simultaneous and identical) Syrian evacuation. The pursuit of these negotiations should not interfere with the implementation of President Reagan's plan, announced on September 1, 1982, on the assumption that the Lebanese crisis was safely on the road to a satisfactory solution.

In the course of the next eighteen months, the assumptions on which this policy was based were proved false and its goals unattainable.[9] It took seven months to negotiate the Lebanese-Israeli agreement of May 17, 1983. The Israeli government sought both to satisfy the country's security needs and to achieve diplomatic gains that would mitigate some of the growing public criticism in Israel of the 1982 war. The Lebanese government, partly for its own reasons and partly in the hope of making the agreement acceptable to Syria, resisted. The Reagan administration exerted pressure mostly on the Israelis. This, coupled with the tense relations between the American Marines and the Israeli military in the Beirut area, produced unusual acrimony between the two countries in the winter of 1983.[10]

Efforts to implement the Reagan plan could not, of course, be divorced from the course of events in Lebanon. King Hussein and Yasir 'Arafat made considerable apparent progress in their negotiations. Armed with 'Arafat's endorsement, Hussein might possibly have overcome the 1974 Rabat resolutions and entered into negotiations with Israel (under American auspices) on the future of the West Bank. But Syria cut the expectations short. When King Hussein demanded a crucial clarification from 'Arafat in April, Syria, taking advantage of the PLO's dependence on it, dictated a negative answer.[11]

The temporary demise of the Reagan plan did, however, expedite the signing of the Lebanese-Israeli agreement, which then enjoyed the administration's single-minded attention. The incremental progress made in earlier weeks and the appointment of a new Israeli defense minister, Moshe Arens, who maintained an excellent relationship with the Reagan administration, were at least as important in effecting the breakthrough. But the agreement was stillborn and that this would be the case should have been clear to the signatories, who knew that Syria opposed it and was likely to obstruct it. We do not know what Washington's emissaries told their government about their efforts to win Syria's endorsement, nor do we know how the American and Israeli governments in their own discussions evaluated Syria's position and its import. But the account of Secretary of State George Shultz's meeting with leaders of the Labor opposition party on May 6 is most revealing. As the Israeli press reported it, Yitzhak Rabin told Shultz that an agreement that had not been endorsed by Damascus was an exercise in futility. Angered, the secretary asked whether Rabin wanted him to go to Damascus to discuss the issue of the Golan Heights.[12] This brief reported exchange revealed a weakness which underlay American policy in Lebanon, then and during the following months. The Reagan administration realized that Syria opposed its policies in Lebanon and was bent on obstructing them. It also deemed prohibitive the price demanded by Syria in Lebanon and in the larger Middle Eastern area for shifting to a more cooperative policy. Because the administration did not intend to use military force against Syria, it must have relied on a dramatic political breakthrough in Lebanon or on the Israelis' willingness to bring their military superiority to bear, directly or indirectly.

No such expectations materialized as Syria mounted its successful campaign against the May 17 agreement. Amin Jumayyil failed to broaden his political base of support, Saudi Arabia exerted no restraining influence on Syria, Israel withdrew from the Shuf, and American troops were attacked from various quarters. It was difficult to retaliate against the organizers of the suicide attacks on the American embassy and the Marines, and the shelling of Druze positions in the Shuf by American ships, even if construed as justified retaliation, still presented the spectacle of a superpower battering a small, determined community and thus added nothing to U.S. prestige.

When the Reagan government finally decided to retaliate against Syria, its action was unsuccessful because two conflicting outlooks existed within the administration. Curiously it was the secretary of state who took the apparently more militant line while the secretary of defense seemed to oppose military action. The State Department's view was that the United States had to bring its military power to bear somehow if its policies were to be effective. The Pentagon was against exposing American forces in any position in which they could be compromised. This dichotomy had been reflected in Washington's conduct in Lebanon well before the end of 1983, and when the decision to act against Syria was made, the result was a compromise—antiquated planes were sent on a bombing mission on December 4, 1983. Two were shot down and one pilot was captured. The administration's embarrassment was subsequently deepened by the fact that Jesse Jackson, the black contender for the Democratic nomination, obtained his release.

Indeed, as the November 1984 elections drew nearer, the danger that a lingering and unsuccessful involvement in Lebanon, not to mention a potential fiasco, could affect President Reagan's prospects loomed increasingly large to his strategists. By February 1984, the Reagan administration's illusions regarding the Lebanese crisis had all been destroyed, and the Shi'i victory in West Beirut provided both a further motivation and a convenient occasion for withdrawing the American military presence from Lebanon.

It is, of course, impossible to assess the long-term consequences of the Reagan administration's Lebanese debacle. The administration itself emerged almost unscathed, but its standing in the Middle East and its own outlook on the region were bound to be affected. For a decade, since 1974, the United States had enjoyed the position of being the one superpower able to orchestrate Arab-Israeli settlements. The dividends were considerable. But in 1984 yet another Middle Eastern government which had rested on American support tottered, and for the first time in a decade an Arab-Israeli agreement sponsored by the United States was destroyed by a local ally of the Soviet Union. After the election the president and his foreign policy team might conceivably have sought to redress the balance. In fact, however, the mood of men like the secretary of state and the national security adviser worked against any such attempt. Less than a year after the abortive efforts to implement the May 17 agreement and the Lebanese army's entry into the Shuf—their formative experiences in the Middle East—they felt no urge to launch or even endorse a far more complex process of negotiation between Israel and Syria or Israel and Jordan. Nor did they believe that they could seriously rely on such allies as Saudi Arabia to exert effective influence on Washington's behalf.[13] The reticence and trepidation that have characterized the second Reagan administration's initial outlook on the Middle East were shaped largely, though not solely, by his first administration's role in the Lebanese crisis.

Syrian Policy

Syria's policy in Lebanon since September 1982 can be seen in two ways: as a continuation of its earlier policy as shaped in 1976–

82, and as a more specific effort to undo the consequences of the 1982 war. It was a successful policy that at least temporarily enhanced Syria's standing as a regional power and for a brief moment endowed the country and its president with international importance.[14]

As described in previous chapters, Syrian policy toward Lebanon since the end of the 1975–76 civil war had aimed at consolidating Syria's ascendancy over its weaker neighbor. Syrian control was to rest on the cooperation of the central Lebanese government, on Syria's influence on the army and the security apparatus, on its role as arbiter between feuding communities and politicians and, finally, on a security pact legitimizing its present military deployment and its right to intervene in the future. With all these guarantees Syrian military presence could subsequently, it was hoped, be reduced to a minimum.

The gradual implementation of this policy suffered a serious setback in the summer of 1982. But the assassination of Bashir Jumayyil marked the transition to a new phase during which Syria's position in Lebanon was restored and subsequently enhanced. As has been shown above, the assassination of Bashir Jumayyil set in motion a chain of events that neutralized Syria's principal adversaries in Lebanon. Asad excelled in locating their weaknesses and in exploiting them to the full. He understood that in the Lebanese arena it was sometimes better to remain passive and let the contradictions inherent in his rivals' positions work for him.

Asad's efforts were helped significantly by the Soviet Union's decision at the end of 1982 to replace the ground-to-air missile system destroyed the previous June with a more sophisticated system, to be manned in part by Soviet personnel. The decision bolstered Asad's self-confidence and added a confounding element to the American and Israeli outlooks on the Lebanese crisis: the danger of a direct conflict with the Soviet Union in case of another round of Syrian-Israeli fighting had to be taken more seriously.

As 1983 wore on, the main lines of Syria's policy appeared more clearly—the central government had to accept Syria's ascendancy or be brought down. Rival external influences—American, Israeli, or European—must be eliminated. Israel must not enjoy any advantages accruing from the 1982 war. Any agreement between Lebanon and Israel arranging for Israel's withdrawal from Lebanon must not confer any such advantages, should not have a political character, and should not suggest that Syria's presence in Lebanon could be compared to Israel's.

Since the imminent danger to Syria's very standing in Lebanon was over, Asad could turn his attention to ways of using his country's improving position in Lebanon and the Lebanese crisis to further Syria's regional policies. One such effort was directed at the PLO and sought to take advantage of 'Arafat's weakness and his increased dependence on Syria so as to subdue him once and for all to Syria's authority. In the same vein Syria organized Abu Musa's rebellion against 'Arafat in the Fath's ranks and then besieged him in Tripoli, forcing him and his supporters (in December 1983) to leave Lebanon altogether. But Asad's success was limited; domestic constraints and his limited influence in Arab politics (where he could obstruct others' policies but had difficulty in implementing his own) prevented him from consummating his victory over 'Arafat. As in 1976–77 Asad defeated, weakened, and humiliated 'Arafat but was unable to have him deposed and replaced with a Syrian proxy.[15]

Syria's other regional aims in Lebanon were pursued with greater success. By obstructing Jordan's negotiations with the PLO in April 1983, Syria demonstrated to the United States that Damascus could not be ignored when a new policy was contemplated for the region.

Syria's criticism of the May 17 agreement has been explained above in the Lebanese and Israeli contexts. It was seen as an instrument forged in defiance of Syria, granting Israel excessive privileges and rewarding it for the 1982 war. But these drawbacks, weighty in themselves, were augmented by considerations of a regional order. Syria viewed the May 17 agreement as a (paler) duplication of the Camp David accords—an Arab-Israeli agreement of a political nature, orchestrated by the United States and excluding Syria. It had to be destroyed so that its destruction could serve to prefigure the future rectification of the "original sin" perpetrated at Camp David. Furthermore, Lebanon's insistence that

it possessed the sovereignty to make such agreements contra-
dicted Syria's claim that there was a collective Arab will, superior
to those of individual Arab countries—of which Damascus was,
naturally, the interpreter. The dangers inherent in Lebanon's defiance of that will were expounded by a variety of Syrian spokesmen. Perhaps the most instructive was the comment published on
July 18, 1983, by the official newspaper *Tishrin*:

> When 'Arafat sheds tears about independent decision-making, he cer-
> tainly wants to lend legitimacy to the independent decisions of others.
> Al-Sadat's treasonous decision was an expression of such sover-
> eignty. Similarly, the Lebanese Phalangists' decision to conclude an
> agreement with Israel is an independent decision and an expres-
> sion of sovereignty according to the 'Arafatist concept of independent
> decision-making. Wasn't the Lebanese regime's main excuse for con-
> cluding the agreement in which they submitted [to Israel] that it was
> an independent Lebanese decision based on Lebanese sovereignty?[16]

By the fall of 1983 it had become clear that in the course of the
preceding year Syria had come more than full circle in Lebanon.
The defeated power of September 1982 had not only reestablished
its hegemony there but had increased its influence and used the
centrality and saliency of the Lebanese crisis to enhance its regional standing and prestige. Nonetheless, at the zenith of its success the sense of achievement was marred by both contradictions
inherent in Syrian policy and accidental factors. One accidental
development was the illness of President Asad, who apparently
suffered a heart attack in mid-November 1983. During the period
of nearly a year that it took him to overcome the illness and its
political by-products, Syrian leadership was unable to devote full
attention to the Lebanese crisis, and its effectiveness vis-à-vis clients and rivals in Lebanon was weakened.[17]

Ironically, it was at Syria's moment of success that the contradictions inherent in its policy in Lebanon surfaced. Organizing a
coalition of Amin Jumayyil's numerous rivals and enemies had
been relatively easy; holding such a diverse group together was
much more difficult when the issue was defense of the status quo,
let alone the pursuit of reforms and settlements. The transition to
this newer phase revealed the cross-purposes at which some of

Syria's allies were working as well as the ambiguities of Syria's own relationship with them. Thus, for Walid Junblatt and the Druzes, Syria was not only an ally against the Maronite president and the Lebanese Forces, but also a potential oppressor, the power seen as responsible for Kamal Junblatt's assassination. As long as Israel remained in or near the Shuf, a semi-clandestine relationship with Israel offered a certain guarantee against Syrian domineering. But with Israel's withdrawal, an outlet to the sea became crucial. One could be obtained at the Iqlim al-Kharoub region at the Maronites' expense, but in the long run the problem pitted the Druzes against the Shi'is since Druze control of a coastal strip south of Beirut interferes with Shi'i plans to develop an autonomous region in southern Lebanon contiguous to the Shi'i neighborhoods in the southern part of West Beirut. Nor was this the only issue separating Druzes from Shi'is. When constitutional and political reforms were discussed in Geneva and Lausanne, a significant divergence appeared. The Shi'is, a large and an underrepresented community, naturally demanded that political power in Lebanon be distributed according to demographic strength. The Druzes, whose importance is determined by location, cohesion, and military prowess and not by numbers, took a different view.

Syria is ambivalent about such antagonisms between its allies and clients. They do obstruct the implementation of policy and render the patron's task difficult, if not impossible. At the same time Syria continues to seek and foster in Lebanon a balance of weakness. Drawing a lesson from its failures in Lebanon in the late 1970s and being fully aware of its limited power and resources, Syria no longer seeks to control every detail of Lebanese politics, but chooses to operate indirectly through clients and proxies. But most of these are not fully reliable, and it has seemed safer to keep them divided with Syria playing the role of the final arbiter.

Nowhere has this mixture of ambiguity and pragmatism been more evident than in Syria's attitude to Amin Jumayyil. Syria's partners in Lebanon and many external observers were amazed by Asad's willingness to work with and through his former enemy once the latter capitulated. But the key to the apparent paradox can be found in Asad's speech of July 1976 reproduced in the Appendix of this book. Asad had then ridiculed Kamal Junblatt, who, according to him, wanted to subdue the Maronites, saying: "Let us discipline them. We must have decisive military action. They have been governing us for 140 years and we want to get rid of them." To this Asad retorted, "decisive military action in Lebanon is impossible, because the factor of might is not the only condition which must be available" (pp. 218, 220).

This perception did not change between 1976 and 1984, and as long as the Maronites could not be subdued Syrian policy had to be addressed to that community's centrality in Lebanon. The president was the most important Maronite leader, the head of state, and head of the central government, and his cooperation was crucial for effective indirect control. Though surely Syria did not trust him and in working with him antagonized others, this choice was deemed preferable to other options.

In the course of the year following Jumayyil's capitulation, two other developments significantly affected Syria's outlook on Lebanon. One was a decline in the importance of the Lebanese crisis as a regional issue. The United States departed, Israel lowered its sights, and the locus of decision shifted elsewhere. Yasir 'Arafat, despite the decimation of his power, succeeded in convening the Palestinian National Congress in Amman. Jordan reestablished diplomatic relations with Egypt and an Egyptian-Jordanian-Iraqi axis was forming. Syria felt threatened by the prospect of a fresh effort to renew the Arab-Israeli peace process that would rely on that axis and on the PLO's manifest desire to escape Syria's pressuring embrace. In the event, for reasons partly explained above, no such serious efforts were made, but in contradistinction to the April 1983 veto, nor were any foiled by a Syria using for that purpose its predominant position in Lebanon.

The other development was Israel's decision to withdraw from Lebanon. In 1983 and 1984 Syria's attitude toward the prospect of an Israeli departure from southern Lebanon had been the subject of debate and speculation. There were those who argued that Syria wanted Israel to remain and bleed further. Others held that for a small price Syria would be interested in having Israel leave southern Lebanon, particularly its eastern part. As it turned out, Syria was not asked in 1985 to pay any price and for its part did not seek to obstruct Israel's departure.

Israel's withdrawal from southern Lebanon inaugurated a new phase in the Lebanese crisis. It released a sizable portion of Lebanon's territory and turned it into an object of competition among several parties. It raised the prospect of a Palestinian attempt to return to southern Lebanon and reopened the question of Syria's attitude toward attacks upon Israel launched from the area and toward Israel's informal presence there in order to prevent and preempt such attacks. More subtly, as Amal began to establish itself as the dominant power in southern Lebanon, Syria had to address itself to the potential for conflict between an external power and a community on the march, both seeking hegemony.

Israeli Policies

When Israel's National Unity government decided in January 1985 to withdraw the IDF to the Lebanese-Israeli border without any satisfactory security arrangements in southern Lebanon, it was, in fact, seeking to break out of the vicious circle in which Israel had found itself since September 1982. Israel's predicament resulted from the combined effect of several factors—the inherent flaws of the 1982 war plan, the divergence of American and Israeli interests and outlooks, the growing criticism and skepticism in Israel, and the awkwardness of Israel's relationship with both Amin Jumayyil and the Lebanese Forces (see above, pp. 154–57). The abortive efforts of three successive Israeli governments to escape that circle unfolded through four principal phases.

September 1982–March 1983

During the six months following the war's end, the government led by Menachem Begin and Ariel Sharon tried to cope with a number of simultaneous challenges. It sought to salvage as much as it could from its Lebanese investment, to oppose the Reagan plan without getting into acrimonious conflict with the Reagan administration, and to cope with the ominous shadows that the Kahan Commission's work cast on the political future of its leading members. The fighting in the Shuf Mountains and the military superiority of the Druze militia over the Lebanese Forces created a further strain on the conduct of Israeli policy in Lebanon and the maintenance of its relationship with its one trusted Lebanese ally.

The government's main effort was directed toward achieving an impressive agreement with the Lebanese government. An agreement that fell short of a peace treaty could still—if it put Lebanese-Israeli relations on a new level and provided adequate security arrangements in southern Lebanon—turn the 1982 war into an almost successful enterprise and enable Israel to withdraw the bulk of its troops. The formal negotiations between Lebanon and Israel, through American mediation, began in October. Direct negotiations began in December and were conducted in Khalde, south of Beirut, and Kiryat Shmone. As has been mentioned above, the negotiations were arduous and acrimonious.

It later emerged that simultaneous informal and secret negotiations were being held between the Israeli government and one of Amin Jumayyil's confidants, a private businessman devoid of any official capacity. This was made public on December 17 by Ariel Sharon himself, in a press interview in which he announced that he had actually reached an agreement with the Lebanese government.[18] Both the announcement and its formulation had a clear anti-American tone. They implied that while the Reagan administration's efforts had obstructed a Lebanese-Israeli agreement, direct negotiations between the two countries produced a genuine understanding. Whatever his motivation, the defense minister's move proved counterproductive. Amin Jumayyil and his government dissociated themselves from the informal emissary and from whatever commitments he had made to his Israeli interlocutor. The whole affair was reminiscent of the abortive effort to negotiate a treaty between the Jewish Agency and the Maronite church in 1946 (see p. 104).

The negotiations continued solely in Khalde and Kiryat Shmone, their lack of progress producing new tensions in Israel's relations with the Reagan administration. This phase ended in March 1983, after the publication of the Kahan Commission's report led to Sharon's resignation from the Defense Ministry and his replacement by Moshe Arens, who for the previous year had been Israel's ambassador in Washington.

March 1983–September 1983

The change of ministers served to expedite other changes in the conduct of Israel's policies in Lebanon. First came the decision to reduce Israel's demands in the negotiations with the Lebanese government, a decision prompted by the state of American-Israeli relations rather than by Israel's position in Lebanon. Having lowered its expectations in Lebanon, the government calculated, correctly, that the practical significance of its concessions was limited, while on the other hand it stood to gain considerably by improving its relations with Washington. This remained the pattern during the following year: The May 17 agreement was stillborn, and the attempted coordination of Israel's withdrawal from the Shuf failed, but Israel's relations with the Reagan administration and its foreign policy team remained close.

The second change was apparently technical—a new position, that of coordinator of Israel's policies in Lebanon, was created. The coordinator, Ambassador Uri Lubrani, was appointed jointly by the prime minister and the ministers of defense and foreign affairs. By appointing him the government sought both to reduce bureaucratic confusion and rivalries, one of the ills of Israel's Lebanese policies, and to generate new ideas. One novel direction was taken by the early summer of 1983: Israel ended its exclusive relationship with the Maronite community and sought to develop dialogues with other communities as well. The Maronites, as represented chiefly by the Lebanese Forces and their supporters, were to remain Israel's prime ally in Lebanon, but efforts to establish cooperation with the Druzes, the Shi'is and, perhaps, others were to be pursued, in response to a lesson belatedly drawn from the experiences of the previous years.

The initiative taken with regard to the Druze community was eminently successful in the short range. It facilitated Israel's subsequent withdrawal from the Shuf, helped prevent Palestinian operations against Israel, reduced tension between the Israeli state and its own Druze community, and stood out as the one dimension of Israel's involvement in Lebanon marked by a bold and creative approach. But it had its price: it was construed and presented by Israel's Maronite allies as a shameful desertion of them.

It also had its limitations: it ran its course in about a year. When Israel decided to withdraw further rather than invest greater efforts in Lebanon, Walid Junblatt practically severed his community's relations with Israel and turned to Syria.[19] The Israeli effort to develop a comparable dialogue with the Shi'i community failed, as we saw earlier.

Israel's most crucial decision had to be made in the summer of 1983, when the failure of the May 17 agreement became obvious. Arens and the other authors of Israel's Lebanese policies identified the fundamental fact that was sapping their efforts—Israel had lost its deterrence capacity vis-à-vis Syria in Lebanon. Asad had understood in the winter of 1982–83 that his Israeli rivals no longer had the will, political capacity, and moral authority to use their military advantage against him. He could, therefore, go to the brink in Lebanon, bring his own considerable advantages to bear and destroy Israeli (and for that matter U.S.) efforts to gain a settlement. Since Arens, for perfectly good reasons, would not go to war against Syria, he found himself in the same predicament as his predecessor. Nor would he and the government choose the other extreme alternative and withdraw to the international border. Writing off the 1982 war and Israel's subsequent investments in Lebanon was not a viable political option even if one believed in its merits. The dilemma was exacerbated by the unending stream of Israeli casualties sustained in the south, in the Shuf, and in the Beirut region.

The policy that was finally chosen in August 1983 in an effort to break the deadlock was a unilateral withdrawal from the Shuf Mountains and the environs of Beirut to a line running along the Awali River. This move amounted primarily to a statement renouncing Israel's ambitions to act on the central stage of Lebanon's national politics and to take part in shaping them. Israel would now seek to address its security interests in southern Lebanon in a more limited sense of the term. By so limiting the scope of its deployment, the Israeli government hoped, fewer troops would be required, a smaller financial investment would be called for, and fewer casualties would be exacted. It also hoped that Israel's credibility vis-à-vis Syria would be improved.

These assumptions were to be tested during the next few

months. More immediately the effort to coordinate the withdrawal with Amin Jumayyil's administration failed, as we saw above. Israel's withdrawal was followed by Druze-Maronite fighting in the Shuf, massacres, and a Druze takeover. Israel insisted on strict neutrality, a stance that was not appreciated by its Maronite allies.

September 1983–September 1984

The next phase began with Israel's withdrawal from the Shuf and ended with the formation of the National Unity government headed by the Labor party's leader, Shimon Peres. (The earlier change of prime ministers, Begin's replacement by Yitzhak Shamir, had been accomplished within the Likud and had not resulted in a change of line in Lebanon.)

Even the more modest aims defined for Israel in Lebanon did not produce a new consensus. The government's policy as represented by Prime Minister Shamir and Defense Minister Arens was to bring the IDF back to the international border only after providing adequate security arrangements in southern Lebanon. Another school of thought, represented most notably by Shimon Peres, then leader of the opposition, argued that the quest for such arrangements would prove futile and counterproductive and that Israel's security interests would best be served by a quick withdrawal from Lebanon. A third school reached the opposite conclusion from the same premise: since Israel's security could not be secured through any proxy, it held, Israel should stay inside Lebanon along a line running some thirty kilometers north of the border. The debate sometimes cut across partisan and bureaucratic lines but could not be divorced from partisan considerations, particularly in view of the July 1984 elections. Still, Shamir and Arens continued to lead the government, and their views shaped Israel's policy—which consisted essentially of a series of efforts to find a cooperative partner that would hold the territory of southern Lebanon and prevent it from becoming once again a launching base for anti-Israeli operations.

The expectation that Lebanon's army would prove to be such a force foundered as that army disintegrated after February 1984.

Another effort was invested in expanding and upgrading Major Haddad's militia into an entity called the South Lebanese army. Haddad himself died of cancer in January 1984 and was succeeded by Brigadier General Antoine Lahad, a retired Lebanese army officer considered close to the Chamounists. His force was expanded to a size of about 3,000 and assumed an increasing share of the policing duties in southern Lebanon with some IDF supervision and support. But as 1984 wore on and the Shi'i population's opposition and resistance grew fiercer, the Israelis became increasingly doubtful that a militia perceived as Christian could control the area in the teeth of Shi'i opposition.

All efforts to mitigate that opposition were to no avail. Talks could be opened with some local leaders in the south but it soon developed that they were fully subordinate to Amal's leadership in Beirut, which then forbade them to maintain contacts with the Israelis. The Amal leadership refused consistently to enter even into indirect dealings with the Israeli government. The Israelis must leave first. Amal's legitimacy would be undermined by talking to the Israelis and had instead to be built by fighting them.

The suggestion was also made that Israel attempt to deal with the numerous Shi'is in the south on a local basis, relying on its own control of the territory and on the passive accommodationist streak in the Shi'i political tradition. Implementing this course of action, however, would have required a manifest Israeli decision to stay in southern Lebanon, and it was never really tried. In the absence of any political progress, Israel and the Shi'is became locked in a vicious spiral of violence.

September 1984–May 1985

On September 13, 1984, in the absence of a clear-cut decision in the July elections, a National Unity government was formed by Shimon Peres. The two principal tasks set for the new government were to rehabilitate the economy and to bring the IDF out of Lebanon. Israel's Lebanon policy was entrusted to the defense minister, Yitzhak Rabin.

Rabin's first move was directed at gaining Syrian cooperation.

Indirect Syrian-Israeli dialogue was conducted through two channels: American mediation and Lebanese-Israeli military talks at
Naqura. But despite initial indications to the contrary, Syria refused to become partner to an agreement facilitating Israel's withdrawal. By December 1984 the efforts had foundered.

The failure of the Syrian gambit prompted the Israeli government to decide in January 1985 on a three-phased withdrawal to
the international border. Along the border itself a security zone
was to be maintained by local militias that would not be necessarily identical with the South Lebanese army. While deployed
on the Israeli side, the IDF would be ready, as it used to be before
June 1982, to operate north of the border if the militias proved incapable of coping with their adversaries. Clearly these were not
the satisfactory security arrangements sought earlier, but the government decided that such arrangements were not attainable and
that Israel's overall security would best be served by its leaving
Lebanon. The Likud ministers, Sharon included, supported the
decision.

Israel's hopes for maintaining a calm border in the north now
lay with Amal. The Israelis were no longer looking for a friendly
neighbor but for effective authority. Their argument was that
Amal, interested in building such authority over the territory
evacuated, should also be interested, for the same reason, in preventing the region from becoming a battleground between Israel
and its opponents, be they Shi'i or Palestinian. In the long run,
these hopes may prove to be well founded. But during the implementation of the first two phases of the IDF's withdrawal from
the Shi'i areas in the western and central sectors of southern Lebanon, a vicious cycle of Shi'i-Israeli violence erupted that could not
be checked before the end of April.

The completion of Israel's withdrawal from southern Lebanon
certainly marks the end of an important phase in the history of
the Lebanese crisis, but unfortunately it does not signify the ending, or even the attenuation of the struggle for Lebanon. The conflict over the future of southern Lebanon continues, and so does
the contest for control of Beirut and the national political stage.

The principal participants in the struggle over Lebanon's character and future enter this new phase with their outlooks and

capacities affected by the developments of the past three years. Israel is in a soul-searching mood, its population and political and military establishments now reluctant to invest further efforts in Lebanon and acutely aware of the discrepancy between military power and political nuance. Of the Lebanese communities, the Maronites and the Sunnis, many among whom enjoyed an illusory sense of power in the final months of 1982, have suffered a distinct loss of power and position. What was lost by Israel and these two communities has apparently been gained by Syria, the Shi'is, and the Druzes. But no one is more acutely aware of the ephemeral nature of power and success in the context of the Lebanese crisis than the apparent winners themselves.

Appendix

THE FOLLOWING, a speech by Hafiz al-Asad, president of Syria, to members of the newly elected Syrian provincial councils, was monitored from Radio Damascus by Foreign Broadcast Information Service on July 20, 1976. Words in brackets are supplied by FBIS. A question mark preceding these words indicates they were not clearly heard but are appropriate to the context.

Brother citizens and brother members of the local administration councils: I am very happy to meet with you today after the completion of the local administration's elections. You have won the confidence of the people when they elected you as their representatives in these councils. The precious confidence of the people which you have gained is the most precious thing you could obtain. The precious confidence of the people which you won is the most precious thing you must preserve because this confidence is a continuous source of power, action and inspiration. Its continuation is necessarily a firm guarantee for the soundness of action and safety of the march forward.

Brother members of the councils: Congratulating you today on the confidence the people placed in you and wishing you success, I sincerely hope that you will do your utmost to rise to the level of the confidence and deserve the confidence your voters placed in you.

The local administration which we began more than 4 years ago is a pioneer experiment in the field of popular democracy. We must act to consolidate this experiment by practicing it daily and continuously so that this experiment may become more positive and effective in our daily public life in all fields.

Today, as we begin the second stage of the local administration, we can say that we are satisfied with the results of the first stage of this experiment. On this occasion, we must thank those brothers who participated in the local councils—the provincial councils—in the past stage. We will definitely continue to say that the first stage we completed in the experiment of the local administration was a pioneer experiment. Therefore, we will continue to remember and also thank these brothers for the good deeds they carried out in that first stage.

I do not doubt, brothers, that you will add to the achievements of the first stage because life is a renewed giving and continuous movement toward what is better. You undoubtedly were aware of the size of the responsibility which will be placed on your shoulders when you were struggling to win the people's confidence and were also optimistic and confident that you would achieve success when you shouldered this responsibility. This will make you happy because your success in your duties will produce good results for all the citizens who placed their confidence in you. All of us constitute a part of these citizens.

I must refer to a new phenomenon, which deserves mention in this stage of the local administration. This phenomenon is the emergence of women and their participation in the local administration's councils. It is a phenomenon which deserves to be noted. This is a new victory which women in our country have achieved. It is a victory for them to stand alongside men in this field to play their role in pushing the wheel of development and progress. It is a victory for women and society. Welcome to the mother, as I have previously said, the wife, the sister and the daughter in the new field of action. [cheers and applause]

Brothers: Your role is very big. You live with all the citizens in every city, quarter and village. This enables you to feel the pains of the citizens and work seriously; you must seriously work to deal with these pains within your abilities. You must understand the hopes of the citizens and act to achieve whatever possible by working continuously and exploiting the available means and by also working continuously to develop these means.

Brothers, you must act to make all citizens participate in your work and exploit every available means in the interests of the people. [cheers and applause]

Brothers, we must contemplate what we can do everywhere and in every city and village. We must think how to provide the essential and necessary capacities to complete what we intend to do. We must exploit the resources—all human, economic and financial resources—to the maximum. I wish to say here that you must not always depend on the central authority to provide your requirements. You must search for these requirements in whatever city or village you may be in. There are many various hidden resources here and there. We must search for them and utilize them for our service.

I and you, I believe, feel optimistic. We must couple this optimism with continuous action to realize greater success in the next stage of the local administration. The resources of our country are boundless but most of them are latent. You must search for them and set them to work so that we may benefit from them everywhere and in every field. There are certain matters connected with the local administration which are under study, such as the financial law of the administrative units and the new executive bill of the local administration and other matters. For my part, I very much encourage the expansion of the powers of the local administration. [applause]

We must do everything to push forward this experiment. We must issue the orders and laws necessary to push forward this experiment and make it, as I said a short while ago, more effective, positive and vital in our daily life. On this occasion, I wish to point that we at the center must also do a lot at the level of the central government. I have previously mentioned this from this very place. Undoubtedly we are late in doing much of what must be done. Some external matters delayed us. I do not want to say, I will not accept and I do not want to persuade anybody that there is any justification for any failure. We must be up to a standard of vitality, ability and efficiency enabling us to effectively respond to our external and domestic concerns at the same time. [applause]

Brothers, we meet today at a time when the incidents taking place in Lebanon occupy a great deal of our interest as well as the interest of the area and the world, because the incidents taking place in Lebanon—as much as Lebanon means, in its positive and negative aspects—concern us and concern our Arab nation. In this period, as we can see, things are getting mixed up, roles are becoming intertwined and goals are almost lost. This is what was planned by those who planned the incidents in Lebanon. They planned for things to get mixed up, for roles to become intertwined, and for goals to become lost. Nevertheless, despite all this, your role, the role of the Syrian people and the role of valiant Syria, can be understood by anyone as the decisive and basic role, because it is the national role which is based on the historic heritage of the Arab nation and on all the cultural values of the noble Arab nation. [applause]

Brothers, perhaps I should have spoken about this question some time ago. I was late in speaking because I depended first on the conscientiousness of the Syrian Arab citizen and on his vast and enormous understanding of these incidents, their motives, and objectives. Second, I was depending on the confidence that you have given me. Third, I was depending on my feeling that I express the conscience of all of you in all the decisions I make regarding these incidents. [applause]

Brother citizens, like you, I hear the radios and the rumors reiterated here and there. Believe me, had I felt for one moment that the confidence of this people in me has been shaken, I would not have stayed in power for one minute. [applause]

Brothers, many of those dealing with us outside this country, both in the Arab and international spheres, do not yet know our true nature despite the many experiences we have been through, which should have been sufficient to reveal the nature of the people and the nature and the ethics of government in this country. Those who cry out from afar should know that I have no lust for power. I am only a member of this people. [applause] Nothing will prevent me from sensing the feelings of this people and taking the decision, which, I think, represents the feelings and desires of the citizens in this country.

The conspirators wanted to confuse us, but we confused them. They used various crooked means, but they failed. They failed to achieve a single objective. They tried to pull strings, but we cut them, and we will cut all the strings. The values and ideals we teach everywhere in the field and the factory throughout the years, the values we uphold, express, and speak about on every occasion, are not just for local consumption—they are values and ideals which express our true feelings, selves, and sanctities. This is what the conspirators outside the border cannot understand, because they do not understand our true nature and values; and because they are conspirators, they failed and they will fail in their plotting.

When we speak about Lebanon's incidents, we must go back a little. I will try to include in my talk only a sufficient amount of detail to give a clear picture. When the events in Lebanon began many months ago, we had an explanation of these events. We shared this explanation with many Arab forces which claim nationalism and progressivism. We also shared this explanation with many parties which call themselves the nationalist parties in Lebanon and with the groups of the Palestinian resistance. We used to say that events in Lebanon are the result of an imperialist plan which aims, first, at covering up for the Sinai agreement; second, at embroiling and striking at the resistance and liquidating its camps and confusing Syria; and third, at partitioning Lebanon. This is what we used to say, and this is what they used to say.

In my opinion, if we ask them today, perhaps they will repeat the same words. At this point a person may ask, Why confuse Syria? How is Syria connected with events taking place in Lebanon? Brother compatriots, I want you to pay heed to this matter, because there are those who are raising it from the outside in order to infiltrate our ranks in the interior. They ask what we have to do with events in Lebanon. Why is Syria involved in Lebanon's events? First, one of the objectives of the plot is to strike at an issue which is the issue of every citizen in this country. If the conspiracy has the aims I spoke about, including striking at the Palestinian resistance and partitioning Lebanon, how can Syria stand by as a spectator to a plot aimed at achieving these objectives? We are concerned about this conspiracy. We must prepare ourselves as much as we can to repulse the conspiracy and the conspirators. The matter concerns us, and there is no escape from the confrontation.

Second, through history, Syria and Lebanon have been one country and one people. The people in Syria and Lebanon have been one through history. Genuine joint interests ensued. This matter must be known by everybody—genuine joint interests. A genuine joint security also ensued. Close kinship between the people in the two countries also ensued. Many thousands of families in Syria have relatives in Lebanon. Many thousands of families in Lebanon have relatives in Syria.

Today we see before us, as a result of this joint history and geography and these events, that prior to the events there were approximately a half million Syrians in Lebanon in various jobs: merchants, doctors, workers, lawyers, and so forth. As a result of the events, they returned to Syria. At present, there are at least a half million Lebanese refugees in Syria. Half a million of our people in Lebanon have come to Syria. A total of approximately 150,000 Palestinians of the brother Palestinians residing in Lebanon have entered Syria. As a result of the events, approximately one million people have entered Syria.

I think we can imagine the magnitude of the problem caused by the entry of one million persons into a country whose population is less than nine million. It helps for us to remember at this point that India was unable to bear the pressure of ten million refugees—ten million refugees from Bangladesh. We all recollect that the ten million refugees were the cause of the Indian-Pakistani war. India is a big state. Its population exceeds 500 million. It was unable to bear the burden of ten million refugees. It was unable to bear entry of one-fiftieth or one-sixtieth of the population of India. How about us, where the rate is one-ninth of the population? Let us imagine the magnitude of the problem. Even if it were one-eighteenth, one-twentieth, or one-thirtieth, the problem would still be a big problem.

Brothers, none of you should think that I am saying these words—or that these words might be said by any citizen in Syria—as grumbling against these brothers who have come to Syria. The country and land is theirs. This country belongs to all the Arabs. I have said this to describe a problem which has resulted from the events in Lebanon, to describe the magnitude of this problem, and to highlight a living problem—which is an answer to those who are saying from outside the borders: and why Syria?

The partitioning of Lebanon is an old Zionist aim, as you know. Perhaps many of you have read the letters exchanged between the Zionist leaders, or some of them, in the fifties on this subject, stressing the importance of partitioning Lebanon.

The partitioning of Lebanon, brothers, is not sought by Israel because of Lebanon's military significance. Whether Lebanon is united or fragmented, it does not constitute a military problem for Israel at present and is not expected to constitute a military problem in the foreseeable future, as far as Israel is concerned. Israel is not seeking to partition Lebanon because it constitutes a military burden. Israel wants the partitioning of Lebanon for a political, ideological reason. It is only natural that Israel wishes the establishment of sectarian statelets in this area so that Israel can remain the stronger state. We learned this and said it in the past, and we will continue to say it.

Israel seeks to partition Lebanon in order to defeat the slogan of the *democratic secular state*—the slogan which we raise. Perhaps not all of us believe in this slogan, but it is the slogan which is raised and can be discussed in this or that part of the world. Naturally, it is a slogan which is greatly different from a slogan previously raised by some of us—and perhaps most of us—that we would throw the Jews into the sea. At that time we were rendering great service to Israel. This is not a secret. Some people might say that the Israelis are listening to what I say. But this is not a secret, and we can speak freely about it.

To say that we are demanding a democratic state in which Moslems, Christians, and Jews can live, whether they are Arabs or not, is a question which can be reasoned about. But when Lebanon is partitioned, the Israelis will say we do not believe these Arabs: if they could not coexist together, if the Moslem Arab could not coexist with the Christian Arab, how then can they coexist with the Jews and the non-Arab Jews who came from all parts of the world, from the West and the East. This slogan will then fall. Israel wants partition to acquit itself of the charge of racism. The United Nations adopted a resolution saying that Zionism is a racist movement, and this is a great victory for the Palestine issue and the Arab struggle. Why is Zionism a racist movement? Because it gathers people from everywhere, with religion the only link among them, to make a people out of them and to establish a state for these people. When Lebanon is partitioned between Christians and Moslems, Israel will say, Where is racism? Israel is based on religion, and in Lebanon there would be states or statelets based on religion. Either we are racists or not racists.

The partitioning of Lebanon would acquit Israel of the charge of racism. The partitioning of Lebanon would constitute a stab at the idea of Arab unity and would look as if we are living proof that Arab nationalism is not the appropriate tie linking all of us in a manner that enables us to live under the banner of Arab nationalism. [applause] When the Arabs in Lebanon fail to live together in one state, despite the long years they have lived together, it would be the practical and material proof they want to prove that the idea of Arab nationalism is invalid. Furthermore, I want to say that the partitioning of Lebanon is a big blow to Islam, the religion of the sweeping majority of the Arab nation, because they want to present Islam as a rigid religion, which prevents its followers from living with others, even if they are the sons of the same people.

This is a plot against Islam and the Moslems. I want to assert this point and not to be hesitant with anyone about it. I have said it in many of my conversations with those concerned, in Lebanon and outside Lebanon. It is a plot against Islam and Arabism and serves the interest of the enemy—Zionism and Israel. [applause]

Naturally, brothers, Arabism and Islam are stronger than these plotters. They will be unable, under the guise of Arabism and Islam, to strike at Arabism and Islam, because we are lying in wait for them. I can say here—although I would be diverging from the subject to some extent—that the plot in Lebanon, as far as this question in particular is concerned, is a plot against Islam and Christianity. The struggle in its essence, not form, is not between Christianity and Islam but between Christianity and Islam on the one hand and their joint enemies on the other. [applause]

This was our interpretation of the incidents in Lebanon, in which we participated with others. We said that this plot cannot achieve its objectives except through fighting. Therefore, in order to foil the plot, we had to stop the fighting. It is a clear mathematical formula. The way the plot can achieve its objective is through fighting, and in order to prevent the plot from achieving its objectives, we had to stop the fighting. We proceeded to work for this. We made political and military efforts. We gave weapons, brothers, in order to stop the fighting. We gave ammunition, brothers, in order to stop the fighting. At one time, the balance of forces was not equal, and fighting could not have stopped. This is why we were compelled to give weapons and ammunition. We gave weapons to those who are attacking us and denying our efforts and sacrifices—those who denied and are denying the past and present efforts and sacrifices of this people, although these efforts and stands are clear like the sun and are known, remembered, and realized by every child not only in Syria but also in most countries of the Arab homeland. We gave weapons and ammunition to them. At one time, we took the arms from our soldiers and our formations and gave these arms to them.

We have offered everything we could. This political decision of ours, our political decision to seek to stop the fighting, had an Arab and international dimension. We tried to narrow the problem in Lebanon as much as we could because we believed, and they believed as well, that widening this problem on the Arab and international levels is in the interests of the conspiracy and not vice-versa. You are now seeing what they are doing.

Despite this, despite our political and military efforts as far as offering arms and ammunition in large quantities and in various types, one day the front of the nationalist parties and the front of the Palestinian resistance collapsed. One day the front of the parties in Lebanon and the front of the Palestinian resistance in Lebanon collapsed. They were unable to stand on their own feet. They sent us cries for help, so we tried and exerted greater efforts.

One day—in the middle of January, if I remember correctly—the foreign minister contacted me and said that they had contacted him by phone from the 'Aramun summit. I do not know Beirut well, but as far as I know, 'Aramun is a place which includes the house of the Mufti, where meetings were held by the Mufti, the Imam, prime ministers, other Islamic personalities, and certain party leaders, including Kamal Junblatt. They contacted the foreign minister and pleaded with him to ask me to contact President Suleiman Faranjiyya so that he would stop the fighting, because the situation was very bad. I told the foreign minister that I was not going to make contact and they must do so. Less than fifteen minutes later, he contacted me for the second time and said that they had contacted him again to say that their situation was very bad and certain quarters had fallen. The Phalangist gunmen were storming the houses, and everything was falling before them. I told him I would not make contact and they must do so. When I said this, brothers, it was not out of hesitation or lack of desire to exert efforts. But I wondered at such requests, because I knew—and naturally we are the ones to know—that the resistance and the nationalist parties—and not only the Phalangists and the national liberals—had arms that did not belong to the Lebanese Army. The resistance and the parties had a lot more arms and ammunition than the Phalangists, the national liberals, and the Lebanese Army put together. The Lebanese Army was not in the battle; it was absolutely not a party in the battle. After a short while, he repeated the contact for the third time and said, Matters are very bad, and they plead that you accept. Indeed, reports reached us on the fall of al-Maslakh, al-Karantina, and other places. They said then, If you do not make quick contact, the Phalangists will outflank western Beirut. The road is open before them. The western sector is now under the control of the organizations, the parties, and armed men.

At this point I said, "Poor western sector." I realized that I had to make contact. I contacted President Faranjiyya and told him, Brother President, you face a dangerous massacre, which will have repercussions everywhere. I wish you would act quickly to stop it and avoid its consequences. Children, women, the unarmed, everybody is being attacked. This matter will have grave results. Please, look into the matter and do your best. We are waiting for the results of your efforts. There was a discussion on the phone between me and President Faranjiyya. We finally agreed on a cease-fire for a specific hour that night. I think it was at 2000 or 2100 hours.

After this, reports came to say that fighting was escalating and that matters were going from bad to worse. We held a meeting here in Damascus. I met with certain brothers in the command and began to think of what we could do to save the situation. We exerted political efforts. We gave arms and ammunition. All this was happening, and yet it was not enough to save the situation.

Hence, we had no choice but to intervene directly. Of course, we discussed the issue from various angles. We also discussed the dangers of intervention and the eventualities of war between us and Israel. We had two alternatives then: either we do not intervene and the resistance in Lebanon collapses and is liquidated in light of this military situation and in light of the cries for help; or we do intervene and save the resistance.

We discussed the possibility of a war. It was possible but not inevitable, for reasons I do not want to mention in detail at this point. However, the conspiracy in Lebanon has aims. Had Israel obstructed us and war occurred, this war would have been the opposite of what the conspiracy aims at achieving. Despite this, war was a likely possibility, and the lack of war was also a likely possibility.

We thus said we must go in to save the resistance. We decided to go in under the name of the PLA. The PLA began to go into Lebanon, and nobody knew of this. Those who are speaking now in the name of Palestine, who live under illusions and deny every effort we exerted for their sake, did not know of the decision to send the PLA. They did not know of the army until it was inside Lebanese territory. We did not consult them nor did we consult the nationalist parties. As a matter of fact, none of them was prepared to argue with us regarding any measure. They were asking for any measure we could take to save them.

Following the 'Aramun contact and on the same day the leaders of the nationalist parties came to Syria, they spent a long time in the Foreign Ministry building. They were here in the Syrian Foreign Ministry building looking for a solution to the problem and a dignified exit from what they were in, while we were moving the army into Lebanon to defend them and the Palestinian resistance.

On the morning of the next day, I received them in my house. Kamal Junblatt was with them. Kamal Junblatt was in 'Aramun when they contacted the foreign minister by telephone. He came to Syria the next morning. I received him and the leaders of the parties. I remember, and those of them who are now listening to me will remember, how their morale was then. At any rate, their morale was not good. I made them understand and told them, We are with you and with the Lebanese people. We will oppose the massacres. We will oppose liquidations because this is in the interests of all the parties in Lebanon.

We sent in the PLA and other forces, and matters were supposed to return to normal.

While I was talking to them, President Suleiman Faranjiyya contacted me. I spoke to him over the telephone. The conversation dealt with several issues, but there is no reason to repeat the whole conversation, although I can even recall the whole conversation. Here I must apologize to Brother President Suleiman Faranjiyya for mentioning these matters. I hope that he will excuse me, because the matter is important and is related to placing the facts before the people.

I say before you that he was an honest man in his dealings and upheld his word to us. He told me that Syrian forces were entering Lebanon. I reminded him of the conversation that had taken place the day before and told him that the matter was serious and I hope, brother president, that all the Arabs would understand us. I told him that our stand toward the Palestinians was consistent and that as far as the Palestinians were concerned, there was a red line that we would absolutely not allow anyone to go beyond. This was what I said to President Suleiman Faranjiyya, while knowing that such talk between two heads of state is more than is necessary and more than what is acceptable. However, it is a fateful issue. Again, I apologize to Brother President Suleiman Faranjiyya, because the matter is related to placing the facts before the people. [applause] We ended this telephone conversation by agreeing that a committee should go to Lebanon to work for a cease-fire. This was done. You will recall that a Syrian delegation went to Lebanon and held discussions and numerous meetings. What is important is that a short while after the delegation went to Lebanon, firing ceased, as is known, and we began to work quickly to create a positive atmosphere and constructive climate which would help everyone embark on fruitful, joint work. Firing ceased, and we said that we had to consolidate the cease-fire.

Let us ask what the resistance wants. We sent for the resistance leaders to come to the Foreign Ministry in Damascus—foremost of whom was Yasir 'Arafat. . . . We told them to write down what they wanted from Lebanon. They wrote down what they wanted. We took what they wrote down to the authorities in Lebanon. We discussed the matter, and the Lebanese authorities agreed to everything that they had written down without omitting one single letter from it. I say and admit that not everything that was written down and demanded was necessary to protect the resistance or to enable it to exercise its role of struggle against the occupying enemy. Nevertheless, the Lebanese authorities approved everything that had been written down without omitting one single letter. The agreement is in front of me now. I would like to read the agreement to you. These are words written down by the resistance leaders themselves:

"One, the PLO is the sole representative of the Palestinian people in Lebanon, and no other side can be recognized." What was intended by this was to consolidate the position of the PLO in such a way that no one could challenge it and the state could not recognize any side but the PLO. "Two, the PLO is responsible for the affairs of the Palestinians inside the camps. Three, the PLO has the right to take measures inside the camps to safeguard its security against any foreign, external aggression. Four, the PLO has the right to exercise all the rights given to it according to the Cairo agreement and its appendixes. Five, the Palestinian presence in Lebanon shall not be harmed or harassed. Six, the security or presence of the Palestinian resistance in Lebanon shall not be harmed or harassed."

What does the resistance want after all this, and what does the PLO want? This is the section related to Lebanese-Palestinian relations. Is all this necessary for the resistance to carry out its activities against Israel? I say no. Nevertheless, the Lebanese authorities agreed to everything that I read out. Nonetheless, they seek now— as we hear over the radios, to confuse the Arab public and perhaps the world—to defend and protect the Palestinian resistance, while the truth is that there are forces inside Lebanon and in the international scene which are seeking to exploit the Palestinian resistance for the sake of their tactical or strategic objectives. The Palestinian resistance is currently fighting for the accomplishment of the objectives of others and against the interest and goals of the Palestinian Arab people. [applause]

After this agreement, we said that there were several national questions [to be discussed]. Motivated by a spirit of fraternity and because we realized that several things could be averted by the Lebanese authorities in that phase—because of all this, we said we had to make a fraternal effort in the hope of achieving some useful results. Furthermore, there were numerous discussions and meetings, and agreement was reached on a number of measures, which were called national reforms, which were documented and written down on a paper.

The paper was later called the constitutional document. This document included at least ninety-five percent of what was demanded by the nationalist parties. I say here that we in Syria added several points which had not been demanded by these parties. The provision for the Arabism of Lebanon was not demanded by the nationalist parties. However, Lebanon's Arab affiliation was stated in the constitutional document. [applause] The Lebanese authorities agreed to that. Therefore, agreement was reached to regulate Lebanese-Palestinian relations, and agreement was reached on the constitutional document, which included the national reforms.

As for us in Syria and through our contacts with these parties, we regarded the constitutional document as a great national victory and a victory for every Lebanese without any exception. There are thousands in Lebanon who do not have Lebanese nationality. Most Arab leaders have known this fact about Lebanon for many years. Many interceded, fought, and struggled to resolve this problem, but it was not resolved. This problem was resolved in the constitutional document, and agreement was reached to give Lebanese nationality to everyone. Job sectarianism, which all Lebanese citizens were suffering from and only one class of leaders was benefiting from—it was agreed to abolish job sectarianism. It became evident to me later that this move constituted a problem and a reason for bringing the situation to a head later on, because the end of job sectarianism has canceled privileges.

This cancellation was the reason for the flare-up of the situation later—because the cancellation of the sectarian structure of government posts canceled the privileges of some people. These people once demanded the cancellation of the sectarian structure of government posts, but when the cancellation was made, or when an agreement was reached on the cancellation, they were shocked to have lost their privileges.

You realize that I have tried and I will continue to try not to mention names except when necessary. There were provisions on equality for all, the establishment of a constitutional court, economic and social reforms, the Arabism of Lebanon, giving citizenship, canceling religious sectarianism, and many other things which, as we know, were part of the problems in the past. But there are people who want to keep these problems, because they thrived on them. Some of the armed people in Lebanon today are against security. If security is achieved, they will be out of work. This is a problem.

When agreement was reached on these matters, the president of Lebanon came to Damascus. Everything was agreed on, finally, and he returned to Beirut. All these matters were discussed at a cabinet meeting. The constitutional document was approved and was broadcast by the president over Beirut radio and television. As we heard, rifle shots were fired everywhere to rejoice in the announcement of the declaration.

A cease-fire really took effect. I remember the situation continued to be quiet for fifty days. Then suddenly a military coup d'etat took place on 11 March. I do not want to question the men who carried out the coup. They might have been good people. I do not know any of them. They might have had Lebanon's interests in mind and nothing else. But if this was the aim, they failed to achieve it. Without discussing the coup, we can say without hesitation that it did not consolidate the cease-fire, the progress of national reforms, or the interest of the Palestinian resistance in securing the continuity of the cease-fire, so that the Palestinian resistance could devote its efforts to engaging the Israeli enemy. The coup came as a challenge, inviting a return of fighting in Lebanon. The coup came to raise a problem which had not been raised. It raised the problem of the resignation of the president of the republic, particularly as the term of the president would end in some five months, as I recall. Yasir ʿArafat came to me a few days after the coup—three or four days after the coup. He appealed to me to make an effort to persuade the president of the republic to resign. I do not conceal the fact that I found this request strange. I said then that I would not make any effort and that I believed that what had been raised by the coup was unrelated to the Lebanese national interest and that the resignation or nonresignation of the president of the republic was not a major problem for the Lebanese masses. Yasir 'Arafat left without any promises from me to make any efforts.

On the morning of the next day, we found out that our duty dictated that we not sit back or despair as long as the matter was related to brothers of ours, who were part of our people, and that we had to make efforts to keep things under control, prevent the resumption of combat operations, and foil any attempt aimed at resuming combat operations.

We decided to contact the sides concerned. Syrian delegations went to Lebanon and Lebanese delegations came to Syria. I discussed the matter in all its aspects. Again I say that President Suleiman Faranjiyya was noble and honorable. We reached an agreement, which I spoke about in this place previously, in light of these contacts and in light of preserving the legitimacy, which everyone upheld, including the coupists—as was mentioned in their communique number one—and naturally the parties that call themselves the nationalist parties.

In light of all this, the following was agreed on: One, to amend the constitution or an article of the constitution allowing the election of a new president of the republic six months prior to the expiration of the term of the old president; two, to elect the new president; and three, to move on then to the resignation of the current president. When we reached this agreement, the situation came to a head violently. The coup came and raised the question of the resignation of the president, and it was adopted by several nationalist parties. They asked us to make efforts, and we did make efforts. When we reached agreement on what was requested by everyone in this respect, the situation came to a head. Fighting erupted, and they were saying that the president of the republic must resign.

At the time Yasir 'Arafat asked that we receive Kamal Junblatt. We told Yasir 'Arafat, "Why should we receive Kamal Junblatt while he is insisting on continuing the fighting and while we in Syria feel the same as you do—and still do, as you say—that fighting is the means for achieving the objectives of the plot?" Why should we receive Kamal Junblatt while he was insisting on continuing the fighting, and what was the use of such a meeting? Yasir 'Arafat said, "No, these are statements intended for local consumption, the Lebanese way. Do not pay attention to them. Everything is all right."

We received Kamal Junblatt. I had a lengthy meeting with him, which lasted for many hours. We reviewed Lebanon's incidents from the beginning. We analyzed Lebanon's incidents—the analysis which I am giving now. I told Junblatt that "we agreed with you on the analysis of Lebanon's incidents. We all worked for the cessation of fighting, and we helped you politically and militarily, and by militarily I mean supplying you with arms and ammunition. Nevertheless, you could not hold out, and we entered Lebanon, taking the risk of a war with Israel. We achieved for the resistance all the guarantees it wanted—guarantees providing for the freedom of action of the resistance. Then we discussed the national reforms, and the constitutional document was agreed upon, and the document included ninety to ninety-five percent of your demands. Then the coup came to raise the question of the resignation of the president of the republic, although this question had not been under discussion and we did not support it. You supported the coup and its objectives regarding the resignation of the president of the republic. We discussed the matter, and we made contacts and efforts and reached an agreement on this question. But when we reached this agreement, you brought the situation to a head. Up to now, we are satisfied with what we have done. We were satisfied because we were walking in the light and knew where we were heading. We thought that we were proceeding together with you on one line and for one objective. However, now after what has happened, we want you to tell us what you really want. The rights of and guarantees for the resistance are no longer a problem. The national reforms, inasmuch as Lebanon's circumstances permit, are no longer a problem. The question of the presidency—the resignation of the president—is no longer a problem. What else do you want?"

We discussed the constitutional document. I believe that there were no major objections [by Junblatt]. I can cite some examples to you. Junblatt said that we agreed on six points; the constitutional document contains seventeen points. I told him in brief that what was important was not the number of points or whether they were six or seventeen. What was important was the contents of those points which were not in harmony with your demands and of your demands which were not included in these points. This was what was important, not the number of the points. He said a committee had been formed which studied the document and concluded that it was ambiguous. I told him that the document was an outline for future action and that every point in the document needed decisions, decrees, and laws. At this point, meanings would become very clear, and you could include all the details you wanted. It is impossible to do this now, and there is no justification for going into more details or specifics now.

He spoke about secularism. I told him that the Phalangist Party is enthusiastic about secularization. When the leadership of the Phalangist Party, headed by Sheikh Pierre al-Jumayyil, visited us, I asked him in person about this matter. He told me, "I do not accept a substitute to secularization. I insist on and cling to a secular state in Lebanon." I raised this matter with the Moslems, with Musa al-Sadr, with certain prime ministers, and with certain speakers of the house. They rejected it because the matter deals with the essence of Islam.

This is something which you in our country, brothers, must know. It is misleading. The Moslems in Lebanon are the ones who do not want secularization and not vice-versa, because the matter deals with the essence of Islam. The Phalangists cling to secularization, and Kamal Junblatt clings to secularization. I told him, "The Moslem ulema are the ones who do not agree to secularization." He replied, "Do not pay attention to them; they do not represent anything." I told him the matter is not one of representation. (At this point I would like to repeat and say that I would not have said what I am saying had not the matter dealt with the clarification of certain facts.) He said they do not represent anything. I told him, "The matter is not one of representation but an issue which touches on Islam—when a matter deals with Islam, it must not be taken lightly." This is what I said at the meeting: "the matter is not one of representation—whether they represent or do not represent—but one dealing with Islam." [applause]

He said, "Let us discipline them. We must have decisive military action. They have been governing us for 140 years, and we want to get rid of them." At this point, I realized that all the masks had fallen. Therefore, the matter was not as we used to say it was and not as we were told. The matter was not between the right and left or between a progressive and a reactionary. It was not between a Moslem and a Christian. The matter was one of vengeance, a matter of revenge, which dates back 140 years. Of course, if I am going to proceed from the fact that I am a Moslem, I must be against this trend, because Islam is love and justice and not hatred and animosity. Islam is for justice for all and against injustice to anyone. Islam has prohibited vengeance and revenge. If I am a true Moslem—and I am a Moslem, with God's help—I have to be against this trend. [applause] If I were to proceed from the fact that I am a revolutionary, the matter is the same. A revolution is justice for all. A revolution is against all kinds of injustice. [applause] A revolution is correction and reform. A revolutionary does not remove injustice from one to place it on another. He removes injustice from himself and from others. This is a revolutionary. This is a Moslem. The true Moslem is the true revolutionary. Islam is the greatest revolution in the history of our Arab nation and of humanity. [applause]

Brothers, Kamal Junblatt emerged from this meeting and left me with the impression that he insisted on fighting. I told him, "Do not count on any help. We cannot march with you on a path which we both agree upon in advance is the path of the conspiracy." On the next day, rather on the same day, I invited Yasir 'Arafat. I received him the next day. He was accompanied by some brothers. I talked with them at length. I repeated to them a lot of what I said during my meeting with Brother Kamal Junblatt. I repeated to them what I just said. I discussed with them the dangers of the decisive military action which he [presumably Junblatt] called for.

At this point, I would like to say something about decisive military action. Decisive military action in a country like Lebanon, decisive military action between two parties in one homeland, is impossible. Decisive military action regarding any problem means the final liquidation of this problem; it means finding a drastic solution to this problem. Decisive military action in this sense in a country like Lebanon is impossible, because the issue does not depend solely upon the factor of might but also upon the availability of other elements, which are not present in Lebanon. I am not philosophizing on the subject. In brief, I want to say: this is what decisive military action means; and decisive military action in Lebanon is impossible, because the factor of might is not the only condition which must be available. There are other factors and conditions which must be available but are not at present.

However, if decisive military action was intended to create a state of repression in the Lebanese arena, then this matter, if achieved, would have extremely grave repercussions. If we strike at the conspiracy from one end, decisive military action, if achieved, would bring about the objectives of the conspiracy from the other end. Decisive military action in this sense, if achieved, would first result in a new problem in Lebanon and in this area. A problem would arise, and we now do not know what it might be called—the problem of a people, the problem of a religion, the problem of Lebanon, the problem of part of Lebanon. It is difficult to know now what this problem might come to be called if it ever arose. However, we can unreservedly and without hesitation assert now that if we had decisive military action, a big and grave problem would arise which would (?preoccupy) us, the area, and the world. This problem would have a special characteristic. It would be the problem of those who are oppressed. The world would sympathize with the problem, because the world always sympathizes with the oppressed. This is the first result that would ensue from decisive military action as they want it—if they can achieve it.

The second result is that the world would seek to find a solution to this problem. As you can see, the world tries its best to find solutions to all problems, particularly big problems, the problems of peoples, the problems of the oppressed. The world, the entire world, struggles to find solutions to the problems of the oppressed.

The world will seek to find a solution to this problem. What could this solution be? We can all guess that a solution would not take place without the partitioning of Lebanon. But it will be a partition of violence and oppression.

This partition would result in ever greater additional dangers than the ones which would result if partition took place without violence. A state for those who are oppressed would be established—a state filled with rancor, a state whose sons would inherit rancor as a result of the oppression from which they suffered. They would disavow all the Arab values and all the values of Islam, since Islam, as I have said, is the religion of the majority in the Arab homeland.

I say frankly and clearly, a state more dangerous and more hostile than Israel would be established—not because the people who would live in this state would be Israelis or aliens. No, they are an essential part of our people. It is not because of this that they and their state would be more dangerous and hostile than Israel. They would be so as a result of the series of oppressions they had suffered. As a result of this oppression, this state and those in it would be more dangerous and hostile than Israel.

The third result: A decisive military action in this way would open doors to every foreign intervention, particularly Israel's intervention. Let us all visualize the magnitude of the tragedy which might ensue if Israel were to intervene and save some Arabs from other Arabs.

The fourth thing: Numerous negative repercussions (which would be caused by such decisive action on the Palestinian issue), both from the Palestinians and from world public opinion and its support for the Palestinian cause and the Arab struggle.

The fifth thing: We can all imagine the many negative repercussions which would take place in the Arab homeland—repercussions on the Arab conscience would ensue from such a solution. We can also visualize an image, consequent on a solution, of the relations that would be formed in this area—an ugly picture detrimental to Arab interests and objectives.

What was important in this meeting was that I asked Brother Yasir 'Arafat to appreciate the gravity of these circumstances and the seriousness of continuing the fighting, particularly the gravity of the participation of Palestinian fighters in this fighting. I told him then and I say now, I cannot imagine what the connection is between the fighting of Palestinians in the highest mountains of Lebanon and the liberation of Palestine. I cannot imagine any such a relationship. The Palestinian fighting in Jabal Lubnan is definitely not fighting for Palestine. He wants to liberate Jounieh and Tripoli and does not want to liberate Palestine, even if he so claims. This is what they used to say in 1970. Brothers, remember what was being said in

Jordan in 1970. They raised slogans, such as *all power for the resistance, all power for the revolution*, and *we will liberate Palestine through Amman*. In essence, the matter is being repeated in Lebanon.

At that meeting, Yasir 'Arafat promised to withdraw from the fighting. He went directly to Lebanon to inform the others of this. At this point, I do not want to discuss details, but I must say that the order was not completely implemented. At any rate, the fighting stopped after a few days, but, if you remember, the fighting stopped after the arrival of Dean Brown in Beirut. Let us go back in memory: The fighting stopped after Dean Brown's arrival in Beirut. Certainly, as an Arab, I thank any person in the world who can stop the firing in Lebanon. What is important is for the tragedy and the conspiracy to end. However, it is surprising that the firing was suspended only after Dean Brown's arrival. By these words I would like to say that if the United States wants to stop the firing and seeks to end it, we welcome this. If any foreign or Arab state is seeking to stop the firing and can end it, we welcome this. [applause]

At any rate, cries arose after this. Cries arose saying that Syria has stopped sending aid. We all remember these cries. Syria has stopped sending aid! As if Syria has to extend aid to whoever wishes it, to offer arms, ammunition, and even soldiers to whoever asks for them, irrespective of its national interests and irrespective of our national objectives and aspirations as well as our opinion about national interests. Syria is against the suspension of firing [as heard], yet they expect us to offer them arms so that they will continue the firing. Syria believes that the path being followed is the one of conspiracy; yet they want, expect from Syria, and assume that Syria must offer them, arms to continue on this path, which is detrimental to them, to us, and to our national interests.

It is obvious that this is not possible. It is obvious that Syria does not move without conviction. It is obvious that nobody can drag Syria into a position it does not want. This must be clear everywhere. We will not move without conviction. We will not compromise our principles and objectives. We will not adopt any decisions without giving due consideration to our national and Pan-Arab interests. [applause] Syria is the land of steadfastness. Whoever supports steadfastness must support Syria. Syria is the land of liberation. Whoever supports liberation must support Syria. Syria is the land of nationalism and progress. Whoever supports nationalism and progress must support Syria. Syria is the land of Palestinian struggle. Whoever supports the Palestinian struggle must support Syria. [applause] Any talk about war, any talk about the liberation of Palestine without Syria, is ignorance and misleads the masses.

During this period, our contacts with the resistance continued, proceeding from the slogan of *no despair and no surrender* in combatting the enemies of the nation and the conspiracies aimed against the issues and aspirations of the nation. Our contacts with the resistance continued; about the middle of the fourth month, we held a meeting with the resistance leadership. The meeting continued all night, as I remember. In the morning of the following day, we announced the points that were agreed on. This is the statement we announced on 16 April 1976. The time noted on the statement was 0400.

Those who attended the meeting were PLO Executive Committee Chairman Yasir 'Arafat, Zuheir Muhsin [head of the PLO military department], Faruq Qaddumi [head of the PLO political department], Nayif Hawatimah [leader of the Democratic Popular Front for the Liberation of Palestine], Salah Khalaf [member of the al-Fatah Central Committee], and Abu Salih. 'Abd al-Halim Khaddam [Syrian foreign minister], Najo Jamil [Syrian deputy defense minister and air force commander], and Hikmat ash-Shihabi [Syrian army chief of staff] also attended. The situation in the area in general and the situation in Lebanon in particular were reviewed. The aspects of the crisis in Lebanon and the perils of its continuation were assessed and analyzed. The viewpoints were in agreement on the various matters; the viewpoints were in agreement on the various matters—that is to say, we were agreed on what I have just said. The two sides asserted their concern for the fraternal Lebanese people, their security, the safety of their territory, and their stability. On this occasion, the two sides appealed to the fraternal people to end the fighting and bloodshed. The two sides agreed on the following:

1. To halt the fighting and adopt a unified stand against any side which resumes combat operations. (Therefore, we agreed to take effective measures against any side that resumes fighting opera-

tions. Of course, the same people who agreed with us and made such statements were the ones who resumed the fighting operations.)

2. To re-form the tripartite Syrian-Palestinian-Lebanese Higher Military Committee, so as to achieve a halt to the fighting, and to implement and supervise it until a new president is elected. The new president will decide on the security measures as he deems fit in accordance with his constitutional powers.

3. To resist partition in all its forms and any action or measure that harms the unity of Lebanon's territory and people.

4. To reject the American plans and solutions in Lebanon.

5. To adhere to the continuation of the Syrian initiative.

6. To reject internationalization or the entry of any international forces into Lebanon.

7. To reject the Arabization of the crisis in Lebanon.

This agreement did not see the light as far as its implementation is concerned. What happened was that on 6 June—after this agreement—the al-Fatah organization, some other Palestinian groups, and some of the parties which call themselves nationalist parties in Lebanon, launched a planned all-out attack on the offices of the Union of the People's Working Forces, the offices of al-Sa'iqa, the offices of the Ba'th party, the positions and offices of the Palestine Liberation Army, and the offices of the other groups of the National Front in Lebanon—this without any preliminaries. At that time I had in my office Libyan Prime Minister Maj 'Abd as-Salam Jallud— he is still in Damascus, as you know. With him was Algerian Foreign Minister Abdelkrim Benmahmoud. We received a report that al-Fatah and the aforementioned groups were launching a large-scale attack in all parts of Beirut.

We had agreed to take measures against any side which started fighting operations. It was they who started the fighting operations but against Palestinians, national Lebanese groups, and the Palestine Liberation Army. We pushed some of our forces in the direction of Beirut in order to restore things to normal. We then halted the advance of these forces before reaching Beirut, as a result of the urging of our brother Algerians and Libyans. The resistance leaders who staged the operation cried and became angry when they learned that we were advancing toward Beirut. They contacted the brothers, the Libyan prime minister and the Algerian minister, who asked us to halt the advancing forces, saying that things would return to what they were before and that we should view what had happened as a temporary matter. We welcomed this idea; we welcomed this idea. The same night, they [resistance leaders] informed us that they had released the detainees and left the offices they had occupied, that they would allow Brother Kamal Shatila, secretary general of the Union of the People's Working Forces, to appear on television and deny the statement they had issued in his name, and they said that what had happened was a temporary matter. We were glad about that. We had not wished to reach Beirut. We wanted the solution to that problem and any problem, and we still have the same wish—the wish that every problem may be solved without our being compelled to reach Beirut.

However, what happened was, regrettably, the reverse. And it so happened that what they had said was untrue. They had occupied the offices, arrested whoever they did arrest, and killed whoever they did kill from all the aforementioned groups. They had also attacked the Syrian soldiers who had earlier gone there to help them. They mercilessly attacked those soldiers and tried to do all they could to harm them. They tried to do all they could to harm the Syrian soldiers who had entered to help them and to contribute to thwarting all the crises to which they were being subjected in more than one place. Despite this, we continued to halt the [Syrian] forces. We continued to halt the forces and gave orders to the soldiers that they should only defend themselves and that, in their own defense, their action should be most limited. Brothers, they were infantry soldiers who have no artillery, tanks, or any means of support that are usually found in army formations. We did not give them support at all. Despite the presence of the Syrian Air Force over Beirut, we did not permit the air force to fire a single shot either in Beirut or in any part of Lebanon.

At this juncture, we remember how much they talked about the air attacks. Up to this time the Syrian Air Force has not attacked any place in Lebanon, nor hit any target, fired a single shot, dropped a single bomb, or fired a single rocket in any place in Lebanon. Moreover, we could have given support to those soldiers from other positions in which we were present, but we did not do so. Of course, we are confident of our soldiers' effectiveness and of the fact that no one can go beyond certain limits in harming them. However, had we dealt with the matter with a purely technical military logic, we would have given them quick support irrespective of the destruction which would have befallen the others. We preferred bearing the harm and our soldiers' tolerating the harm to destroying and killing the others.

It appears sometimes that they misinterpreted our position and did not understand it as it really was. In my estimation, it sometimes appears that they have not understood our position as yet. The offenses they have committed against Syria through their offenses against the Syrian soldiers have not been committed by anyone else. They have offended not just the soldiers who were present in Beirut airport. In the camps there are brothers. Three years ago, we sent our soldiers to defend the Palestinian camps in Lebanon; we sent materiel with the Syrian soldiers three years ago, to defend the Palestinian camps in Beirut, in the south, and in Tripoli. These soldiers, who have been living in the camps for three years now, have been gravely harmed.

We have brothers from Lebanon in our midst, and they are aware how much harm has been done to those soldiers, some of whom have been killed and some have been arrested. Everybody is aware that those soldiers have had nothing to do with all that has happened. The fighting is taking place in Beirut among the factions; but the eyes of these soldiers are watching the Israeli Air Force, to fight it should it attack the Palestinian camps. Some of them have been detained, and others have been killed, even in Tel al-Za'tar, of which they are now talking. A number of Syrian soldiers are still being detained in the Tel al-Za'tar camp even now; that is, unless they have already killed them—unless they have already killed them. In the south, in Sidon also, Syrian soldiers who were defending the area and the camps have been detained, and some of them have been killed.

Earlier, we chose those soldiers from the various sectors of the Syrian Army. We deliberately chose them.

We deliberately wanted soldiers of every formation of the Syrian Army to go there for Pan-Arab reasons—to defend the camps so that we might strengthen the spirit of the defense of the Palestinian cause and the camps in every one of our Syrian formations. We had a small number of individual rockets. We spared whatever possible of this small number of rockets and sent them with our soldiers to defend the Palestinian camps in Lebanon. However, that was how they treated these soldiers. Perhaps we can now say, This is the reward of [word indistinct]. How remote these actions are from the manners of the Arabs. How far these actions are from the character of the Moslems.

When the forces advanced—we had pushed a brigade toward Sidon—the brigade was preceded by an advance detachment of company strength. This detachment and this brigade were applauded by the people all along the road in every village and town, and roses were tossed at them everywhere. There was a distance between the detachment and the brigade. The detachment arrived in Sidon and the people of Sidon received it. The soldiers stood in one of the squares, and the children and women approached them, carrying pictures and ornaments. Our soldiers alighted from their vehicles and joined the people, reciprocating their welcome and embracing them as if they had returned to their family after a long absence. [applause] As they were in such a situation—our soldiers with the compatriots in Sidon, with the women and children—the gunmen of the organizations poured fire on our soldiers and the children and women, as well as on the vehicles, killing whoever they could and destroying whatever they could. These are facts, brothers, examples of actions this people must be aware of so that they may know who the people are who are now disavowing every value and every effort and sacrifice this people and the heroic army of Syria have made. [applause]

Naturally, all of us realize—all of you realize—that we could easily counter such actions with decisive and crushing measures. We could have destroyed whatever we liked and purged every place of these persons, killed whomever we could and whomever we wanted. But we did not do so. The orders remained: Do not strike except in self-defense and within the narrowest limit. Why? Because I believed and I continue to believe that the plot is much bigger than those small people who are implementing such small treacherous actions.

I say frankly, brothers, that there is no military problem in Lebanon. We wish that every member of the resistance were equal to a whole army and that every individual in some of the Lebanese parties were equal to a whole army. We would then have fought Israel, liberated the land, and enjoyed much welfare and prosperity. But this is one thing, and reality is something else.

There is no military problem in Lebanon. If we intended to settle our accounts militarily, it would be an easy matter. If we wanted to follow the course of settling accounts militarily, then the matter would have been settled long ago. But we did not follow this course—first, because, as I have already said, the plot is bigger than those; and second, because we wanted the misleaders to know the limits of how far they can go and at the same time we wanted to give the misleaders enough time to discover the facts for themselves, particularly that Syria has given them the breath of life and nurtured and supported them with the blood of its dutiful sons.

Who is it that now stands up in Lebanon and says no to Syria in Lebanon? This is an odd and strange thing. Those who speak in the name of Palestine stand up and say, Do not enter Lebanon. They forget, or try to disregard, or want us and the world to forget or disregard, the fact that Lebanon is not Palestine and that Beirut is the capital of Lebanon and not of Palestine. Who complained when we entered Lebanon? It was not the president of Lebanon, its foreign minister, prime minister, or speaker of the Chamber of Deputies. It was the PLO's foreign minister, the chief of the PLO's Political Department, or the PLO Executive Committee's chairman, or so-and-so, speaking in the name of Palestine. Naturally, such a person must carry a rifle to complain against Syria. By what ethical, patriotic, and legal logic do these persons stand and say, Leave Lebanon, withdraw from Lebanon and have no connection with Lebanon. How does a Palestinian stand up in Lebanon to tell the Syrian, Do not enter Lebanon.

I am saying this, brothers, to reveal the facts. This is what is actually happening. We in Syria will always remain the heart of Arabism. [cheers and applause] Because we are the heart of Arabism, we cannot understand how a Palestinian Arab citizen and a palestinian fedayeen can stand up in Lebanon to tell the Syrian soldier, Get out of Lebanon. If the argument is that the Palestinian fears this soldier, then why does he fear him in Lebanon and not in

Syria? The Palestinian fedayeen goes from Syria to Lebanon to tell the Palestinian [as heard] soldier, Get out of Lebanon. He then returns to Syria to meet with the Syrian soldier. This is strange and odd. Who is it who tells us, Leave such and such a place. Leave Sawfar, leave Sidon, and leave Tripoli, or any other place. Not the official or the citizen in Lebanon but the Palestinian Arab citizen. Is this being done in the name of Palestine? Is this done for the sake of the liberation of Palestine? Of course and definitely not. It is being done for the sake of everything other than Palestine. [applause] We in Syria accept it if the president of Lebanon should tell us, Get out or do not get out. We accept it if the prime minister of Lebanon should tell us, Get out or do not get out. We accept this from the speaker of the Chamber of Deputies and even every citizen in Lebanon. But we cannot accept this from any Palestinian Arab citizen. We absolutely refuse to allow any Palestinian Arab citizen to tell us, Get out of Lebanon. It is not only us but also all the Arabs who refuse this.

Syria's sacrifices for the sake of Palestine were not made for the sake of so-and-so and will not be for their sake in the future. If they want us to disavow the Palestinian cause, then they have erred in their judgment. If they want us to disavow the idea of the resistance, they have erred in their intentions. The issue is sacred, as far as we are concerned. The issue is ours, and it is not an issue of individuals, particularly when they behave in a manner harming this issue.

I am not reviewing the sacrifices this country made for the sake of the Palestinian question since its emergence, but let us remember only some of the actions that Syria carried out in the past few years, not for the sake of Palestine or its question, because this is something inevitable and undebatable, but also for the sake of the resistance groups. How much did we sacrifice for the sake of the resistance in the past few years? Fifty percent of the Syrian war planes that fell in clashes with the enemy before the 1973 war fell in defense of the positions of the Palestinian resistance. Thirteen planes fell in just one day in al-'Urqub in defense of the resistance. These planes were manned by the elite of our pilots, including the hero martyr, Fayiz Mansur. [applause]

I remember some of the outstanding events. We lost five hundred Syrian soldiers in one day. We lost them in a fight with the enemy, because the enemy had hit a fedayeen base somewhere in Syria. The battles we fought against the enemy for the sake of the Pale_tinian resistance are numerous. These battles continue daily. Our relations with our Arab brothers had always deteriorated because of our attitude toward the resistance.

Who has done for the resistance what Syria has? Who has sacrificed for the resistance as much as Syria sacrificed? What Arab country other than Syria entered in warlike operations with another Arab country? All of us remember our fighting with our brothers in Jordan, who are our closest brothers. All of us know now the amount of cooperation and confidence between us and fraternal Jordan and what we aspire to do jointly. We entered into violent fighting with these close brothers in 1970 and 1971. Syrian and Jordanian soldiers were killed and Syrian and Jordanian tanks were destroyed for the sake of the resistance. Who, other than us in Syria, did such a thing?

In 1969, we adopted a stand in Lebanon by which we saved the resistance. In 1973, we alone adopted a stand in Lebanon by which we saved the resistance. In 1976, we entered Lebanon, as I said a short while ago, for the sake of the resistance and saved it. [applause] It is fit to apply to their present attitude toward all this the proverb which says, This is the reward for [word indistinct]. Naturally, when Syria adopts such stands, it asks for no rewards or gratitude and does no favor to anybody. It adopts these stands on the basis of its firm belief that they serve its national cause and not any individual. This was Syria's position in the past, this is its present position, and this will be its position in the future. [applause]

Who has done—I realize that I am repeating some expressions and I must repeat them—what Syria did for the sake of the resistance? Who has sacrificed as much as Syria sacrificed for the sake of the resistance? Why did we not enter into negotiations after the Sinai agreement and regain a part of the Golan? Why did we oppose the step-by-step policy? If we wanted to serve Syria's regional interests, we should have entered into negotiations, regained a part of the land, and moved within the framework of the step-by-step policy. But for the sake of the Palestinian question and those who say that they represent the Palestinian question, and so that they may not be isolated and the Palestinian question may not be aborted, we refused to negotiate, despite the fact that such negotiation would have restored to us part of our occupied territory under acceptable conditions.

We were given the offer to negotiate through the United States and to regain a large part of the land. We said no, because our estimate was that the step-by-step policy's final aim was to liquidate the Palestinian question. We viewed this policy as follows: A step in Sinai in return for concessions, a step in Syria in return for concessions, and a step afterward or earlier in Jordan in return for concessions, and then another round of one step and concessions, another step and concessions, and a third step and concessions, to be followed by a fourth and fifth round. The result after many rounds would be that we give everything to the enemy without reaching the 1967 borders, and in the best of circumstances that we give everything to the enemy when we reach the 1967 borders, and the Palestinian question is liquidated. This is how we viewed the step-by-step policy, and this is why we opposed this policy, because it did not take into consideration the rights of the Palestinian Arab people and consequently did not take into account the role of those people who claim to embody, represent, and work for the rights of the Palestinian Arab people. This is why we refused to negotiate. [applause]

Moreover, when we refused to negotiate, we were made the offer of withdrawal without negotiations—that Israel withdraw from a part of the Golan. This could have been a small part, and indeed it was small, but nevertheless it was an offer for withdrawal from a part of the Golan without negotiations. When I told the person who made the offer that we do not agree, he said, "You are not required to say you agree or do not agree." I told him, "No; we will say we do not agree." [applause] Why? It is because we believed that this withdrawal, although not the result of negotiations, would constitute a step and provide a justification for repeating the round and bringing on the same dangers we wanted to avoid.

Who in this area will do such a thing for the sake of Palestine? Who in this area will do such a thing for the sake of Palestine and the Palestinian resistance? Nobody. The leaders of the Palestinian resistance are aware of these offers. They know what we are offered and our attitude toward these offers. Despite this, they have adopted their present stands. Our stands will not change. They are firm, principled stands, on a just cause, which is in essence our sacred cause. Our stands will never change. At a time, however, when the papers are piled up and are shuffled, we must refer to certain stands. We must refer to certain sacrifices that Syria has made and is making. We wish that the Arab brothers would compete with us in real sacrifices for the sake of Palestine and the Palestinian resistance and not in so much talk for the sake of Palestine and the Palestinian resistance. Syria's sacrifices are clear and bright. It is sacrificing its sons, economy, land, and everything so that the Palestinian question may continue, the struggle for the Palestinian question may continue, and so that we can provide impregnability and strength for all Arabs and the Palestinian resistance and ultimately restore our occupied land and the rights of our displaced people. [applause]

What is tragi-comic are those persons who want to conceal their imperfections—cover themselves and conceal their imperfections—by levelling accusations at Syria. You have heard, I believe, those who say that Syria is plotting with the United States in Lebanon. They say it is an American-Syrian plot. I can very clearly, frankly, proudly, and confidently say that if Syria agreed to the U.S. plans in the area or even if Syria adopted a neutral stand in these plans, they would have faced no problems in the Arab area. [applause] Our stand on Lebanon and the Lebanese problem or issue is as firm and principled as it is on the Palestinian question. We will be neither courteous nor will we bargain.

We had many contacts with several states during the Lebanese crisis. I would like to give you examples of these contacts so that those who are not yet aware may know how Syria deals proudly and honestly with all people—foes and friends. I would like to read passages from the minutes of two separate communications to give you an idea how we deal with others and the course or inclination of our communications. The first communication between us and the Americans took place on 16 October 1975.

Naturally, the minutes are long, as you can see. I will not read them in full. But I will read some of the passages. The U.S. ambassador saw me on that date with a message, of course. He said, "First, I would like to correct the impression among some people in Syria that the United States supports the Christian diehards and extremists in Lebanon. This does not mean that we do not care about the situation of the Christians in Lebanon. But there is a clear difference between the position of the extremists and the position of the moderate Christians in Lebanon. It seems clear to us, and this is a U.S. stand, that a stable solution must be acceptable to the Christian moderates and must not disrupt their security, because this feeling of security is to them a major factor in a stable solution. We would like to know how Syria views the development of the situation. We would like to know Syria's diagnosis. Our careful view, in short, and I would like to make sure that we are not misunderstood in this, is that Israel will consider the intervention of foreign armed forces a very grave threat, so that no matter what we say to it, it might intervene. This means that the United States supports Syria's intervention in Lebanon, especially the armed intervention. I repeat this passage: Our careful view, in short, and I would like to make sure that we are not misunderstood in this, is that Israel will consider the intervention of foreign armed forces a very grave threat, so that no matter what we say to it, it might intervene. This is a situation which we clearly want to avoid.

I believe that all the brothers clearly understand what this statement means. We want to avoid this situation—Israel's possible intervention "despite our advice." I would like to make it very clear that this does not represent any joint discussions between Israel and the United States. This was the fundamental idea on this subject at the interview.

I will now also read to you my reply. Naturally, my reply is long, and I will read to you the passages which constitute a reply to the idea: "On our position on Lebanon, we proceed from the fact that we are the sons of a single Arab nation. What prompts us to show serious concern toward what is happening in Lebanon is our anxiety over the tragedies there. We are concerned about all Lebanese— Christians and Moslems—because they are the sons of our Arab nation and come under the flag of Arab nationalism. It is with this understanding that we tackle what is going on in Lebanon. It is on this basis that we are seeking to stop the fighting through understanding and cooperation with various political forces in Lebanon and to create the right atmosphere to solve their other domestic problems democratically and through dialogue among them. As for

the impression you said existed" (he told me, 'We want to remove
the impression that the United States supports the Christian extremists') "as for the impression you said existed among some people about the U.S. attitude, that it supports Christian extremists—as
far as I know, this impression does not exist. What exists is that the
United States is playing a role in the fighting in Lebanon for other
political reasons, primarily to help the Sinai agreement.

"All in the area have the impression that the United States does
not care for matters of religion in the world. Were this not so, or in
other words if the United States builds its strategy on the basis of
defending the Christians in the world, as you say, then it should
have first defended Christ himself and fought Israel, because it is
the Jews who crucified Christ, as you yourselves say. How can this
deep paradox be explained if we were to believe that the United
States cares for religious affairs? In one place you show interest in a
problem involving the Christians, and in another place you give
every support to those who crucified Christ. Therefore, we cannot
give any U.S. opinion on Lebanon a religious interpretation; rather
we give it a political interpretation.

"Regarding Israel, as I said a while ago" (of course this is further
to my talk with him) "we, as I said a while ago, believe that the
problem in Lebanon is connected with the Arab nation and therefore is an internal Arab problem. Israel, even in the event of its being
a state with an old history in the area—that is if we make such a
supposition, which is absurd—Israel has no right to interfere in the
internal affairs of the Arab nation. Israel is a foreign presence as far
as Lebanon, Syria, Egypt, and Jordan are concerned. As for Syria, it
is not a foreign presence as far as Lebanon is concerned, and Lebanon is not a foreign presence as far as Syria or Jordan or Saudi Arabia
and so forth are concerned. The Arabs are one nation, and Israel is a
stranger to this nation, and it has no connection with its aims. This is
a self-evident matter, which needs no debate. If Israel wishes to
intervene, it is only because since it was established—brothers, of
course this is my reply," (because it is clear that he is saying that
Israel will intervene and fight), "if Israel wishes to intervene, it is
only because since it was established it has been looking for suitable
means to exploit for further expansion and aggression. Any time it
sees the circumstances opportune to expand and commit aggres-

sion, it will expand and commit aggression. This is what experience has confirmed ever since Israel was established. In our position, regarding the events in Lebanon, we will in no way take into consideration what Israel might do. We will perform our duties toward Lebanon fully at all times, and we will do everything in our power to halt the fighting, because it is a fight among factions of our kinsmen and family. If our brothers in Lebanon wish to seek the assistance of our military capabilities and our armed forces, we shall place at their disposal everything they want in any part of the Lebanese territory, from the southernmost part to the northernmost part of Lebanon. What Israel intends to do will not prevent us from performing this duty. [applause]

"Any time Israel seeks to confront us, we will not feel any anxiety because we will be ready to confront Israel, not only on the territory of Syria alone but anywhere in the Arab homeland." [applause] This is my reply to the American stand. This is a concrete proof. Some claim that Syria is proceeding according to an American plan and that Syria's stand in Lebanon is an American-Syrian conspiracy.

Another communication was dated 14 April 1976. I believe that on 9 April 1976 we dispatched a force to the al-Masna [Syrian-Lebanese border post]—just to al-Masna. We did not enter the al-Beqa or any other area beyond that. The communication took place after this move. It was obvious that there was a warning against intervention and also a threat—*do not intervene.* On 14 April 1976 they brought us this ultimatum. Again the minutes are long, but the substance is clear: "On the twelfth of this month" (that is three days after we moved troops to al-Masna, we moved these troops in the evening of 9 April 1976, and by the morning of 10 April 1976 our move was known) "the Israeli government informed us that it considered that the Syrian actions in Lebanon had reached a point at which Israel would find itself compelled to take its own measures if this point was transcended. This is very clear. We in the United States are concerned that Syria might get the impression that the absence of an open Israeli reaction means lack of Israeli concern regarding the Syrian actions, contrary to what we constantly communicated to Damascus during the past weeks—that is to say, this matter is not just a question of a communication which took them one hour to convey to us—contrary to what we constantly communicated to

Damascus during the past weeks." This message was given to my political adviser, Adib ad-Dawudi. I read the message he sent me, and I wrote my reply on a piece of paper so he would convey it. I said: First, Syria feels that the contents of the message constitute an ultimatum. It categorically rejects this ultimatum. [applause] Second, Syria is not ready now and will not be ready in the future to accept any ultimatum from any quarter in the world. [applause] Third, what is happening in Lebanon is an internal Arab affair. The Arabs alone are entitled to deal with this matter. Fourth, the only consideration which has defined and defines, now and in the future, the dimensions of the Syrian intervention in Lebanon, including the size and the positions of the Syrian forces—including the size of the Syrian forces and the positions of the Syrian forces—is the interest of the people of Lebanon, because our history is one, our future is one and our destiny is one. [applause] This was my reply to the message we got from the United States, to the ultimatum we received from the United States. The reply is clear. I have read out these two communications to you and I do not want to comment. It is up to the people to judge after this and to understand how Syria deals with all peoples with honor and sincerity. [applause] Syria will remain a bright beacon to guide all the strugglers of our Arab nation. [applause] We in this country shall remain noble and dignified, acting on the basis of our principles and ideals. We do not flatter or compromise our aims and principles. We embody the pride, dignity and message of our Arab nation. [applause] Every hand that attempts to harm the dignity and pride of this great people, who are sacrificing all they have for the sake of their pride and the pride of their nation, shall be severed. [applause] I shall relentlessly and unhesitatingly struggle as long as I live to safeguard the trust you have placed in me. [applause] Whoever traverses the path of the people will not get lost. Whoever traverses your path—the path of the people—will not get lost because the path of the people is the road of right and reality. Brothers, let us have faith in God and have confidence in the people. Whoever believes in God and has confidence in the people and works for the sake of the people, he will inevitably triumph. Peace be upon you. [applause]

Notes

Chapter 1. The Lebanese Paradox

1. See Iliya Harik, *Lebanon: Anatomy of Conflict* (Hanover, N.H.: American Universities Field Staff, 1981).

2. On this point, see the instructive criticism by Albert H. Hourani of Kamal Salibi's book, *The Modern History of Lebanon* (London: Weidenfeld, 1965). The review was published under the title "Lebanon from Feudalism to Modern State," *Middle Eastern Studies*, 2 (1966), 256–63. Salibi's interpretation of Lebanon's modern history can also be found in two of his essays: "The Lebanese Identity," *Journal of Contemporary History*, 6 (1971), 76–86; and "The Personality of Lebanon in Relation to the Modern World," in L. Binder, ed., *Politics in Lebanon* (New York: Wiley, 1966), pp. 263–70. In Salibi's later work on the origins of the civil war, *Crossroads to Civil War: Lebanon, 1958–1976* (Delmar, N.Y.: Caravan Books, 1976), a change of perspective can be discerned.

3. On the history of the autonomous Mutasarifiyya, see John P. Spagnolo, *France and Ottoman Lebanon, 1861–1914* (London: Ithaca Press, 1977).

4. On the demands of the Maronite nationalists, see John P. Spagnolo, "Mount Lebanon, France and Dâûd Pasha: A Study of Some Aspects of Political Habituation," *International Journal of Middle Eastern Studies*, 2 (1971), 148–67; Meir Zamir, "Smaller and Greater Lebanon—The Squaring of a Circle?" *Jerusalem Quarterly*, 23 (Spring 1982), 35–53; and C. M. Andrew and A. S. Kanya-Forstner, *France Overseas* (London: Thames & Hudson, 1981), pp. 177–79.

5. See Zamir, "Smaller and Greater Lebanon," and E. Kedourie, "Lebanon: The Perils of Independence," in his *Islam in the Modern World* (London: Mansell, 1980), pp. 85–91.

6. Quoted by Meir Zamir, "Emile Eddé and the Territorial Integrity of Lebanon," *Middle Eastern Studies*, 14 (May 1978), 232–35. On Emile Eddé's role in Lebanese politics in the interwar period, see Salibi, *Modern History of Lebanon*, pp. 171–78.

7. In a meeting of the directorate of the Jewish Agency on February 11, 1945, Weizmann, the president of the agency, reported that, "The son of the former president came to me. A Christian under a strong French influence—he came with a proposal . . . that he would like to hand over to us, to the national home, Tyre and Sidon . . . because there are there a hundred thousand Muslims. I responded by saying that my grandfather used to say that he would not receive a 'biting' gift; but he would not relent, and said that he will come again" (minutes of the Jewish Agency Directorate General; I am grateful to Dr. Z. Ganin for bringing this quotation to my attention).

8. Compare Salibi, "Lebanese Identity"; N. A. Faris, "Lebanon, Land of Light," in James Kritzeck and R. B. Winder, ed., *The World of Islam* (London: Macmillan, 1960), pp. 336–50; and Albert H. Hourani, "Ideologies of the Mountain and the City," in R. Owen, ed., *Essays on the Crisis in Lebanon* (London: Ithaca Press, 1976), pp. 33–41.

9. The standard work on the evolution of Lebanon's political institutions is still Pierre Rondot's *Les institutions politiques du Liban* (Paris: Maisonneuve, 1947).

10. See Arnold Hottinger, "Zuʻama in Historical Perspective," in Binder, ed., *Politics in Lebanon*, pp. 85–105.

11. Peter Gubser, "The Zuʻama of Zahlah: The Current Situation in a Lebanese Town," *Middle East Journal*, 27 (Summer 1973).

12. Ibid., p. 181.

13. When it was still considered a success story, the Lebanese political system was often cited as a distinctive example of a consociational democracy at work. See particularly David R. Smock and Audrey C. Smock, *The Politics of Pluralism* (New York: Elsevier, 1975). On the concept of consociational democracy, see Arend Lijphart, "Consociational Democracy," *World Politics*, 21 (January 1969), 207–25.

14. See Michael Hudson, *The Precarious Republic: Modernization in Lebanon* (New York: Random House, 1968), pp. 105–8.

15. On the 1958 civil war, see Salibi, *Modern History of Lebanon*, pp. 198–204; Hudson, *Precarious Republic*, pp. 108–16; Malcolm Kerr, "Lebanese Views on the 1958 Crisis," *Middle East Journal*, 15 (Spring 1961), 211–17; and Camille Chamoun, *Crise au Moyen Orient* (Paris: Gallimard, 1963).

16. On Shihab's presidency and reforms, see Kamal Salibi, "Lebanon under Fouad Chehab 1958–1964," *Middle Eastern Studies*, 2 (1966), 211–26; and Hudson, *Precarious Republic*, pp. 297–331.

17. Titles of works on Lebanon published in the late 1960s and early 1970s reflect the same extremes of optimism and pessimism. See Leila Meo, *Lebanon, Improbable Nation: A Study in Political Development* (1965; rpt. Westport, Conn.: Greenwood Press, 1976); Hudson, *Precarious Republic*; and Elie A. Salem, *Modernization without Revolution: Lebanon's Experience* (Bloomington: Indiana University Press, 1973). The state-of-the-art volume on Lebanese politics in the mid-1960s is the collection of essays edited by Binder, *Politics in Lebanon*.

18. J. Zuwiyya, *The Parliamentary Elections of Lebanon, 1968* (Leiden: Brill, 1972); H. Zamir, "The Electoral Campaign and the Elections (Jan.-Apr.)," in D. Dishon, ed., *Middle East Record*, 4 (1968), 624–42.

19. On the Faranjiyya family, see Hottinger, "Zu'ama in Historical Perspective."

20. Halim Barakat, *Lebanon in Strife: Student Preludes to the Civil War* (Austin: University of Texas Press, 1977), pp. 185–99; and Barakat, "Social and Political Integration in Lebanon: A Case of Social Mosaic," *Middle East Journal*, 27 (Summer 1973), 301–318.

21. Iliya Harik, "The Economic and Social Factors in the Lebanese Crisis," *Journal of Arab Affairs*, 1 (1982), 209–241. Ironically, Harik mentions that his conclusions derive in part from a study he conducted together with Halim Barakat.

Chapter 2. The Second Civil War, 1975–76

1. The most comprehensive description of the events that led to the Lebanese civil war of the mid-1970s is Kamal Salibi, *Crossroads to Civil War: Lebanon, 1958–1976* (Delmar, N.Y.: Caravan Books, 1976).

2. See Iliya Harik, *Lebanon: Anatomy of Conflict* (Hanover, N.H.: American Universities Field Staff, 1981).

3. *Death in Beirut*, tr. Leslie McLoughlin (Washington, D.C.: Three Continents Press, 1978).

4. Fuad I. Khuri, "Sectarian Loyalty among Rural Migrants in Two Lebanese Suburbs: A Stage Between Family and National Allegiance," in R. Antoun and I. Harik, eds., *Rural Politics and Social Changes in the Middle East* (Bloomington: Indiana University Press, 1972), pp. 198–213.

5. See Itamar Rabinovich, "The Limits of Military Power: Syria's Role," in P. E. Haley and L. W. Snider, eds., *Lebanon in Crisis: Participants and Issues* (Syracuse, N.Y.: Syracuse University Press, 1979), pp. 55–73; and Adeed I. Dawisha, *Syria and the Lebanese Crisis* (London: Macmillan, 1980).

6. See *Al-Hayat* (Beirut), February 24, 1973, April 4, 1973, and July 6, 1973; and *Al-Nahar* (Beirut), July 6, 1973.

7. Jean Aucagne, "L'Imam Moussa Sader et la Communauté Chiite," *Travaux et Jours* (October-December 1974), pp. 31–51; Tom Sicking and Shereen Khairallah, "The Shi'a Awakening in Lebanon: A Search for Radical Change in a Traditional Way," *Ceman Report 1974* (Beirut: Center for the Study of the Modern Arab World, 1976), pp. 85–126. On the connection between the Iranian revolution and southern Lebanon, see Joseph Alpher, "The Khomeini International," *Washington Quarterly*, 3 (Autumn 1980), 54–74.

8. Quoted in Sicking and Khairallah, "The Shi'a Awakening in Lebanon: A Search for Radical Change in a Traditional Way."

9. See Michael Hudson, "The Palestinian Factor in the Lebanese Civil War," *Middle East Journal*, 32 (1978), 261–78; and Michael W. Suleiman, "Crisis and Revolution in Lebanon, *Middle East Journal*, 26 (1972), 11–24.

10. Kamal Salibi, "Right and Left in Lebanon," in G. Stein and U. Steinbach, eds., *The Contemporary Middle Eastern Scene* (Opladen: Leske, 1979), pp. 97–103. See also Salah Khalaf, "Changing Forms of Political Patronage in Lebanon," in E. Gellner and J. Waterbary, eds., *Patrons and Clients in*

Mediterranean Societies (London: Duckworth, 1977), pp. 185–205; and M. Johnson, "Political Bosses and Their Gangs: Zu'ama and Qabadayat in the Sunni Muslim Quarters of Beirut," ibid., pp. 207–24.

11. See F. Stoakes, "The Supervigilantes: The Lebanese Kataeb Party as Builder, Surrogate, and Defender of the State," *Middle Eastern Studies*, 11 (1975), 215–36.

12. See Rabinovich, "Limits of Military Power."

13. Thus Emile Eddé in 1932 wrote in a memorandum to the Quai d'Orsay that "France has a great economic and political interest in consolidating her position, at least on the Syrian coast. . . . In order to reach this kind of consolidation it would be wise to keep and develop French administration at both Alexandretta and the Alawi region and expedite the territorial reduction of Lebanon." See Meir Zamir, "Smaller and Greater Lebanon—The Squaring of a Circle?" *Jerusalem Quarterly*, 23 (Spring 1982), 35–53.

14. Itamar Rabinovich, "The Greater Syria Plan and the Palestine Problem—Historical Roots, 1919–1939," *Jerusalem Cathedra*, 2 (1982), 259–71; Elizabeth Picard, "L'évolution récente du Parti Populaire Syrien," *Maghreb Machrek*, 78 (1977), 74–76.

15. Kamal Junblatt, *Hadhi-hi Wisayati* (This is my legacy) (Beirut, 1978), p. 28.

16. *Observer* (London), March 6, 1977.

17. See Galia Golan and Itamar Rabinovich, "The Soviet Union and Syria: The Limits of Co-operation," in Y. Ro'i, ed., *The Limits of Power: Soviet Policy in the Middle East* (London: Croom Helm, 1979), pp. 213–31; I. Kass, "Moscow and the Lebanese Triangle," *Middle East Journal*, 33 (1979), 164–87; and R. Freedman, "The Soviet Union and the Civil War in Lebanon, 1975–76," *Jerusalem Journal of International Relations*, 3 (Summer 1978), 60–93.

18. See "The Syrian Invasion of Lebanon: Military Moves as a Political Instrument," (in Hebrew) in the Israeli army's monthly, *Ma'arachot*, July 1977.

19. Radio Damascus, July 20, 1976. On April 12, Asad had delivered on Radio Damascus another revealing speech in which several of the themes that were fully developed in July appear in an embryonic form. For the text of the July 20 speech see the appendix to this volume.

Chapter 3. Political Parties and Factions

1. See the interesting characterization of the Maronite community by Walid Khalidi, *Conflict and Violence in Lebanon* (Cambridge, Mass.: Center for International Affairs, Harvard University, 1979), pp. 68–72; and Elizabeth Picard, "Rôle et évolution du Front Libanais dans la guerre civile," *Maghreb Machrek*, 90 (1980), 16–39.

2. On the Phalange see John P. Entelis, *Pluralism and Party Transformation in Lebanon: Al-Kata'ib 1956–1970* (Leiden: Brill, 1974); F. Stoakes, "The Supervigilantes: The Lebanese Kataeb Party as Builder, Surrogate, and Defender of the State," *Middle Eastern Studies*, 9 (1975), 215–36; and Marius Deeb, *The Lebanese Civil War* (New York: Praeger, 1980), pp. 21–25. *Note:* the Western press transliteration of Jumayyil is Gemayel. In rendering Arabic

and Israeli names I have used an intermediate system, not quite as loose as that employed by most of the Western press, but not so rigid as academic systems.

3. Quoted by Fuad I. Khuri, "Sectarian Loyalty among Rural Migrants in Two Lebanese Suburbs: A Stage between Family and National Allegiance," in R. Antoun and I. Harik, eds., *Rural Politics and Social Changes in the Middle East* (Bloomington: Indiana University Press, 1972), pp. 198–213.

4. *Greater Lebanon—A Half Century's Tragedy* (in Arabic), University of Kaslik, October 1975.

5. See Deeb, *Lebanese Civil War*, pp. 25–28.

6. Chamoun's account of the civil war is given in *Crise au Liban* (Beirut, 1977).

7. An interesting and ironic description of Faranjiyya's modus operandi can be found in a PLO leader's account of the deterioration of Palestinian-Lebanese relations. See Abou Iyad, *Palestinien sans patrie: Entretiens avec Eric Rouleau* (Hebrew edition, Jerusalem: Mifras, 1978).

8. See Itamar Rabinovich, "Syria," in C. Legum and H. Shaked, eds., *Middle East Contemporary Survey 1976–77* (New York: Holmes and Meier, 1978), pp. 604–21; and Elizabeth Picard, "La Syrie de 1946 à 1979," in A. Raymond, ed., *La Syrie d'aujourdhui* (Paris: Editions du Centre National de la Recherche Scientifique, 1980), pp. 143–84.

9. Qassis has been replaced by Father Bulus Na'aman.

10. On the earlier phases of Lebanon's military politics, see J. C. Hurewitz, *The Middle East Politics: The Military Dimension* (New York: Praeger, 1969).

11. See Deeb, *Lebanese Civil War*, pp. 30–31.

12. Kamal Junblatt, *Hadhi-hi Wisayati* (This is my legacy) (Beirut, 1978), p. 102.

13. On the history of the Lebanese Communist party, see Elyas Murqus, *A History of the Communist Parties in the Arab Homeland* (in Arabic) (Beirut: Dar al-Tali'a, 1964); and J. Coland, "Le Parti Communiste libannaise 50 ans après," *Maghreb Machrek*, 68 (1975), 61–75. On the more recent developments of the 1970s, see *The Lebanese Communists and the Tasks of the Present Phase* (Beirut: Lebanese Communist Party, 1972).

14. See John F. Devlin, *The Ba'th Party: A History from Its Origins to 1966* (Stanford: Hoover Institution Publications, 1976), pp. 110–11 and 204–06.

15. See Walid Kazziha, *Revolutionary Transformation in the Arab World* (London: C. Knight, 1975).

16. On the history of the PPS in Syria and Lebanon, see Labib Zuwiyya Yamak, *The Syrian Social Nationalist Party: An Ideological Analysis* (Cambridge, Mass.: Harvard University Press, 1969); M. Van Dusen, "Political Integration and Regionalism in Syria," *Middle East Journal*, 26 (1972), 123–36; and Hisham Sharabi, *Ashes and Embers* (in Arabic) (Beirut: Manshurat Ibn Rushd, 1978), a memoir of the author's membership and activity in the party in the 1940s.

17. A detailed description of the abortive coup can be found in Y. Oron, ed., *Middle East Record*, 2 (1961), 398–404.

18. See Elizabeth Picard, "L'évolution récente du Parti Populaire Syrien," *Maghreb Machrek*, 78 (1977), 74–76.

19. See M. Farouk-Sluglett and P. Sluglett, "Aspects of the Changing Nature of Lebanese Confessional Politics: Al-Murabitun, 1958–1979," *Liban, Remises en Cause Peuples Mediterranéens*, 20 (1982), 59–73.

20. Later in the 1970s, a rivalry developed between the Palestinian organizations in southern Lebanon and Mustafa Sa'd and other local leaders who refused to accept the hegemony of the Palestine Liberation Organization.

21. The traditional political system of Tripoli is described in J. Gulick, *Tripoli, a Modern Arab City* (Cambridge, Mass.: Harvard University Press, 1967).

22. For an illuminating study of the Sunni politics of Beirut, see M. Johnson, "Factional Politics in Lebanon: The Case of the 'Islamic Society of Benevolent Intentions' (Al-Maqāsid) in Beirut," *Middle Eastern Studies*, 14 (1978), 56–75.

23. See Salah Khalaf, "Changing Forms of Political Patronage in Lebanon," in E. Gellner and J. Waterbary, eds., *Patrons and Clients in Mediterranean Societies* (London: Duckworth, 1977).

24. Kamal Junblatt, *Hadhi-hi Wisayati*, p. 105.

25. Legum and Shaked, eds., *Middle East Contemporary Survey 1976–77*, p. 185.

26. See Khalidi, *Conflict and Violence in Lebanon*, pp. 79–82.

Chapter 4. The Lingering Crisis

1. See W. Quandt, *Decade of Decisions* (Berkeley: University of California Press, 1977), pp. 281–84; and R. Stookey, "The United States," in P. E. Haley and L. W. Snider, eds., *Lebanon in Crisis: Participants and Issues* (Syracuse, N.Y.: Syracuse University Press, 1979), pp. 225–48.

2. Quoted in Fuad Ajami, *The Arab Predicament* (Cambridge: Cambridge University Press, 1981), p. 157.

3. On the evolution of the Reagan administration's outlook on Israel and the Lebanese crisis, see the revealing piece by Z. Schiff, "The Green Light," *Foreign Policy* (March 1983), 73–85.

4. U.S. International Communication Agency press release, Tel Aviv, April 6, 1981.

5. Itamar Rabinovich, "The Foreign Policy of Syria: Goals, Capabilities, Constraints and Options," *Survival* (July 1982), 175–83.

6. *TASS* (Moscow), May 22 and 28, 1981.

7. See Ali E. Hillal Dessouki, "The New Arab Political Order: Implications for the 1980's," in Malcolm Kerr and El Sayed Yassin, eds., *Rich and Poor States in the Middle East* (Boulder, Colo.: Westview Press, 1982), pp. 319–47.

8. Dina Kehat, "Syria," in C. Legum and H. Shaked, eds., *Middle East Contemporary Survey, 1977–78* (New York: Holmes and Meier, 1979), pp. 732–38.

9. Itamar Rabinovich and H. Zamir, "Lebanon," in ibid., pp. 603–27. This interpretation is different from the one presented by Walic Khalidi in *Conflict and Violence in Lebanon* (Cambridge, Mass.: Center for International

Affairs, Harvard University, 1979), pp. 121–43, where he argues that the process of reconstruction and reconciliation was impressive and that it was Israel's Litani operation that obstructed this development.

10. Elizabeth Picard, "Rôle et évolution du Front Libanais dans la guerre civile," *Magreb Machrek*, 90 (1980), 16–39.

11. See for instance *Al-Mauqif al-Arabi* (Beirut), June 8, 1981; and *Sabah al-Khayr* (Beirut), September 12, 1981. See also the illuminating piece by Percy Kemp, "La stratégie de Bashir Gemayel," *Hérodote*, 29/30 (1983), 55–82.

12. For accounts of Tony Faranjiyya's murder, see *New York Times*, June 14, 1978; and *International Herald Tribune* (Paris), same date. The Phalangist version was given by their radio station on June 13, 1978.

13. *Al-Nahar* (Beirut), July 7, 1980; *As Safir* (Beirut), July 7, 1980; *Washington Post*, July 10, 1980.

14. A. Drysdale, "The Asad Regime and Its Troubles," *Merip Reports*, 12 (1982), 3–11.

15. This analysis of the PLO's buildup in southern Lebanon draws on a study conducted in Palestinian refugee camp by Zvi Lanir of Tel Aviv University's Center for Strategic Studies. See his "The PLO's concept of 'Armed Struggle' as Tested in the 'Peace for Galilee' War" (in Hebrew) *Ma'arachot*, September 1982.

16. See Dan Schuftan, "The P.L.O. and the Lebanon War—An Interim Assessment," in *The Lebanon War—Between Protest and Compliance* (Tel Aviv: Hakibbutz Hameuchad, 1983), pp. 80–98; and Matti Steinberg, "Trends and Changes in the P.L.O.," in ibid., pp. 61–79.

17. On these relationships, see the memoirs of two Arab experts of the Jewish Agency's political department: Eliahu Elath, *Zionism and the Arabs* (in Hebrew) (Tel Aviv: Dvir, 1974), pp. 294–314; and Eliahu Sasson, *On the Road to Peace* (in Hebrew) (Tel Aviv: Am Oved, 1978), pp. 122–29. The heads of the Maronite church in Lebanon spoke to the United Nations commission that looked into the future of Palestine, supporting the notion of a Jewish national home in Palestine. See A. Podet, "Husni al-Barazi on Arab Nationalism in Palestine," in E. Kedourie and Sylvia Haim, eds., *Zionism and Arabism in Palestine and Israel* (London: Frank Cass, 1982), pp. 171–81 and particularly pp. 180–81. On the Jewish relationship with the Lebanese Sunni politician Khair al-Din Ahdab, see Sasson, pp. 115–16. David Ben-Gurion's recently published diaries of the 1948–49 period (Tel Aviv: Ministry of Defence Publishing House, 1983) indicate a close cooperation between the Jewish Agency and Riad al-Sulh, Lebanese prime minister and prominent Sunni leader.

18. M. Brecher, *The Foreign Policy System of Israel* (London: Oxford University Press, 1972), pp. 45–58.

19. On the Maronite-Jewish treaty of 1946, see Bernard Joseph, *A Faithful City* (Hebrew edition, Tel Aviv: Schoken, 1960), pp. 215–16. The text of the treaty can be found in the Central Zionist Archives.

20. See E. Oren, "The Battles for the Galilee in the War of Independence," in A. Shmueli, A. Sofer, and N. Kliop, eds., *The Book of the Galilee* (Tel Aviv: Aretz Geographic Research, forthcoming). The essay sheds an interesting light on the Lebanese army's attitude to Christian and Muslim Arabs in the Galilee.

21. See chapter 6.

22. A cryptic account is found in Yitzhak Rabin's memoirs, *A Service Diary* (in Hebrew) (Tel Aviv: Maariv Books, 1979), pp. 502–04. During the public debate on the war in Lebanon in 1982, Ariel Sharon, an adviser to Rabin in 1976–77, criticized the Israeli government's attitude of 1976.

23. The assassination of Salim al-Lawzi is depicted by Fuad Ajami (*Arab Predicament*, p. 2) as a symbol of a qualitative change that had taken place in Arab politics in the late 1970s.

24. Compare Zvi Lanir, *Israel's Involvement in Lebanon: A Precedent for an "Open" Game with Syria?* (Tel Aviv: Tel Aviv University, Center for Strategic Studies, paper no. 10, April 1981); and R. Avi-Ran, "Is a Syrian-Israeli Settlement in Lebanon Possible? The Israeli-Syrian Understanding of 1976, a Possible Model for the Future" (in Hebrew) *Ma'arachot*, February 1983.

25. Later evidence revealed that in the fall of 1978 the Lebanese Front had exerted strong pressure on Israel to intervene on its behalf, arguing that otherwise the Front was likely to collapse under Syria's pressure.

26. See Kehat, "Syria."

27. See Itamar Rabinovich, "The Problem of South Lebanon," in Legum and Shaked, eds., *Middle East Contemporary Survey 1978–79* (New York: Holmes and Meier, 1980), pp. 673–76.

28. Picard, "Rôle et évolution du Front Libanais"; and also Kemp, "Le stratégie de Bashir Gemayel."

29. See chapter 6 for detailed discussion.

30. See Itamar Rabinovich, "The Lebanese Missile Crisis of 1981," in Legum and Shaked, eds., *Middle East Contemporary Survey, 1980–81* (New York: Holmes and Meier, 1982), pp. 167–81.

Chapter 5. War, June–September 1982

1. Statement by cabinet secretary Dan Meridor in Israeli government press bulletin, Jerusalem, June 6, 1982.

2. See, e.g., "The I.D.F.'s Action in Lebanon—Defence of the Peace of Israel and Her Citizens," background material issued by IDF, June 1982.

3. See David Shipler, "Israel Likely to Seek Power Shift in Lebanon," *International Herald Tribune*, June 11, 1982. Sharon discussed the subject in an interview on Israeli television on June 16, 1982.

4. For a critic of the Israeli government's aims see Yitzhak Rabin's two pieces *The War in Lebanon* (in Hebrew; Tel Aviv, 1983), and "Political Illusions and Their Price," in *The Lebanon War—Between Protest and Compliance* (Tel Aviv: Hakibbutz Hameuchad, 1983), pp. 13–22.

5. On the PLO's doctrinal approach to the nature of the prospective armed conflict with Israel in southern Lebanon, see the findings of the study conducted by Zvi Lanir, in *Ma'arachot*, September, 1982. For an essay expounding the view that nothing short of an operation reaching as far as Beirut would have removed the PLO challenge to Israel from southern Lebanon, see Dan Schuftan, "The PLO and the Lebanon War—An Interim Assessment," in *The Lebanon War*, pp. 80–98.

6. *Davar* (Tel Aviv), May 13, 1982; *Maariv* (Tel Aviv), May 17, 1982.

7. *Maariv*, April 18, 1982, April 6, 1982, and June 1, 1982.

8. See Sharon's interview with Oriana Fallaci, *Washington Post*, August 21, 1982.

9. See *Al-Amal* (Beirut), May 27, 1982; and *La Revue du Liban*, May 5, 1982.

10. Z. Schiff, "The Green Light," *Foreign Policy* (March 1983), pp. 73–85.

11. See "The War That Almost Was," Israeli government press office "Selections from the Hebrew Press," February 7, 1982. On General Sagi's visit to Washington, see *Haaretz* (Tel Aviv), February 10, 1982.

12. See Z. Schiff, "The Green Light."

13. U. S. *Department of State Bulletin*, July 1982, pp. 44–47.

14. For Begin's interpretation of the Camp David accords and for criticism of his approach by a former supporter, see Shmuel Katz, *Lo 'Oz velo Hadar* (Neither valor nor splendor) (Tel Aviv: Dvir, 1981) and Uzi Benziman, *Rosh Memshala Bamatzor* (Prime minister under Siege) (Jerusalem: Adam, 1981).

15. Sharon's views on the policy to be conducted in the West Bank were spelled out in an interview published by *Der Spiegel* (Hamburg), April 5, 1982.

16. Cf. Mordechai Gazit, "The Middle East Peace Process," in *Middle East Contemporary Survey 1981–82* (New York: Holmes and Meier, 1984).

17. General Sagi made this point on more than one occasion. See for instance his interview in *Bamahane*, the IDF's weekly magazine, May 5, 1982.

18. *Haaretz*, March 30, 1982. For an earlier version see Z. Schiff, "Sharon's Red Lines," *Haaretz*, November 22, 1981.

19. Sharon's text, originally prepared as a lecture, was published in the Israeli press. For criticism of his approach, see *Maariv* and *Yedioth Ahronoth* (Tel Aviv), December 18, 1982; and M. Amit, "There Is Nothing New in Ariel Sharon's Strategic Gospel," *Maariv*, December 25, 1981.

20. For the evolution of the war plan see Amir Oren, "The Road to Beirut," in *The Lebanon War*, pp. 35–41.

21. Sharon alluded to these aims in several interviews and pronouncements during the summer of 1982; see, for instance, *Maariv*, September 17, 1982.

22. *Maariv*, September 17, 1982.

23. A particularly detailed and accurate report was given by John Chancellor on NBC News. For an Arab scenario, see *Al-Mustaqbal* (Beirut), May 22, 1982.

24. The most notable effort by Syria to signal its intentions to Israel was made on February 12, 1982, through Louis Fares, Radio Monte Carlo's correspondent in Damascus. The Ba'thi regime has used Fares on numerous occasions to transmit its outlook.

25. Politically the Israeli government was aided in its decision to fight Syria in Lebanon by the fact that Syrian forces opened fire on Israeli troops. Still, the scale was so small as to justify the argument that Syria was not interested in full-fledged fighting.

26. See *Yedioth Ahronoth*, June 10, 1982; *Haaretz*, June 10 and 11, 1982.

27. A decision made by the Israeli cabinet on June 15 entrusted that role to the Lebanese Forces. See the Kahan Commission's Report.

28. Since its contacts with Israel began in 1976, the Phalange presented the Palestinian problem in Lebanon as an "Israeli" problem. From their vantage point, Israel was responsible for the "injection" of the Palestinian refugees into the Lebanese body politic in 1949 and had a special responsibility to help Lebanon deal with the refugees as a necessary step in a reconstruction of the Lebanese state. See the interviews granted by "senior sources" in the Phalange to Israeli journalists in *Maariv* and *Haaretz*, June 23, 1982. See also David Hirst's piece in the *Guardian* (Manchester), July 3, 1982.

29. See B. Gwertzman on Haig's resignation in the *New York Times*, June 28 and July 2, 1982, and the list of Haig's grievances in *Middle East Policy Survey* (Washington), July 2, 1982.

30. *The Times* (London), June 18, 1982.

31. See Yair Evron, "United States and the War in Lebanon," in *The Lebanon War—Between Protest and Compliance*, pp. 99–114.

32. Galia Golan, "The Soviet Union and the Israeli War in Lebanon," and Amnon Sella, "The Soviet Attitude Towards the War in the Lebanon—Mid-1982," The Soviet and East European Research Center, Hebrew University of Jerusalem, Research Papers 46 and 47, October and December 1982.

33. See the statement published by the Syrian Progressive National Front; also the information minister's statement, Radio Damascus, June 19 and 20, 1982.

34. The dissatisfaction with the Soviet Union was expressed through Louis Fares, Radio Monte Carlo, June 25, 1982.

35. This point of view was articulated by Salah Khalaf in an interview granted to *al-Huriyya* (Beirut), May 17, 1982.

36. *The Economist* (London), February 13, 1982, p. 55.

37. See *Al-Nahar* (Beirut), June 30, 1982; see also the evasive position taken by al-Amal's leader, Nabih Beri, in *Agence France Presse*, July 1, 1982 and *Le Matin* (Paris), July 5, 1982.

Chapter 6. An Interim Assessment

1. See Cecil Hourani's two interesting pieces on Bashir Jumayyil and his policies in *Al-Majalla* (London), August 28, 1982, and *Middle East International* (London), September 3, 1982.

2. In the weeks following his election, Amin Jumayyil presented his views in several speeches and interviews. See his speech of September 30 (Radio Beirut), his address to the UN Security Council on October 18 (Radio Beirut), and the interview broadcast by Radio Beirut on November 30, 1982. The views of a prominent member of the president's inner circle can be found in Ghassan Tweni, "Lebanon: A New Republic?" *Foreign Affairs* (Fall, 1982), pp. 84–99.

3. See Sa'ib Salam's interviews with *Al-Mustaqbal* (Beirut), September 11, 1982, pp. 28–32 and on Voice of Lebanon radio the same day.

4. G. H. Jansen, "Quenching the Chouf and Tripoli Fires," *Middle East International* (London), December 23, 1982, pp. 6–7. *The Economist*, November 13, 1982.

5. See A. H. Hourani, "Ideologies of the Mountain and the City," in Roger Owen, ed., *Essays on the Crisis in Lebanon* (London: Ithaca Press, 1976), pp. 33–41.

6. From file of documents on Israeli Foreign Ministry contacts with the Phalange through Rababi, recently released to the Israeli State Archives. These files were studied by Benni Morris who published some of his findings in the *Jerusalem Post Magazine*, July 1, 1983.

7. Ben-Gurion's position is reflected in several places in Moshe Sharett's *Personal Diary* (Tel Aviv: Maariv Books, 1978), most fully in the exchange of letters between the two, published as an appendix to the diary on pp. 2397–2400.

8. Ben-Gurion's letter to his son Amos, July 27, 1937, published in his *Memoirs* (Tel Aviv: Ami Oved, 1974), vol. 4, pp. 324–333.

9. Sharett, *Personal Diary*, pp. 996, 1024.

10. App. to Sharett, *Personal Diary*.

11. See note 6, above.

12. *Divrei HaKnesset* (minutes of the Israeli parliament), June 3, 1981.

13. See the Kahan Commission Report.

14. *Maariv*, September 17, 1982.

15. See Fuad Ajami, *The Arab Predicament* (Cambridge: Cambridge University Press, 1981), and Malcolm Kerr and El Sayed Yassin, eds., *Rich and Poor States in the Middle East* (Boulder, Colo.: Westview Press, 1982).

Chapter 7. The Lebanese Crisis, 1983–85

1. For general assessments of Amin Jumayyil's administration and policies, see G. Bayram's article in *Al-Mustaqbal*, December 4, 1982, and the January 1983 issue of *Middle East Insight* (Washington, D.C.).

2. Radio Damascus, July 23, 1983. As for the reference to "little Lebanon," cf. pp. 158–59 above.

3. For a detailed and very sympathetic description of the Lebanese Forces see L. W. Snider, "The Lebanese Forces: Origins and Role in Lebanon's Politics," *Middle East Journal*, 38 (1984), 1–33.

4. Itamar Rabinovich, "Israel and Lebanon in 1983," in C. Legum, H. Shaked, and D. Dishon, eds., *Middle East Contemporary Survey, 1983–84* (New York: Holmes and Meier, 1985).

5. See Thomas L. Friedman, "The Power of the Fanatics," *The New York Times Magazine*, October 7, 1984.

6. On Amin Jumayyil's desperate message to Israel see *Maariv*, February 16, 1984.

7. On the Shi'i community in post-1982 Lebanon, see Helena Cobban, "The Shia Community and the Future of Lebanon," *The Muslim World Today*, Occasional Paper of the American Institute for Islamic Affairs (Washington, 1985); Augustus R. Norton, "Political Violence and Shia Factionalism in Lebanon," *Middle East Insight*, 3 (August–October 1983), 9–16, and Fouad Ajami, "Lebanon and Its Inheritors," *Foreign Affairs*, 63 (Spring 1985), 778–99.

8. For a perceptive analysis of Israel's failure to build bridges to the

Shi'i community, see Moshe Shemesh, "Shi'i Terrorism: A Different Angle," *Haaretz*, March 12, 1985. Uri Lubrani, by then appointed coordinator of Israeli policy in Lebanon, himself explained this policy in a revealing interview that appeared in *Koteret Rashit* (Tel Aviv), February 22, 1984, pp. 11–13.

9. For critiques of U.S. policy in Lebanon written from two contradictory vantage points, see R. G. Neumann, "Asad and the Future of the Middle East," *Foreign Affairs*, 62 (Winter 1983/84), 237–56, and Michael Ledeen, "The Lesson of Lebanon," *Commentary*, May 1984, pp. 15–22.

10. For manifestations of this tension in the American and Israeli press see, for instance, *The Baltimore Sun*, January 20, 1983, *Washington Post*, February 3, 1983, and *Maariv*, January 21, 1983.

11. An unusually detailed and authoritative account of this episode was published in the *Wall Street Journal*, April 14–15, 1983.

12. *Maariv*, May 7, 1983. Rabin's full-fledged analysis of this issue in the Knesset's Foreign Defense Affairs Committee was reported by Israel's radio on April 29, 1983.

13. Cf. *The International Herald Tribune*, June 4, 1983, and March 1, 1984.

14. The most authoritative political profile of Asad at the height of his success was published by the Phalangist leader Karim Pakradouni, who had been his party's emissary to and liaison man with Syria, in *Le Monde* (Paris) on November 20/21, 1983. The article, titled "Hafiz al-Assad—the Arabs' Bismarck," was distilled from the author's illuminating book *La paix manquée* (Beirut, 1983).

15. Cf. Asher Susser, *The PLO after the War in Lebanon* (Tel Aviv, 1985).

16. Cf. Itamar Rabinovich, "The Politics of Fragmentation and Anticipation: Inter-Arab Relations in the Early 1980's," Occasional Papers Series (The Dayan Center, Tel Aviv University, 1984).

17. See A. Drysdale, "The Succession Question in Syria, *Middle East Journal*, 39 (1985), 246–57.

18. The lengthy interview was published by *Maariv* on December 17, 1982.

19. For an analysis of the rival schools of thought in the Israeli government regarding policy vis-à-vis the Druzes, see Amir Oren's "The Last of the Firemen," *Koteret Rashit*, September 20, 1983.

Glossary

ALAWIS (OR NUSAYRIS): A Muslim sect, an offshoot of Shi'a Islam. Most of the Alawis live in Syria, where they form some 12 percent of the population. Once a marginal, rural, underprivileged community, Syrian Alawis have undergone a dramatic transformation in the past twenty years, as members of the community advanced through the army and the Ba'thi party to positions of dominance.

AL-AMAL (HOPE): A Shi'i political movement cum-militia. It developed originally as the military arm of the Movement of the Disinherited, the radical organization formed by Imam Musa al-Sadr, the religious leader who transformed Lebanon's Shi'i politics in the 1970s. After his disappearance he was replaced by Nabih al-Beri and the movement was taken over by al-Amal.

BA'TH (RENAISSANCE): A Pan-Arab socialist party with branches in several Arab countries, most notably Syria, Iraq, Lebanon, and Jordan. The party emerged during World War II, was formally established in 1947, and has been influential in Arab politics since the early 1950s.

CAIRO AGREEMENT: An agreement reached in November 1969 between the Supreme Commander of the Lebanese Army and the PLO in an effort to regulate the relationship between the Lebanese government and the PLO and the latter's activity in and from Lebanon.

DRUZE: A Muslim sect, an off-shoot of Shi'a Islam. The Druzes are divided into two roughly equal communities in Syria (where they constitute some 3 percent of the population) and Lebanon (some 6 percent of the population), with a smaller group in Israel. In all three states, because of their territorial concentration, solidarity, military skill, and political acumen, they enjoy a political influence well beyond their numerical strength.

ERETZ ISRAEL: The Hebrew term designating the Land of Israel, the ancestral homeland distinct from and larger than the State of Israel. The term is sometimes used as the Hebrew equivalent of Palestine.

AL-FATH: The largest and most important of the organizations that make up the PLO. Fath, which means conquest in Arabic, was founded in secret in the late 1950s and appeared publicly on the scene in 1965. In 1968 it took over the PLO, and its leader Yasir 'Arafat became the organization's chairman. Unlike its Marxist rivals/partners, the Fath focuses on Palestinian issues and does not seek to revolutionize Arab politics.

HARAKAT AL-MAHRUMIN: The Movement of the Disinherited or Dispossessed, Shi'i protest movement formed by Imam Musa al-Sadr.

IDF: Acronym for Israeli Defense Forces, the official English-language designation for Israel's armed forces.

AL-ISHA 'A AL-LUBNANI (Lebanese illumination): A concept developed by Lebanese intellectuals who sought to bolster the notion of a supracommunal Lebanese entity which has made a special contribution to human civilization as a mediator between East and West.

JEWISH AGENCY: Organization formed in 1929 as the formal representative of the Jewish community vis-à-vis the British mandatory government. It gradually acquired the attributes of a proto-government for the Jewish community. After the establishment of the State of Israel, the Jewish Agency shifted its focus to issues common to the State and to Jewish communities abroad.

LABOR PARTY: Israeli political party formed by the union of three parties: Mapai, Achdut Ha'avoda, and Rafi. It is aligned with a fourth party, Mapam, in the Labor Alignment. Until the 1977 elections, the Labor party (under different names) had held power since independence and had dominated Jewish public and political life in mandatory Palestine.

LEBANESE FORCES: The military arm of the Lebanese Front, formed in August 1976, which brought four militias—the Phalanges, the National Liberals, the Tanzim, and the Guardians of the Cedar—under a joint command. The Lebanese Forces subsequently became the power base of Bashir Jumayyil.

LEBANESE FRONT: The political backbone of the status quo coalition in the Lebanese civil war. It was formed in 1976 by a group of Christian leaders, including Camille Chamoun (its president), Pierre Jumayyil, Father Bulus Naʿaman, head of the permanent congress of the Lebanese monastic orders and two intellectuals, Charles Malik and Fuʿad Ephrem Boustani.

LEBANON'S ARAB ARMY: A group of predominantly Muslim officers and soldiers who under the leadership of Lieutenant Ahmed al-Khatib seceded from the Lebanese army in 1976 and fought with the revisionist militias in the Lebanese civil war. Originally anti-Syrian, it eventually became a pro-Syrian force.

LIKUD: Israeli political alignment, including the nationalist populist Herut party and the centrist Liberal party, plus several smaller parties. The Likud has been in power in Israel since 1977.

MALKERT AGREEMENT: An agreement made in 1973 as one of several abortive attempts to implement the 1969 Cairo Agreement.

MANDATORY PERIOD: The period of direct French control in Lebanon, 1918–45. Formally France had a mandate from the League of Nations to prepare Lebanon for independence.

MARONITES: Members of the largest Uniate church in the Arab world. The Uniate churches at various periods accepted the Vatican's authority but retained a measure of autonomy. The Maronites who migrated to northern Lebanon from inland Syria drew closer to Latin Europe and to Catholicism after the Crusades. By the eighteenth century the Maronites' growing numbers, early modernization, and effective church organization and leadership made them the leading community in Mount Lebanon. The same century saw the community's southward expansion and the emergence of a proto-national consciousness in its ranks.

MUJTAHIDUN: Shiʿi men of religion.

MUTASARIFIYYA: A subprovince in the Ottoman Empire. In the Lebanese context, the autonomous subprovince of Mount Lebanon, 1861–1915.

NATIONAL BLOC: A small Maronite political party representing the outlook and influence of the Eddé family.

NATIONAL LIBERALS: A Lebanese political party established by Camille Chamoun, which reflects his style and policies. In recent years his son Dany has played an increasingly prominent role in its leadership.

NATIONAL PACT: The oral agreement made in 1943 by Bishara al-Khuri and Riad al-Sulh, leaders of the Maronite and Sunni communities in Lebanon, on the nature and governance of the Lebanese state: Lebanon was neither part of Catholic Latin Europe nor was it an Arab state, but it did have an "Arab face"; political and administrative power was divided among the major communities according to their estimated numerical strength.

PALESTINE LIBERATION ORGANIZATION (PLO): Umbrella organization, a coalition of groups including the Fath, the Marxist Popular Front for the Liberation of Palestine, and several others. The PLO was formed in 1964 by the first Arab summit conference as the embodiment of the notion of a Palestinian entity. It was originally controlled by the Arab states but after the 1967 war was taken over by genuine Palestinian nationalist groups and became autonomous.

PHALANGES LIBANAISES (al-Kataib al-Lubnaniyya): The largest and most important Christian-Maronite party in Lebanon. Founded in 1936 by Pierre Jumayyil as a vigilante youth movement dedicated to the preservation of a Christian Lebanon, it later developed into a political party with a sophisticated and elaborate organization and a quite complex concept of the Lebanese entity and its problems.

REAGAN INITIATIVE OR PLAN: The plan for settling the Palestinian dimension of the Arab-Israeli conflict, issued by President Ronald Reagan on September 1, 1982. It sought to return the bulk of the West Bank to Jordan. Both the plan's timing and its essence were influenced by the course of the war in Lebanon.

REDLINE AGREEMENT: The informal and indirect understanding negotiated in 1976 by the United States between Syria and Israel, which defined the limits of Syria's intervention in Lebanon and made it acceptable to Israel.

SHI'IS: Adherents of Islam's heterodoxy, the Shi'a (literally, faction). The Shi'a originated among the supporters of Ali, the Prophet's cousin and son-in-law, and his descendants. Eventually, important doctrinal differences developed between the Shi'a and the Sunna. Shi'is are divided into Zaydis, Twelvers, and Isma'ilis. The Alawis and the Druzes are offshoots of the Isma'iliyya.

SIX DAY WAR: The third Arab-Israeli war, fought from June 6 to June 11, 1967.

SUNNIS: Adherents of Islamic orthodoxy, the largest group in Islam. Sunnis accept the Islamic tradition (sunna) and the legitimate authority of the caliphs as the Prophet's successors.

SYRIAN SOCIALIST NATIONALIST PARTY: A political party established in the 1930s that advocated secular, territorial Syrian nationalism. It had branches in Lebanon, Syria, and Palestine, and has undergone several transformations in the past fifty years. Its largest faction in Lebanon is a pro-Syrian force.

TREATY OF FRIENDSHIP AND COOPERATION: One of a series of treaties that the Soviet Union has signed since the early 1970s with its clients and friends in the Middle East. The treaty with Syria was signed in October 1980.

AL-WATAN AL-BADIL: The Alternative Homeland, a sardonic term used by Lebanese opponents of the PLO to refer to the establishment of a Palestinian state in southern Lebanon.

ZA'IM (PL. ZU'AMA): Literally a leader; a term referring to a rural or urban notable who mediates between his clientele and the formal political structure.

Index

255

119; Israel's withdrawal, 125, 128–30; return to Egypt, 178
Six Day War, 31, 165; description, 252
Six Parties Summit. *See* Riyad conference
South Lebanon. *See* Lebanon, southern
Soviet Union: and Lebanese crisis, 93, 126, 147–48, 186; Middle East policies, 119; and Syria, 48, 54, 92, 93–94, 147–48, 150, 155. *See also* Treaty of Friendship and Cooperation
Sulh, Riad al-, 24
Sunni(s), 18, 22, 24; description, 252 opposition to Syria, 55, 78; political role, 25, 32, 35, 37, 38, 39, 52, 176, 181, 199; politicians, 66, 83–84, 155, 156; religious leadership, 84
Syria: claims for Lebanon, 36–37; control of Lebanon, 59, 91, 92, 99; fighting against Phalanges, 114–18; intervention in second civil war, 48–54, 87; invasion of Lebanon, 54–56; and Israel, 49, 59, 100, 105–7, 111, 116, 131, 137–38, 146, 148–50, 173, 187–88, 195, 197–99; and Amin Jumayyil, 175, 177, 179, 189–90; and Lebanese Front, 74, 100, 110–11, 113, 114, 115–18, 124; and Maronites, 51, 55, 73; military buildup, 131–32; opposition to, 51–52, 55, 77–78, 97; vs. PLO, 10, 49, 86–88, 89, 102, 110, 184–85, 188, 191; political strength, 36, 37, 48; postwar position, 186–87; presence in Lebanon, 89, 91, 93, 109–11, 155, 190–92, 199; quest for hegemony, 99–101, 188–89; reform document, 50–51, 77; and Soviet Union, 48, 54, 92, 93–94, 147–48, 150, 155, 187; and U.S., 48–49, 87, 90, 91–92, 117, 119, 125, 150, 184; and war of 1982, 148–50; withdrawal from Lebanon, 101, 113. *See also* Asad, Hafiz al-; Syrian-Israeli missile crisis; Treaty of Friendship and Cooperation
Syria, Greater, notion of, 48, 53–54; and Phalanges, 64; and PLO, 86; support for, 80–82
Syrian-Israeli missile crisis, 92–94, 118–19, 120, 122, 124, 166
Syrian Socialist Nationalist Party, 61; and Ba'th party, 81; description, 253; doctrine, 81–82; Lebanese, 28

Tanzim, 70, 71
Treaty of Friendship and Cooperation (Soviet Union and Syria), 92, 93–94; background, 148; description, 253; test of, 119
Tripoli: fighting in, 44, 82, 125, 156; PLO and, 156; Syrian control of, 172
Tyre, 176; attacks on, 175, 179

Union of Toiling People's Forces, 82–83
United Arab Republic, 28
United Nations Interim Force in Lebanon (UNIFIL), 102, 107
United States:
Carter administration, 90–91, 106
and Israel, 48–49, 106, 125–26, 193–94; ambivalence toward, 140; conflicts with, 130, 184; support for, 128, 132, 135, 145–46
and Lebanon: attitude toward, 35, 59; intervention, 34, 35, 58, 177; policy in, 90–93, 108, 125, 140, 142, 145–47; support of Amin Jumayyil, 177, 178; withdrawal, 175, 186
mediation in Middle East, 53, 92, 119, 120, 125, 137, 150
Reagan administration, and Middle East, 120; changing views, 125, 142, 145; intentions for Lebanon, 91–92, 139–40, 144–45; policy, 91–92, 108, 117, 120, 178, 183–86. *See also* Reagan plan
and Syria, 117, 119, 125, 150, 184–85; dialogues with, 90; denunciation of, 91–92; support for, 48–49, 87

Wakim, Najjah, 36, 82
War of 1982: aftermath, 153–56, 174; background (1977–82), 9–10, 108–20; beginning, 121–32; consequences, 170–73; Israeli concept, 132–34; limited Syrian-Israeli war, 137–38, 146; and PLO, 150–52; significance, 10, 145–47, 158, 168–69; and Soviet Union, 147–48; and Syria, 148–50; and U.S., 139–40, 142–43, 144–47
Wazzan, Shafiq al-, government of, 96, 145, 153
Weizman, Ezer, opposition to Begin, 108, 127
Weizmann, Chaim, 22
West Bank: fighting along, 95; Israel's

Library of Congress Cataloging in Publication Data

Rabinovich, Itamar, 1942–
  The war for Lebanon, 1970–1985.

  Rev. ed. of: The war for Lebanon, 1970–1983. 1984.
  Includes index.
  1. Lebanon—History—1946–1975. 2. Lebanon—History—1975–   . I. Rabino-
vich, Itamar, 1942–   . War for Lebanon, 1970–1983. II. Title.
DS87.R332   1985   956.92′04   85-14891
ISBN 0-8014-1870-4
ISBN 0-8014-9313-7 (pbk.)